Palgrave Studies in Education Research Methods

Series Editors
Patrick Alan Danaher
University of Southern Queensland
Toowoomba, QLD, Australia

Fred Dervin
The University of Helsinki
Helsinki, Finland

Caroline Dyer
School of Politics and International Studies
University of Leeds
Leeds, UK

Máirín Kenny
Wexford, Ireland

Bobby Harreveld
School of Education and the Arts
Central Queensland University
Rockhampton, Australia

Michael Singh
Centre for Educational Research
Western Sydney University
Penrith, NSW, Australia

This series explores contemporary manifestations of the fundamental paradox that lies at the heart of education: that education contributes to the creation of economic and social divisions and the perpetuation of sociocultural marginalisation, while also providing opportunities for individual empowerment and social transformation. In exploring this paradox, the series investigates potential alternatives to current educational provision and speculates on more enabling and inclusive educational futures for individuals, communities, nations and the planet. Specific developments and innovation in teaching and learning, educational policy-making and education research are analysed against the backdrop of these broader developments and issues.

More information about this series at
http://www.palgrave.com/gp/series/15092

Alice Brown

Respectful Research With and About Young Families

Forging Frontiers and Methodological Considerations

palgrave
macmillan

Alice Brown
Faculty of Business, Education, Law and Arts
University of Southern Queensland
Springfield Central, QLD, Australia

Palgrave Studies in Education Research Methods
ISBN 978-3-030-02715-5   ISBN 978-3-030-02716-2   (eBook)
https://doi.org/10.1007/978-3-030-02716-2

Library of Congress Control Number: 2018961481

This Palgrave Macmillan imprint is published by the registered company Springer Nature Switzerland AG
The registered company address is: Gewerbestrasse 11, 6330 Cham, Switzerland

And so she forges towards the new frontiers, although confident, she steps tentatively, for little does she know what is to become of her.
(Brown, 2008 #793, p. 152)

Series Editors' Foreword

Current scholarship about young families is complex, diverse and contested, reflecting multiple and sometimes competing research methods, paradigms and theories. This proliferation manifests equally varied assumptions about and understandings of the characters and constituent elements of children, childhood and families, which in turn reflect broader discourses and disagreements about the meanings and purposes of living and learning in the contemporary world in the first quarter of the 21st century.

The complexity and diversity of this crucial scholarly field generate important questions and accompanying dilemmas for researchers seeking to design, conduct, publish from and evaluate appropriately ethical and empowering research projects with young families. These questions range from defining key terms and mobilising relevant conceptual and methodological resources, to selecting productive paradigms and harnessing the affordances of qualitative research, to striving for reciprocity in interactions with research participants and representing the lives of those participants authentically. The scale and scope of these questions and dilemmas can appear overwhelming and paralysing for researchers in this contested and contradictory intellectual space, not least because they can spring traps for the inexperienced and unwary.

Enter this book, *Respectful research with and about young families: Forging frontiers and methodological considerations*, by Dr Alice Brown,

Senior Lecturer in Early Childhood Education at the University of Southern Queensland, Australia, and an acknowledged expert in researching and publishing about the interplay among early childhood education, health, wellbeing and social ecology. I have known and worked with Alice for the past 14 years, having had the privilege of being the principal supervisor of her excellent and well-received Doctor of Philosophy thesis (Brown, 2012). Alice's thesis demonstrated comprehensively and with consummate skill her capacity to work closely with the research participants in her study to elicit their challenges and opportunities in designing and enacting effective active play opportunities with their young children. In doing so, Alice linked her original and significant research findings with increasingly urgent concerns about the global epidemic of childhood obesity and the associated lifelong personal and public health and wellbeing costs and risks.

In this book, Alice has a larger canvas than her Doctor of Philosophy thesis to display her knowledge of and empathy with young families engaging with the vicissitudes of contemporary life. In painting the variegated panes on that canvas, Alice's central conviction is both the necessity and the possibility of planning and implementing research in close consultation with the young families who have so much to share about their lives and about their formal and informal learning and teaching practices.

This large-scale canvas has been organised around eight comprehensive yet tightly focused chapters. Chapter 1 introduces us to the widely ranging terrain of researching with young families, including changing constructions of families and/or parents. In Chapter 2, Alice explores the dynamic interplay between perspectives and positionality, and highlights recurringly important notions such as strengths-based approaches, situatedness and social ecology. Alice uses Chapter 3 to elaborate the productive power of interpretivism as a method of inquiry and of its interdependence with storying. Chapter 4 articulates several requirements for genuinely ethical research with young families, including respect, multiple layers of participant involvement, and ethical praxis. In Chapter 5, Alice deploys a number of strategies for carrying out research effectively and ethically with young families, ranging from contextual audit tools and photo-documentation to creating mosaics through storying and interviews. Alice uses Chapter 6 to outline the applicability to researching with young families of the three CHE (connectivity, humanness, and empathy) principles. Chapter 7 approaches the vital task of making sense of data through a focus on retelling the stories told originally by the young families. Finally, in Chapter 8, Alice distils some of the wider lessons to be gleaned from the book by emphasising how ethical and empowering research with young families can contribute directly to pushing methodological boundaries and thereby to helping to reframe education research, and research with young families, more broadly.

This book is integrally located in, and also contributes new insights to, current international literature about young families and researching with them. Moreover, each chapter features a scenario that encapsulates the themes to be explored in that chapter, and in combination these scenarios constitute a textual innovation that works well to evoke broader issues. Furthermore, Alice writes engagingly and powerfully, and illustrates vividly the insights garnered from combining rigorous findings from her own and others' research with her considerable experiential knowledge gained from teaching in this field for an extended period of time.

On behalf of the editors of the Palgrave Studies in Education Research Methods book series, I am delighted to welcome *Respectful Research with and About Young Families* into the series. I know at first hand how conscientiously and painstakingly Alice has undertaken the conceptualisation and writing of the book. Even more importantly, Alice has constructed an outstanding synthesis of research in the book, which accordingly constitutes a significant and timely landmark in this diverse and contested scholarly field. I commend Alice for this intellectual achievement, and I commend the book to everyone with an interest in, and a commitment to, researching respectfully and rigorously with young families. I have no doubt that readers will find much of practical utility, as well as of theoretical and methodological sophistication, in this book to support and sustain their own engagements with young families around the world today and in the future.

Toowoomba, QLD, Australia   Patrick Alan Danaher

Reference

Brown, A. (2012). *The new frontier: A social ecological exploration of factors impacting on parental support for the active play of young children within the micro-environment of the family home.* Unpublished Doctor of Philosophy thesis, Faculty of Education, University of Southern Queensland, Toowoomba, Qld, Australia.

Preface

A number of years ago, as a neophyte researcher, I wrote a chapter in a book titled 'Troubling terrains: Tactics for traversing and transforming contemporary educational research' (Brown, 2008). On the cusp of embarking on my doctoral studies, I wrote of my experiences and the importance I placed on the need to regularly pause, to reflect, and to question the problems that were presented to me while engaged in the process of inquiry. I noted that this journey had many parallels to that of an active agent, or an explorer challenged when navigating difficult terrain and often requiring them to take risks and negotiate paths through uncharted territory towards a destination. At the time, in an effort to afford others a sense of the feelings I had experienced in my early inquiry, and the road traversed towards a place referred to as 'the new frontier', I employed active exploration metaphors and verbs at timely junctures in my writing and publications, as a literary style (Brown, 2008).

A number of years later, and in contemplating the approach that I would adopt for this book, on 'respectful research with and about young families', I found myself reconsidering and experiencing similar sorts of emotions and struggles. As I reflected on my journey as a researcher, I appreciated that for myself, and indeed many others who are researching, or contemplating embarking on a journey of inquiry, that in many respects we are not unlike explorers, forging towards frontiers. And perhaps, like myself, others might also find themselves moving through and amongst unchartered territory, and traversing risky and unsettling terrain (Higgs & McAllister, 2001; Youngs, 2003).

This terrain is potentially fraught with unexpected complexities, and broader research and ethical dilemmas, causing one to step cautiously and sensitively, weary that our interactions and the methods we employ may place ourselves, and others, in positions of vulnerability and powerlessness. This is particularly relevant for researchers planning to engage in inquiry with those who have experienced marginalisation or disadvantage (Brown & Danaher, 2017; Gorin, Hooper, Dyson, & Cabral, 2008; Paris, 2011; Vähäsantanen & Saarinen, 2013). This is exasperated by the idiosyncratic nature of young families, the nature of qualitative research, and in entering into the domestic spaces in which families are located.

While researching with or about young families offers an unprecedented opportunity for inquiry, knowing how to proceed, and the balance between the science of inquiry with the practice of interactions and relationships, is not always a well-worn path. Nor are the tracks and steps that others have taken easily sourced, or able to be easily contextualised. This is particularly the case when our intent is to engage in research sensitively from the very onset of a project, cognisant that the rights and wellbeing of each party are considered, and that the methods employed afford for ethical practices, and respectful and meaningful relationships (Hammersley, 2015; Palaiologou, 2014). Being sensitive to these kinds of issues includes being aware of our own and 'the other's' positionality, and the privileged position of researchers being 'custodians of the story'. It also requires us to be respectful of families opening their doors to us, entrusting us with their stories, and sharing a rare insight into the intimacy of their life-worlds (Bergold & Thomas, 2012; Von Unger, 2012).

It is with these sentiments in mind, as well as appreciating that others may also have experienced similar hesitations and concerns, that I considered the types of inclusions, content, and style of book that I deemed important to write. I chose to set the scene for each chapter by introducing a snapshot of an inquiry related to young families, each of these scenarios attempting to capture the theme of the chapter. I also front-ended each chapter by providing a collection of questions that reflect key themes identified in each chapter.

As researchers, we are also very weary of the fact that theoretical paradigms, perspectives, and approaches are never static and continue to evolve, and that research with young families often requires us to manoeuvre around unanticipated situations and ways of thinking. This shifting terrain can both challenge and perhaps cause us to reframe or reposition ourselves and, in turn, our 'ways of working'. I hope this comes through in the book with the inclusion at timely junctures of reflective questions, where the reader might also be fundamentally provoked, and encouraged to 'forge frontiers' in terms of the methodological considerations necessary for embarking in research, and entering into the privileged spaces of researching with young families.

While writing this book, I was also cognisant of the fact that inquiry and the methods we plan to employ are not merely tokenistic efforts to jump on a particular paradigmatic bandwagon, but are intentionally ethical and authentically considered. This is important so as to not perpetuate a dominant discourse that has the possibility of negatively impacting on those whose voices have been traditionally silenced, or who have experienced marginalisation and disenfranchisement historically as a ramification of engaging in social research (Paris, 2011). Over the years, and to this day, I continue to read widely on these topics, consult with my peers, and am vigilant in seeking out meaningful and innovative approaches that are ethical and respectful (Brown & Danaher, 2017).

These themes and approaches permeate this text, foregrounding humanising research principles, and reinforcing the valuing of relationships, integrity, genuine respect for 'the other', and the importance of engaging with others in a dialogic process. A significant part of these efforts tracks back to earlier work my colleagues and I have engaged in, underpinned by the importance placed on supporting participants in feeling more comfortable with the interview process, and investing in efforts to break down initial communication barriers, by building connections, trust, and rapport (Brown, 2012, 2014; Brown & Danaher, 2012, 2017). These methods and considerations have been refined over the years, and have included the development and reference to the CHE principles of 'Connectedness', 'Humanness', and 'Empathy' (note these principles are addressed in Chap. 6 of this text). The intent of these efforts is to continue to explore strategies and seek out methods of interaction that are mutually humanising, and in doing so engage in collaborative meaning-making related to a phenomenon (Paris, 2011).

In developing each chapter, and the associated topics for this text, I have drawn upon not only my own experience and research, but also my deep engagement and reading of related contemporary literature and theory. I continue to be inspired, but also challenged, by the ongoing evolution and innovative research and thinking in these spaces. This has meant that in the process of writing this text I have grown exponentially in my own knowledge, as a researcher and personally, and of course all of these 'learnings' and research have made their way into the various chapters of this text. I am also constantly reminded through my reading and reflections to not lose sight of the potentiality of others, and the recognition of the knowledge, skills, and capacities that participants bring to the table. As such, I embrace and seek out practices and methods that harness this potential, and enter these research spaces sensitively, conscious to treat others with respect and dignity.

I hope that these sentiments and themes emerge and become evident to readers, and that I write this book from a very humbling position in two respects. First, that my writing reflects my deep respect for family members, who bring with them to the research relationship so much knowledge, meaning-making of their context, and lived experiences, and offer multiple and idiosyncratic perspectives to inform our research (Harden, Backett-Milburn, Hill, & MacLean, 2010). I continue to feel very privileged to be invited in and be permitted to 'step through the thresholds' of the very private spaces in which family members work, play, and live. Second, I hope that my efforts in this text, either directly or indirectly, make a contribution to the field, one that is already informed by research giants and legends, early adopters, and so many outstanding academics that have inspired and informed my writing (Greenstein & Davis, 2013; Harden et al., 2010; McCarthy, Doolittle, & Schlater, 2012; Paris & Winn, 2014).

It is also my hope that in reading parts, or all of this text, academics and scholars have the opportunity to reflect deeply on what is shared, perhaps even being motivated to work within a 'brave space', where existing paradigms and discourses are challenged. This book pays tribute to those researchers who are willing to take such a step, researchers prepared to invest the time in exploring ways to embed authentic respect, social justice, democracy, and the acknowledgement of participants' rights and agency into their work.

In writing this book, I am weary that the research landscape is a moveable feast, continually shifting and evolving. This requires researchers to manoeuvre around unanticipated situations in terms of exploring innovative, ethical, and respectful approaches to inquiry. This is particularly evidenced when encountering diverse ethical situations which emerge from different settings, cultures, and in the context of young families with their diverse practices and domestic environments (McCarthy et al., 2012). As such, we should never stop problematising, never stop taking risks and adopting the role of 'active agents' in exploring relatively unchartered territory, including challenging and pushing the boundaries in adopting humanistic approaches to engaging in research with, and of, others.

I invite you, the reader, to join with me on this journey of discovery and that together we might 'forge frontiers' in a legitimate space that still has so far to go. To 'forge frontiers' in pursuing legitimate research with young families, and in doing so, to learn about, from, and with individuals that reside within these domestic spaces. I invite you to step cautiously, but also confidently and with conviction, with the intent of moving towards a more empowering position of challenging existing discourse and adopting counter-narratives. I believe that by engaging in this journey there is the opportunity to transform this research landscape, and in doing so create more humane and enabling research terrain for, and with, young families. This is defined as the 'New Frontier'.

Alice Brown ☺

Springfield Central, QLD, Australia   Alice Brown

References

Bergold, J., & Thomas, S. (2012). Participatory research methods: A methodological approach in motion. *Historical Social Research/Historische Sozialforschung,* *13*(1), 191–222.

Brown, A. (2008). Towards a new frontier in understanding the contextual influences on paediatric inactivity. In R. Henderson & P. A. Danaher (Eds.), *Troubling terrains: Tactics for traversing and transforming contemporary educational research* (pp. 149–168). Teneriffe, QLD: Post Pressed.

Brown, A. (2012). *The new frontier: A social ecological exploration of factors impacting on parental support for the active play of young children within the micro-environment of the family home.* PhD, University of Southern Queensland, Toowoomba, QLD.

Brown, A. (2014, June 5). *CHE principles: A framework for supporting rapport building and new possibilities in authentic and dialogical semi-structured interviews.* Paper presented at the BELA seminar series for the School of Teacher Education and Early Childhood Research, USQ, Springfield.

Brown, A., & Danaher, P. A. (2012, December 2–6). *Respectful, responsible and reciprocal ruralities research: Approaching and positioning educational research differently within Australian rural communities.* Paper presented at the In: Joint International Conference of the Australian Association for Research in Education and the Asia Pacific Educational Research Association (AARE 2012): Regional and Global Cooperation in Educational Research. Sydney, NSW.

Brown, A., & Danaher, P. A. (2017). CHE principles: Facilitating authentic and dialogical semi-structured interviews in educational research. *International Journal of Research & Method in Education*, 1–15. https://doi.org/10.1080/1743727X.2017.13799.

Gorin, S., Hooper, C. A., Dyson, C., & Cabral, C. (2008). Ethical challenges in conducting research with hard to reach families. *Child Abuse Review, 17*(4), 275–287.

Greenstein, T. N., & Davis, S. N. (2013). *Methods of family research* (3rd ed.). Thousand Oaks, CA/Los Angeles: Sage.

Hammersley, M. (2015). On ethical principles for social research. *International Journal of Social Research Methodology, 128*(4), 433–449.

Harden, J., Backett-Milburn, K., Hill, M., & MacLean, A. (2010). Oh, what a tangled web we weave: Experiences of doing 'multiple perspectives' research in families. *International Journal of Social Research Methodology, 13*(5), 441–452.

Higgs, C., & McAllister, L. (2001). Being a methodological space cadet. In H. Byrne-Armstrong, J. Higgs, & D. Horsfall (Eds.), *Critical moments in qualitative research* (pp. 31–43). Oxford, UK: Butterworth Heinemann.

McCarthy, J. R., Doolittle, M., & Schlater, S. D. (2012). *Understanding family meanings: A reflective text.* Bristol, UK: Policy Press.

Palaiologou, I. (2014). 'Do we hear what children want to say?' Ethical praxis when choosing research tools with children under five. *Early Child Development and Care, 184*(5), 689–705.

Paris, D. (2011). 'A friend who understand fully': Notes on humanizing research in a multiethnic youth community. *International Journal of Qualitative Studies in Education, 24*(2), 137–149.

Paris, D., & Winn, M. (Eds.). (2014). *Humanizing research: Decolonizing qualitative inquiry with youth and communities.* London: Sage.

Vähäsantanen, K., & Saarinen, J. (2013). The power dance in the research interview: Manifesting power and powerlessness. *Qualitative Researcher, 13*(5), 493–510.

Von Unger, H. (2012). *Participatory health research: Who participates in what?* Paper presented at the Forum Qualitative Sozialforschung/Forum: Qualitative Social Research.

Youngs, H. (2003). *Getting to the heart of servant leadership: An exploration of multi-strategy methodology.* Paper presented at the NZARE Conference, Auckland, New Zealand. http://www.aare.edu.au/03pap/you03135.pdf

Overview

Raising children is a collective undertaking, and one that is integrally linked to multiple places, and the existing and changing sociocultural milieu (Brown, 2012; Moore & Fry, 2011). Yet families and the domestic spaces in which they are located are still at the heart of this endeavour. Parents and significant caregivers are understood to play a critical role in influencing the short- and long-term health, development, behaviour, and learning of young children (Center on the Developing Child at Harvard University, 2010; Fox, Levitt, & Nelson, 2010). Science also tells us that early life experiences, including nurturing relationships and responsive interactions, can have a cumulative effect on the long-term outcomes for children (Shonkoff, 2012).

There is now an unprecedented opportunity, and some would go so far as to say 'an urgent need', to engage in respectful, ethical, rigorous, and innovative research with, and about, individuals that reside within these domestic spaces. The intent of this book is to build upon and leverage the insights from academics and researchers who have already gained traction in this field, as well as to add to this new understandings and approaches for investigating the lived experiences, and a range of other phenomenon associated with 'young families' (Greenstein & Davis, 2013; McCarthy, Doolittle, & Schlater, 2012). Young families are understood in the broadest and most inclusive sense to comprise of at least two individuals that reside within the same domestic space, or are connected by birth, parenthood, associated biologically or non-biologically, with one of these individuals being a significant carer of at least one child, five years of age or under.

Although ambitious, at the heart of those engaged in researching with young families is a passionate commitment to gain insights into the narratives of another's lifeworld, behaviours, practices, perspectives, and values. Just as importantly, researching with or about families affords opportunities for giving voice to those who have a vested interest in matters which concern them, and issues which impact on their lives (McCarthy et al., 2012). It is also the vision of many scholars choosing to research in this space that, directly or indirectly, their findings will make a difference to the individuals at the heart of these endeavours (Greenstein & Davis, 2013).

This book shares distinctive theoretical and methodological features, and gives particular attention to the considerations and challenges associated with conducting ethical and respectful research with, and of, individuals within these environments. The text adopts an interpretivist lens for inquiry, and offers readers a wide range of contemporary approaches for gathering layers of meaning with and about young families. This volume also seeks to provide insights into a broader repertoire and framing of contemporary understandings of 'participant involvement' in inquiry, and the theory/practice nexus of respectful and ethical inquiry.

A scenario, positioned at the beginning of each chapter, helps set the scene, by weaving in the focus and key topics that each chapter addresses. A number of reflection questions are also positioned at the beginning of each chapter, as a way of provoking thought, and fore-fronting key topics. It is apt, and in line with the theme 'Forging frontiers', that interspersed at various junctures throughout the text are journal entries from the author that share her thoughts and research journey. These passages mark the researcher's struggles, reflections, steps travelled, achievements, and repositioning of consciousness in terms of researching with young families. At times poignant and evocative, the purpose of these are to reveal considerations and reflections that may resonate with others who research, or plan to research in this space.

The book comprises eight chapters, all of which comprehensively interweave considerations for engaging in respectful and ethical research with, and about, young families. The author draws from her own extensive scholarly work, and the various research projects she has engaged in with others. She also extensively examines the reputable, contemporary, and innovative qualitative works of scholars from a range of disciplines, fields, and perspectives, who contribute to the conceptual, paradigmatic, and methodological considerations of embarking on, and engaging in, research with families.

Each chapter offers the reader an opportunity to connect with contemporary literature, perspectives, discourse, and methodological approaches. The goal of this being to motivate readers to reflect critically on their positioning, the positioning of others, and how the decisions, choices, and views of research participants will impact on the territory that they plan to traverse. Indeed, by engaging with the themes addressed in each chapter, it is anticipated that the reader will develop a deeper respect for the individuals within these domestic spaces, and the contributions that their lived experiences make to a more nuanced understanding of context and phenomena. Finally, the intent is that by engaging in the themes and various topics addressed in this text researchers may choose to engage in research with young families, and adopt methodological approaches that are respectful, humane, dialogical, and ethical.

Forging frontiers starts by exploring notions of family, the idiosyncratic nature of 'the family', the complexities of family life, and the richness and pervasive nature of the environments in which individuals are embedded. A rationale is offered for the value of engaging in researching with and about young families, including the recognition of children as significant agents within the domestic space of the family home, and other environments they are engaged in, or move within. Chapter 1 concludes by provoking thought regarding the professional responsibility researchers have for employing methodological approaches that are dialogical and ethical, while also ensuring that alongside our own research agenda we are cognisant that the rights of others are respected.

Readers are then guided through 'an audit of self' and invited to more closely consider their and others' positionality. It is anticipated that this will lead to giving greater consideration for the creation of 'humanised spaces' for researching with members of young families. The chapter concludes by exploring a range of perspectives and paradigms that researchers may wish to consider in terms of the axiological positioning of their research (Chap. 2) (Paris & Winn, 2014).

Storytelling and oral history are embedded in, and are a notable part of, the practices and culture of many tribes, and families across generations, and through time. Chapter 3 is dedicated to exploring the important act of storying, and the potentiality that these narratives afford interpretive researchers as mechanisms for better understanding the everyday lives and the perspectives of members of young families. Adopting such an approach to inquiry calls for a paradigmatic repositioning of the value of storying, of meaning-making, and the recognition that others have something to share (Fenton, Walsh, Wong, & Cumming, 2015; Saleebey, 2012). This chapter concludes by addressing the mechanics of listening, with a particular focus on considerations for the inclusion of 'child voice within family', and the complexity of this task.

Appreciating that each family context is idiosyncratic, later chapters (Chaps. 4, 5, 6, and 7) explore the nuances that are important to consider, in terms of the types of relationships we develop with participants, and how we might build rapport and trust through research practices which are humane and respectful. The 'ethical praxis and participant involvement model' is introduced to encourage readers to think more deeply about their existing practice, methodologies, and techniques in terms of participant's interests, rights and agency, and issues such as power differentials (Chap. 4). Final chapters focus attention on rethinking methods for 'gathering layers of meaning' of individuals within context, yet with the responsibility of being custodians of these stories. A range of popular and innovative qualitative methods are showcased, the careful selection and combination of which potentially support inquiry that seeks to gain a deeper appreciation and understanding of the idiosyncratic experiences and motivations of young families (Gabb, 2010).

Chapter 6 is dedicated to considerations regarding going beyond just acknowledging the importance of building rapport, trust, and the relational dimensions in our work, and research with young families, to exploring key strategies and tools for maximising ethical, dialogical, and meaningful research encounters, and mutually beneficial outcomes

(Brown & Danaher, 2017). This is particularly the case in relation to decision-making pertaining to key elements of rapport-building, and maximising dialogical opportunities with members of young families, including those who may have been marginalised, disenfranchised, or positioned through a pathologised lens (Bermúdez, Muruthi, & Jordan, 2016).

Chapter 7 addresses the role of the storyteller. 'Stories' being loosely referred to as the narratives and other forms of data that help to create a picture of the lived experiences and environments of participants. Discussion is directed towards factors that will impact on researcher decision-making regarding the analysis and 'retelling' of participant stories. This includes the influence of paradigms adopted by the researcher, as well as of the positionality of participants. Attention is then directed towards the importance of considering what stories to tell and to privilege, and the factors that underpin these decisions.

This final chapter captures the direction that a new line of critical inquiry might look like, and the potential for innovation. This journey requires researchers to be open to the process of deconstructing and critically reflecting on existing approaches, methods, and the frames that bind us, as well as being willing to take risks in venturing beyond dominant interpretivist discourse. Innovation and creativity will emerge from those prepared to explore new ways of thinking, some of which are still very much at the fringe of qualitative research, such as that of humanising, decolonising, critical feminist, and post-structuralist research.

While this book draws on the author's own experiences, methodologies, and established works in researching with young families, the intent is not to simply 'repackage' early works. Rather, in the process of writing this substantive text, the author shares her experience of being nudged, provoked, challenged, and many times motivated to push the boundaries, in efforts to reframe her own thinking and approaches. Each chapter therefore draws upon core theory, an extensive body of literature, and the tried and tested approaches adopted by other leaders in the field regarding their efforts to forefront respectful and ethical research. The text integrates innovative and post-foundational themes including critical feminism, indigenous knowledge constructs, decolonizing theory, and post-structuralism.

In a field of uncertainty and constant change, the purpose of this book is to challenge, prod, and perhaps even provoke reflection for those planning on entering the very privileged space, and engaging in inquiry with, of, or about young families. It is anticipated that the book will appeal to both early career researchers that are on the cusp of embarking on their doctoral journey, as well as those more experienced in research. As such, rather than seeing the information shared in this book as a panacea, the intent is that that by engaging with the themes of the book researchers are afforded the opportunity to challenge existing thinking and paradigmatic positions, and to reexamine notions of family, participation, and involvement. As well, the intent is that key themes addressed in the book will encourage researchers to think deeply about the contribution that family members offer to inquiry, and to existing understandings of phenomena.

Finally, in reflecting upon the title of the book, the author sees the content and themes addressed in this book as essential in terms of 'Forging frontiers' in a legitimate space that still has so far to go in terms of exploring innovative methodological approaches that are ethical and respectful. 'Forging frontiers' relates to the untapped potential that awaits us as researchers in learning about, from, and with young families that reside within domestic spaces—a space where much research still needs to be done in order to advance our understandings, yet has the potential of being an untapped resource that in many respects could still be defined as the 'New Frontier'. Forge on...*Alice Brown* ☺

References

Bermúdez, J. M., Muruthi, B., & Jordan, L. (2016). Decolonizing research methods for family science: Creating space at the centre – Decolonizing research practices. *Journal of Family Theory & Review, 8*(2), 192–206.

Brown, A. (2012). *The new frontier: A social ecological exploration of factors impacting on parental support for the active play of young children within the micro-environment of the family home.* PhD, University of Southern Queensland, Toowoomba, QLD.

Brown, A., & Danaher, P. A. (2017). CHE principles: Facilitating authentic and dialogical semi-structured interviews in educational research. *International*

Journal of Research & Method in Education, 1–15. https://doi.org/10.1080/1 743727X.2017.13799.

Center on the Developing Child at Harvard University. (2010). *The foundations of lifelong health are build in early childhood.* Retrieved from Cambridge, MA. https://developingchild.harvard.edu/wp-content/uploads/2010/05/ Foundations-of-Lifelong-Health.pdf

Fenton, A., Walsh, K., Wong, S., & Cumming, T. (2015). Using strengths-based approaches in early years practice and research. *International Journal of Early Childhood, 47*(1), 27–52.

Fox, S., Levitt, P., & Nelson, C. (2010). How the timing and quality of early experiences influence the development of brain architecture. *Child Development, 81*(8), 28–40.

Gabb, J. (2010). Home truths: Ethical issues in family research. *Qualitative Research, 10*(4), 461–478.

Greenstein, T. N., & Davis, S. N. (2013). *Methods of family research* (3rd ed.). Thousand Oaks, CA/Los Angeles: Sage.

McCarthy, J. R., Doolittle, M., & Schlater, S. D. (2012). *Understanding family meanings: A reflective text.* Bristol, UK: Policy Press.

Moore, T., & Fry, R. (2011). *Place-based approaches to child and family services: A literature review.* Retrieved from Parkville, VIC. http://www.rch.org.au/ uploadedFiles/Main/Content/ccch/Place_based_services_literature_review. pdf

Paris, D., & Winn, M. (Eds.). (2014). *Humanizing research: Decolonizing qualitative inquiry with youth and communities.* London: Sage.

Saleebey, D. (2012). *The Strengths Perspective in Social Work Practice* (6th ed.). Boston: Pearson.

Shonkoff, J. P. (2012). Leveraging the biology of adversity to address the roots of disparities in health and development. *Proceedings from the National Academy of Science of the United States of America, 109*(Supp 2), 1–6.

Contents

List of Figures

1

Surveying the Terrain—Realising the Potential of Researching with Young Families

Scenario 1: Integrating Inclusive Approaches to Interpretations of Family Through Action Research

In an urban kindergarten setting, Mario, a doctoral student, sits quietly, observing a group of children huddled in the sandpit chatting about their weekends and their adventures. Mario is working on a collaborative action research project with the services' early childhood teachers, on the integration of authentic inclusive practices within the EC curriculum. Mario listens to Carla sharing her experience of enjoying time with her mum and dad picnicking, and playing in a local park. Samson pipes up and excitedly reminisces about making dinosaur biscuits in the kitchen with his little sister and nanna, while Luke excitedly details his experience of camping with his mothers and catching a Bigggggg fish (which he measures as his arms stretch out widely)!

Carla then remarks, "Did you say your two mums?" "There's no such thing as having two mums!" Mario notes that the excitement drops from Luke's face, instead replaced by embarrassment, as he is visually observed to withdraw from his peers, while he tries to make sense of Carla's words, and contemplates a response.

© The Author(s) 2019
A. Brown, *Respectful Research With and About Young Families*, Palgrave Studies in
Education Research Methods, https://doi.org/10.1007/978-3-030-02716-2_1

Clair (one of the educators at the service) is also outside closely observing the play episode unfold. She is reflecting on the contextual insights she has of each of these children, particularly the traditional views that Carla and Samson's families hold on topics related to 'family', and their role and make-up. Having heard and witnessed the scene unfold, she promptly steps in, in an effort to refocus the children. She offers the children some miniature toy houses, tractors, and animals, prompting the children to consider how they might incorporate these items into their sand play. Distracted by these new resources, the children easily turn their attention to embellishing their creative pursuits, while Claire breathes a sigh of relief, thankful that she has deescalated the situation.

During morning tea, Clair and Mario discuss the scene both having observed, and comment that while changes in modern family dynamics are evidenced in contemporary reality and across public and community spaces, heteronormative stereotypes continue to exist. Unfortunately, these under-standings and appreciations of diverse family structures are not necessarily making their way, or being reflected in early childhood contexts and pedagogy. After chatting to several of their colleagues, the team agree that it would be valuable to move through the next action research cycle of 'plan, act, observe and reflect', with a focus on exploring strategies for authentically integrating more inclusive discourse and pedagogical approaches for supporting multiple interpretations of family, that extend beyond the construct of the traditional nuclear family, including making visible same-sex parented families and non-heterosexuality.

As Clair continues to move about her day with a heightened sense of con-sciousness regarding this issue, she notices evidence of hegemonic family struc-ture throughout the service, from the displays in the dramatic play areas, and books included on the shelves, to the language and examples shared through songs, and discussion during group time, each of these making reference to the 'typical' family. The placement of these resources further marginalising chil-dren like Luke in terms of reinforcing a particular discourse, and membership regarding family, one which Luke is not able to identify with. In doing so, these practices and environments send a dominant message of the valuing of one type of family over another.

Inspired by the research of Alicia Cameron, honours student—University of Southern Queensland.

Chapter Synopsis

This chapter presents a picture of the contemporary landscape in which families with young children are located, and the multiple interpretations of 'the family'. A strong rationale is offered for the value of engaging in researching with, and of, young families, including the recognition that children are significant agents within the domestic space of the family home, and other environments in which they are embedded. Contemporary understandings and constructions of families and their dynamic contexts are introduced in this chapter, while noting the need for being critically aware of the dominant discourse that prevails within these spaces, and which may privilege dominant narratives.

How is 'the young family' defined and understood in post-modernist times?
How have young families changed over time, and across places and spaces?
    What is the impact of 'family change', on a child's development, and long-term life-course trajectory?
    What factors impact on a parenting practices, values, and behaviours?
    What role does the environment play in individual behaviour within young families?
    Why research about, and with, young families?
    What insights can we gain from the lived experiences and narratives of individuals in young families in terms of education, learning, health, and child development?

This chapter draws attention to the idiosyncratic nature of 'the family', and reminds us that families are located within complex social ecological systems. The chapter addresses the richness and pervasive nature of the environments in which individuals are embedded. Much of this terrain is still unchartered, with the environments, the nuances, the factors that influence behaviour, and the perspectives of family members offering legitimate, and unlimited, potential for research.

This chapter concludes by providing a rationale for why we might choose to research 'with' young families in ethical and respectful inquiry, rather than research 'about', or 'on', family members. This section of the text addresses the professional responsibilities we have as researchers for ensuring the rights of participants are respected and protected. This requires investing significant thought and commitment, so that in exploring the lifeworlds and meaning-making of family members we do so sensitively and with integrity (Hammersley, 2015; Palaiologou, 2014; Paris & Winn, 2014).

Journal Entry 1—The Morning Rush

Mary Wagner, a 35-year-old mother to Benjamin, 18 months; Katy, 6 years; and Marcus, 14 years; takes pride in her parenting ability. She feels that despite the daily challenges experienced and faced with raising a busy young family, her husband and herself are managing well and making every effort to provide their children with a good start in life.

This morning is another typically hectic and rushed morning in the Wagner household. Susan is holding down the fort, as her husband Marty has had to leave early for work again today. Her teenage son Marcus is having trouble emerging from his bed and organising himself for the day ahead, so Mary is trying to urge him into the shower, while pressing a uniform for Katy, putting on quick a load of wash, shovelling down her own breakfast, and rinsing the dirty dishes. In the meantime, 18-month-old Benjamin is crying out for attention and pulling utensils out of a kitchen drawer, discovering that the spatula he has in his hand makes a great sound when hit on the leg of the kitchen table. "20 minutes till we need to go!" Susan calls out.

Susan flicks on the television and luckily Peppa Pig *is on, one of Benjamin's favourite shows. She gently nudges Ben towards the TV, while experiencing a brief pang of guilt in using the TV as sort of 'babysitter', weary that her son shouldn't be watching too much TV at his age. However, this feeling quickly dissipates as Ben focusses his attention on the pink pig and starts to sing a song with Peppa that she believes is quite 'educational'. (Adapted from the writing and efforts of Emma Smolenaers, honours student—University of Southern Queensland)*

Background

What happens behind the doors of domestic spaces in which young families live has intrigued many within contemporary society and, indeed, throughout time. In the post-modernist world in which we live, the media and its ability to present a sort of voyeurism into family life have positioned a panopticon gaze, causing a widespread culture of surveillance (Bratich, 2017; Foucault, 1979) on the lives of families. Inherent in this scrutiny is a legacy, or default position for forming opinions, making comparisons and judgements (based on ones' own positionality and perspectives) on topics such as definitions of family, their roles and responsibilities, and parenting practices.

A large body of research confirms the family context as being a significant location where a child's learning, behaviour, and development takes place, with parents, primary carers, and other significant adults recognised as important as a child's first educators (Mannion & Walker, 2015; McMahon & Camberis, 2017). There is also a significant body of empirical studies that confirm the important role that parents of young children play as gatekeepers, and as critical contributors to children's learning, development, and behaviours throughout the life-course trajectory (Eisenstadt, 2011; Emerson, Fear, Fox, & Sanders, 2012; Shonkoff, 2013; Sweeny, 2014; Zubrick et al., 2012). These studies and research affirm the importance of working closely with family, capacity building with families, and investing early in young children to help mitigate the impact, and associated health, development, and intervention costs anticipated for many, later in life (particularly with those identified as vulnerable or marginalised) (Heckman, 2006; Knudsen, Heckman, Cameron, & Shonkoff, 2006).

There is also evidence of a strong neoliberal narrative (Moss, 2015a), and one would even go so far as to say a 'regime of truth' (Dahlberg & Moss, 2005) that attempts to rationalise and normalise the economic benefit of investing early in young children as a proactive step in positioning society as one that is strong and sustainable (Heckman & Masterov, 2007; Mustard, 2008; Save The Children, 2009; Sweeny, 2014). Yet, academics like Moss (2015a, 2015b) raise concerns over universalising claims that "are often cited as evidence of the 'high returns' to be gained from 'investing' in 'early interventions', with claims of anything from up to $17 in benefits for every $1 spent" (p. 92). He cautions that these types of reports, studies, and evaluations provide little attention "to the larger picture" in relation to positioning this discourse within the context in which this research was located and conducted (p. 92).

Positioned against this backdrop, there is now a renewed focus by policy makers, practitioners, and researchers from a range of backgrounds and disciplines, including education (Dockett et al., 2009), physical activity and active play (Brown & Smolenaers, 2016; Mori, Nakamoto, Mizuochi, Ikudome, & Gabbard, 2013), neuroscience, psychology and family studies (Bachraz & Grace, 2009; Center on the Developing Child at Harvard University, 2016a), social science (Bushin, 2009), medicine (including neonatal and obstetrics), sociology and social work (Cowan, Callaghan, Kan, & Richardson, 2016; Montirosso & Provenzi, 2015), asking questions and seeking to investigate a range of phenomena related to family members, and the places and spaces in which families reside and are embedded (Poulton, Moffitt, & Silva, 2015) This book adopts a contemporary and malleable definition of terms such as 'parent', and 'family'. These efforts acknowledge that understandings, and the interpretations of these terms, are situated, context dependent, temporal, and reflect social, cultural, and historical constructs (Grace, Hayes, & Wise, 2017; Greenstein & Davis, 2013; McCarthy, Doolittle, & Schlater, 2012).

Given this, although traditional interpretations of 'a parent' refer to the biological parents of a child, in this text the term 'parent' is interpreted, and refers to those significant adults in biological, non-biological, and adoptive relationships with children (particularly within the domestic space of the home, or living space in which family members reside), but also includes grandparents, extended family members, and legal guardians. So, in reference to the word 'parent'/'parents' within multiple citings and contexts of this text, the author attempts to expand on, and be more inclusive of this term, with the intent of recognising other significant adults responsible for raising, caring, and impacting on the lives, development, learning, and well-being of children.

Questions over understandings of terms such as 'parent' and 'family' raise challenges when engaging in family research, as these contexts and parameters morph and evolve (McCarthy, 2012). As such, it is important that researchers are mindful of the changing dynamics, practices, values, and beliefs of 'familied life', and the individuals that reside within these domestic spaces. There is also a need for greater sensitivity for how ours and others' positions might impact on how families are perceived, and indeed how families may perceive themselves. This is particularly important for those who have experienced, or are currently victims of, marginalisation (Fiese, 2013).

Perceptions of 'family' have implications for those wishing to engage in inquiry with, and of, families, with regard to ensuring that the research methods and practices we adopt are ethical, and honour the individuals located within these domestic spaces (Bermúdez, Muruthi, & Jordan, 2016). This approach requires establishing trust and rapport with participants. It requires us to enter these spaces conscious of the degree to which opportunities are afforded for authentic and respectful research, co-construction of knowledge, and for others to share insights into their worlds and storied lives (Geia, Hayes, & Usher, 2013).

1.1   Changing Constructions of 'Family'

Same-sex parented families, extended families, single-parent families, 'the urban family' adopted or foster families, intact or blended families, childless families, step families, the nuances and interpretations of family continue to evolve and change (Australian Bureau of Statistics, 2016). As such, understandings of 'family' are increasingly understood in broader, more fluid, and organic terms, rather than in modernist terms that are universal and static (Shehan, 2016). Social scientists and family scholars that adopt a post-modernist position suggest that society should embrace more inclusive definitions, ones that extend beyond monolithic interpretations, and that attempt to capture the true complexity of 'family' (Greenstein & Davis, 2012; McMahon & Camberis, 2017).

However, despite the increase of pluralist notions of contemporary family structures, long-standing impressions of 'the nuclear family' (understood to include a membership of a married heterosexual couple, raising their biological child/children under the same roof) remain a modernist legacy, and still remain a 'frame', or automatic point of reference for many (Goldberg, 2014; McCarthy & Edwards, 2011). As a society, we continue to be challenged by what makes up the membership, role, and function of today's family, with the characterisations of the 'average family' still the most visible in public, political, community, and early learning and educational spaces (as evidenced in Scenario 1).

Unfortunately, despite cultural understandings of family and the diversity of family structures evidenced and represented, heteronormative stereotypes, and discourse of the 'average family', often silence and continue to marginalise other conceptions of family and family members (Byard, Kosciw, & Bartkiewicz, 2013; Lohoar, Butera, & Kennedy, 2014). Further, in relation to conducting research about or with young families, Greenstein & Davis (2012) argues that "This uncertainty about what constitutes a family causes major problems for researchers. Without a generally agreed-upon definition of family, how can researchers know who to study or exclude from their research?" (p. 8).

Diverse and dynamic conceptions of family are not a contemporary phenomenon, as historically multiple interpretations and socio-cultural constructions are evidenced (Bushin, 2009). However, despite what many in the population might think, the family is 'not an institution' (Rogers, 2016). Some argue that the term 'family' continues to be disputed and politicised (McCarthy & Edwards, 2011). Others, such as Bermúdez et al. (2016), suggest that it is impossible to agree on a definitive description, or the "existence of the true family" (p. 197), and ponder whether to use the term at all. There are even some who suggest that we should refer to a different term, such as 'families', to better capture the diversity of family make-ups (Lamanna, Riedmann, & Stewart, 2015).

From a functionalist perspective the family still plays an important role in society, including the task of reproduction, and the socialisation of children. Others, such as economists, see families as consumers (including providing material support), with decolonists viewing families as connected to ancestors and ancestral history (Bermúdez et al., 2016; McCubbin, McCubbin, Zhang, Kehl, & Strom, 2013), and those in education viewing families as 'first teachers' (Centre for Social Research and Evaluation, 2011). Finally, from a transactionalist perspective, 'the family' continues to be understood as serving the key function of caring, supporting, and nurturing children, as well as transmitting cultural values, traditions, and knowledge (Baxter, 2016). McCarthy (2012) aptly sums up these sentiments by writing that "family can serve as a symbol around which many features of personal and social lives intertwine and coalesce" (p. 3).

Nevertheless, while progressive ideas and notions of family have started to challenge staunchly held conceptions, traditionally held views of family remain evidenced, and often firmly unchanged and unchallenged.

These views make their way into our communities, social/cultural settings, schools, and even our early childhood settings (as evidenced in Scenario 1). We also continue to witness the legacy these views leave on family members, silencing and marginalising those who don't fit the mould of more traditional notions of family. These evolving perspectives regarding notions of family, or the roles and function of a family, challenge us as a society to question and continue to redefine our assumptions, values, and beliefs regarding this term and its membership.

Researchers are also challenged with the evolving notions of family, causing them to consider their own ontology and epistemology in reference to notions of individual agency, rights, inclusivity, and social justice. As such, there is a need for researchers to engage in an ongoing process of questioning, and renegotiation of interpretations regarding dominant discourse, stereotypes, paradigms of heteronormativity, and long-held biases (Ajandi, 2011). It asks that we hesitate before entering these domestic spaces, and when we do 'knock', that we approach families with a deep respect of 'the other', and their positionality.

In moving forward, although I hesitate to offer a definition of the term 'young family', for the sake of a point of reference for this text, I see a working definition as necessary. In doing so, the intent of this definition is that it is in no way offered as a definitive or static notion. Rather, it is an effort to engage with the reader initially in a 'shared understanding', and to provoke conversation, ongoing dialogue, and, from a post-structuralist perspective, an invitation for others to challenge this term. In the end, this is an attempt, and my efforts to reflect on how to best define the membership of a group of individuals. Therefore, 'young families' in this text will be defined in the broadest and most inclusive sense to comprise of at least two individuals that reside within the same domestic space, or are connected by birth, parenthood, associated biologically or non-biologically, with one being a significant carer of at least one child, five years of age or under (Center on the Developing Child at Harvard University, 2010b; Lohoar et al., 2014).

Young families located in this millennium are growing up, and embedded in a world that is in many ways uniquely and substantially different to that of any previous generation (Moore, McDonald, McHugh-Dillon, & West, 2016; Zubrick et al., 2012). The impact of socio-cultural changes on 'the family' and family life are complex, with services, systems, policy, and legislation often struggling to accommodate for the dynamics of these changes in efforts to support families, or to acknowledge the duplicity in perspectives held (Bushin, 2009). Evolving constructions and shifting dynamics of the family structure include changes in family practices and behaviours; increased rates of family fragmentation; moves to cohabitation and partnerships, instead of marriage; increased age of 'parenting'; changing interpretations of childhood; increased child agency; and increased family mobility (Baxter, 2016). These changes in family dynamics flow directly through to the health, well-being, development, and cognitive capacity of individuals within these environments, as well as family practices, beliefs, values, and behaviours, and socio-culture structures in which they are embedded.

Changes to family structure and circumstances reflect the values of those embedded context, as well being influenced by context. These perspectives and values also have a flow-on effect on other socio-cultural places and spaces, such as early childhood education and care settings, as well as educational priorities, and agendas. For researchers, seeking to investigate and understand the differing needs of today's young families, or the intrinsic and cumulative impact these changes have on the behaviours and practices of young families, these diverse contexts open up a range of possibilities for inquiry, and worthy topics to pursue from multiple fields and disciplines (Wise, 2003).

1.2   Parents as Gatekeepers—The Impact of Young Families on the Health, Development, and Life Course of Children

Parents as Key Players in a Child's Development and Learning

From conception a child's environment impacts on their immediate and future learning, behaviour, development, health, and well-being (Cowan et al., 2016; Grace, Hodge, & McMahon, 2017). The life of an individual is understood to develop longitudinally, and within a complex set of social, ecological, and environmental systems (Bronfenbrenner & Morris,

2006). Although the threads of caregiving may be woven into the fabric of our society, where in many cultures multiple caregivers are the norm rather than the exception, at the heart of this system is the family (as most inclusively defined).

In the critical window of the first years of life, parents and primary carers are understood to be major players and have a 'direct effect', alongside early childhood contexts and other significant adults, in influencing childhood health, beliefs, attitudes, development, and learning (Martorell, 2017; Moore, Arefadib, Deery, Keyes, & West, 2017; Shonkoff, 2017). These factors are particularly associated with parental practices, lifestyle, the environments they move and work within, their past experiences and backgrounds, and their access to different types of capital (economic, human, and social) (Morin, Glickman, & Brooks-Gunn, 2015). From a social ecological perspective, the relationship between child, parent, and/ or main carer/s is understood to be situated, complex, and bi-directional (Bronfenbrenner, 2004).

Through this lens, the child and their characteristics and behaviours, as well as those of the adult/s, are understood to be influenced by, and in turn influence, each other (Moore & McDonald, 2013). For young children, the socially patterned exposure of early life events, particularly those that take place within micro-environments situated close to the child, are understood to impact on their current and future health behaviours, well-being, learning, development, and practices (Arabena, Panozzo, & Ritte, 2016; McMahon & Camberis, 2017). The term 'micro-environment' is understood to reflect 'an ecological niche', or specific location or boundary where an individual is most heavily influenced, or spends significant time (Brown, 2012, 2013).

A life-course perspective reinforces this thinking, and points to early life experiences having a pervasive influence on ongoing life trajectories (Grace, Hodge, et al., 2017; Shonkoff, 2017). Additionally, research reveals that interactions and environments are complex, and that early behaviours, experiences, and habits (particularly those that occur in the first three years of life) are often more difficult, and costly to change and address at a later point (Heckman, 2008; Heckman, Moon, Pinto, Savelyev, & Yavitz, 2010; Siegel, 2015).

Economic Rationalism, and the Trajectory of Early Life Experiences

Within the domestic space of the family home children are recognised to sit within multiple socio-cultural systems where these environments and significant adults and individuals in their lives will expose them to factors that can benefit, or adversely affect, their health, well-being, learning and development, social and cultural practices, and later responses (Martorell, 2017; Moore et al., 2017). The National Preventative Health Taskforce reinforcing this thinking (2009), commenting that "early childhood experiences may place children on health and developmental pathways that are costly and difficult to change. Therefore, children necessarily form the cornerstone of any prevention agenda" (p. 44).

This thinking, and new knowledge emerging from fields such as education, social science, neurobiology, and epigenetics (Cowan et al., 2016; Organisation for Economic Co-operation and Development [OECD], 2015; Shonkoff, 2017), continue to reinforce the significance that life events, genetics, quality experiences, and environments have on establishing the architecture of the brain, and being a key trajectory for future health, learning, and development. Alternatively, stressful experiences and early adversity, particularly in the first 1000 days of a child's life, may possibly change epidemics and can potentially have a 'cascading effect' across the lifespan (Moore et al., 2017). The results of those who have researched the phenomenon of the impact of early experiences tracking to future learning and development vary considerably, particularly in relation to the age group studied, the types of measurements used, and the length of time tracked. Researchers such as Wise (2009) contest the use of metaphors associated with the life-course framework such as 'trajectory', 'embedding', and 'programming', in terms of the highly deterministic path set from the over-reliance and reference to early life interactions. Wise suggests that this view oversimplifies the impact of 'early life exposures' and points out that "these early-life interactions are themselves subject to considerable later influences and therefore, may not be highly predictive of later outcomes" (p. S203).

The implications of this deterministic perspective are that it undermines the relevance of implementing a constructive framework, or a comprehensive policy that seeks to address effective intervention approaches after the critical period of early life. Others, however, are more optimistic, confirming the significance of tracking (Nader et al., 2006). The combination of these efforts attempt to validate a life-course perspective for the prevention of a range of health issues and preventable diseases, and as a significant reason for early health intervention.

What emerges is a paradigm, and a substantiated trend, that reinforces the impact of primary caregivers as pivotal in contributing to a child's early learning and development, and in promoting and sustaining positive, or negative, behaviours, health, and development in young children (Australian Institute of Health and Welfare, 2012; Melhuish et al., 2008; Moore et al., 2017). Although the life-course perspective has its critics, and not all of these views are commensurate, there is strong support for the discourse that early childhood experiences are increasingly understood to have a far-reaching and solidifying effect on the future of individuals (Shonkoff, 2017; Sweeny, 2014).

Of relevance to this chapter, and the rationale for the inclusion of this topic, is reinforcing the importance of being cognisant of contemporary literature, research, and groundwork that has been previously conducted in this space, yet critical in not adopting a universal lens, discourse, or application. This cautionary approach is supported by the likes of Moss (2015a, 2015b) and Wise (2009), who remind us that in entering the space of research with young families, and reviewing the contemporary literature, that we adopt a post-structuralist, post-feminist, and critical lens. This enables us to question, and cautiously assess and document the current discourse that exists, while also considering where the gaps, scope, and potential exist for innovative, respectful, and contemporary inquiry.

1.3   Young Families as Complex and Dynamic Systems

The idiosyncratic nature of young families and their interpretations, perspectives, and functions are located within dynamic systems. These systems, and the individuals that move within them, are ever-changing, and in a constant state of flux. So too are the many factors that impact on family relationships, practices, and in turn child outcomes and development (Fiese, 2013; Zubrick et al., 2012). Over the last two decades growing recognition and attention has focussed on the role of the environment, and the role of context on human behaviour, with 'the family' being understood as located within a dynamic and bioecological system (Brown, 2012; Grace, Hodge, et al., 2017). Building upon Bronfenbrenner's (1979; Bronfenbrenner & Morris, 2006) ecological systems theory, in which the child is positioned at the centre of a number of bi-directional and intersecting systems (including the micro-, meso-, chrono-, and macrosystems), we can also view young families as being located in a similar system with the child and family positioned at the centre of this system.

Adopting this framework, a social ecological, or family systems perspective views families as embedded within multiple systems and networks, and influenced directly and indirectly by a complex range of factors that exist both close to the home environment (at a micro level) and a broader, more distal level (macro/meso level), while being connected through and across time (chronosystem) (Neal & Neal, 2013; Stokols, 2000). We can only truly understand individuals within these places by appreciating their context, located within multiple environments and the wider social milieu (Bronfenbrenner, 1995; Brown, Stokols, Sallis, Hiatt, & Orleans, 2013). Research also needs to be underscored by valuing the contextual nuances that exist within these spaces. Context can be understood as a "unique set of conditions or circumstances that operate on or are embedded in the life of an individual, a group, a situation or an event, which gives meaning to its interpretation" (Brown & Reushle, 2010, p. 37; Oers, 1997).

This perspective recognises the great complexity and wide range of determinants that can impact on parent decision-making and support, even prior to the birth of a child. Some of these factors include: real or perceived concerns, socio-economic factors, time constraints, parenting styles (Schary, Cardinal, & Loprinzi, 2012; Veldhuis, van Grieken, Renders, HiraSing, & Raat, 2014), work-related issues, and level of education (Koplan, Liverman, Vivica, & Wisham, 2007; Lawlor & Mishra, 2009). Factors such as these also impact on specific parenting behaviours, such as parent engagement, the level of attachment, and the proactive support for a child's learning, experiences, and health (Zecevic, Tremblay, Lovsin, & Michel, 2010).

An important feature to recognise, according to both ecocultural and social ecological theory, is that family members are not passive in this process, and individually, as well as collectively, impact on the multiple environments in which they move, work, and live (Brown, 2012). When considering influences on the behaviours and practices of individuals within young families, one has to appreciate the agentic nature of parents and young children in the systems in which they are located, and the dynamic nature in which they make adjustments and adaptions within these environments (Bachraz & Grace, 2009). This is particularly important to keep in mind when engaging with young families in research, and will be addressed further in Chap. 2.

The appreciation that young families are located in context, and that a complex range of factors impact on their behaviours, practices, function, and the development of children in these spaces, is important to keep in mind for a range of reasons (Sameroff, 2009). First, it helps us to be critical about research, our own and others. Further, it helps us to be mindful when reviewing contemporary literature that might make universal claims, and recommendations based on interventions and studies conducted in one location and with particular groups, at a particular place in time (Moss, 2015a, 2015b). Finally, in terms of families as the subject of research, hopefully a greater appreciation of the locatedness of families in multiple contexts and systems increases our consciousness regarding the complexity of young families, and the range of determinants and environments in which they are embedded. This includes the importance of looking at the influence of macro- and meso-system factors, such as the impact of international contexts, policy, and politics.

This topic will be expanded further on further in Chap. 7, where more attention will be given to the embedded and locatedness of families as a framework, or lens of analysis. Adopting a social ecological framework is a powerful tool for helping us make sense of the range of factors that influence and impact on parents and young children. Although a number of key points will be highlighted in the next section of this chapter, key themes will be revisited in a number of other sections and touchpoints throughout this book.

Family and Children Shaped by Social and Cultural Contexts

A growing area of interest for researchers from a range of disciplines, including education and early childhood, are the mechanisms that influence parent values, beliefs, practices, and behaviours, and the flow-on these factors have on early life events, childhood practices, behaviour, development, health, and future life trajectories (Center on the Developing Child at Harvard University, 2010a; Lawrence et al., 2015; Zubrick et al., 2012). There is also great interest in the influence of environmental factors, such as the type of neighbourhood, types of capital, and other significant determinants (such as socio-economic status, level of parent education and employment, and self-efficacy), in shaping parenting practices, and parent engagement with children (Merlo, 2011). Within this space there are still so many unanswered questions, and phenomena to be explored regarding the interplay these variables might have on practices, such as the effectiveness of parenting, parent efficacy in supporting children's learning and development, maternal and child health, optimal learning environments for children, and parenting practices.

There is also a growing body of literature that reinforces the role and pervasive influence that positive family function, and the quality and strength of the relationships of significant adults, have on the development of a child's brain architecture, genetics, and holistic development, health, and well-being (Cowan et al., 2016; Moore & McDonald, 2013; Shonkoff, 2017). A child's cumulative exposure to adversity, adverse environments, and a range of 'risk factors' (such as sustained poverty, abuse, or mental illness) is also recognised to compromise their health, well-being, and development and negative long-term outcomes (Moloney, Weston, Qu, & Hayes, 2012; Moore & McDonald, 2013). Again, the literature points to adverse experiences that occur in the prenatal and post-natal period being particularly pervasive, and manifesting themselves later in life (in areas such as physical and mental health, participation in employment, and cognitive capacity).

Levels of adversity and pervasiveness of determinants appear to be dependent upon the prevalence and length of time of exposure to risk, as well as the presence of protective factors within these environments (Grace, Cashmore, Scott, & Hayes, 2017; Shonkoff, 2012). Moreover, research confirms that children exposed to multiple and/or cumulative risk factors have a greater likelihood of experiencing later developmental, health, and mental health problems. Those who support a prevention approach and positive psychology (Hamilton & Redmond, 2010; Seigman, 2013) reinforce the importance of focussing efforts on maximising protective factors and various types of capital in these environments (Morin et al., 2015) as a way of ameliorating the negative impact of these factors (Reupert, Maybery, & Kowalenko, 2012).

The Family Home: A Significant Micro-environment

Only over recent decades has attention focussed on the domestic space of the family home as a significant site of intervention and research. This environment is increasingly being recognised as a critical leverage point for facilitating, or hindering, the health behaviours, well-being, and the development and learning of children (Emerson et al., 2012; Shonkoff, 2017). For young children, micro-environments are of particular significance, the main of which being 'the family home', or main domestic space in which family members reside. In this space, the construct of family ecology could include: family demographics, the dynamics and family make-up, family rules, the beliefs and values of each of its members, culture, and occupation of parents and the socio-economic status of the family.

Factors that sit within, and amongst, these various systems are recognised to be interconnected, complex, and dynamic. These multiple factors are located within a web of inherent and explicit factors, arrived at from multiple sources, and embedded in parent choices, behaviours, their own life experiences, beliefs, and actions, as well as those of children in these environments (Jamner & Stokols, 2000; McMahon & Camberis, 2017). In this book a number of definitions of 'an environment' have been combined, and will therefore be defined as, 'an objective or perceived context or boundary (either physical or possessing a particular place or space in time) that can include built environments, neighbourhoods, buildings, roads, recreational facilities including places where people work, play and live' (Brown, 2012; Davison & Lawson, 2006; Sallis & Glanz, 2006).

We also need to factor in the temporality in which families are located, which includes recognising that this temporality considers the history of lived experience not only over a life course, and through generations, but also at a particular moment in time. As a 'collective', all of these elements influence the relationships, behaviours, values, and attitudes of parents, and their support for their children (Bronfenbrenner, 1979). Whilst there may be other micro-environments, which includes the extended family, the local neighbourhood, extra-curricular facilities, playgroups, and peers, as well as care and educational setting, the home environment is deemed to be most influential in impacting on experiences, behaviours, development, health, and well-being of young children (Center on the Developing Child at Harvard University, 2016a; McMahon & Camberis, 2017).

It is important at this point to reinforce that it is also acknowledged that each context is complex and idiosyncratic, with no two micro-environments the same. This complexity is illustrated in a study conducted by Salmon and his colleagues (2005), who explored whether there was any correlation or relationship between the amount of children's television viewing and low activity levels. Their findings identified that the relationship between television viewing and activity levels was not linear or one dimensional, but was complex and very distinct in nature. Therefore, overlapping the impact that 'an environment', or multiple environments have on influencing a phenomenon is the intrinsic range of determinants also present which influence the same phenomenon. 'Determinants' are defined as 'a range of factors that significantly contribute to or impact on a phenomenon or complex set of behaviours' (Brown, 2012; Sallis, Prochaska, & Taylor, 2000).

In this text, it is suggested that determinants move within various microsystems and environments, with one of these being the domestic space in which the family resides. These determinants are a powerful force in influencing what motivates, or inhibits, parents' attitudes, dispositions, and practices, as well as those of young children. Further, there is a need to move beyond assuming that all people are affected by similar environmental factors and determinants. The uniqueness and nuances that exist within an associated context can alter the power and the way environmental determinants influence the behaviours, practices, and perspectives of individual families (Hertzman & Williams, 2009).

Parents and Young Families as Sites for Intervention

Young families are increasingly identified as a cornerstone of many interventions and prevention agendas. This is predicated on the premise that the home environment, and other factors, such as parental support, parent or carer's capabilities, positive experiences, and supportive environments, can have a profound impact on affording, or hindering, short- and long-term health, well-being, and development in children (Center on the Developing Child at Harvard University, 2016b; Moore & McDonald, 2013). Further, it is understood that these outcomes can be improved through intervention intended to build parent capacity (Emerson et al., 2012; Walker & Berthelsen, 2010), and optimise the environment in which children and families spend significant time (Cowan et al., 2016; Kiser, 2015). As such, a growing number of studies and interventions are underpinned by parents being significant gatekeepers, and therefore recognised as a critical factor in intervention strategies. This is underpinned by a position that children, particularly in vulnerable settings, have better opportunities for learning and holistic health outcomes when intervention occurs early in the domestic space of the family home settings, and other locations in which they spend significant time (such as early learning settings).

What is interesting to note is that discourse and targeted contextual findings reinforce the value and opportunity for engaging in research with young families, particularly evidence-based practice of targeted populations who are vulnerable or experiencing adversity (Moore & McDonald, 2013). Leaders in the field also reinforce that early intervention applied more universally not only builds capacity with those young families identified as vulnerable, but is a way of capacity building with all young families (Shonkoff & Fisher, 2013).

However, some leaders in the field, such as Moss (2015b), caution against making universal claims, or adopting a 'one size fits all' discourse, such as that of the deterministic and positivist statements associated with early experiences impacting on a life-course outcomes. Moss highlights concerns regarding "assertions of the long-term and widespread benefits of early childhood education" and early intervention based on "iconic studies" which were context specific and temporally different (p. 91). He supports this position by pointing to the Penn report (2006) where "reviewers caution against generalizing from research conducted in such very specific spatial and temporal contexts" (p. 91).

Moss' cautionary position is worthy of consideration when reviewing research and findings related to intervention targeted at children and young families. It is important as researchers when entering into, or engaging in this research space that we do so critically and cautiously, yet open to the possibilities and potentialities of engaging in a range of exciting and valuable research. For example, research in these spaces may enable evaluation of intervention that measures the impact of programs, such as tracking the long-term social and developmental outcomes and capacities of children, and how this intervention impacts on building stronger and healthier communities.

Contributing to the field of intervention research may also enable researchers to build upon the strengths, resources, wisdom, and human/social capital, which already exists, and is evidenced in the family home, associated environments, and education and support services, therefore complimenting and building upon existing capital, with additional tools, connections, and knowledge to support better outcomes for children and families. Finally, despite the critical roles that parents play in the short- and long-term development and health outcomes of children, there is still untapped potential and research that is worth exploring, including "the mechanisms of parental influence" (Trost et al., 2003, p. 277), and qualitative research that seeks to explore the ecological factors that influence parental values, practices, and support particular early childhood behaviours (Brown, 2012; Pearce, 2009).

Young Families and the Home Environment—Critical Spaces for Research

In 'surveying the terrain' of this chapter, hopefully it is conveyed that while raising children is a collective undertaking, young families, parents, and other key adults are at the heart of these endeavours and play a significant role in the health, well-being, and development of young children. As researchers, hopefully we also recognise and appreciate the richness and dynamic nature of the spaces and places in which young families live, work, and play and the insights members of young families can provide of their everyday lives (Harden, Backett-Milburn, Hill, & MacLean, 2010).

The home environment offers so much potential as being a significant environment for affording, or restricting, childhood behaviours, learning and development. The complex, dynamic, and idiosyncratic nature of these domestic environments and the multiple systems, determinants, environments, and contexts in which young families are embedded make this field of research important (Shonkoff, 2012). This includes inquiry, which seeks to investigate the degree to which ecological factors influence parent behaviours and decisions (how they think, value, are motivated, and feel). Also worth investigating are the sites and domestic spaces in which young families are located, and how these environments impact on family behaviours, practices, but also on the learning and development of young children.

The intent of this chapter was to showcase key areas where research is currently being conducted, and areas of current focus, in relation to young families, as well as to highlight the complexity and the richness of these environments. It is hoped that readers develop an increased appreciation for the unprecedented potential of engaging in research with or about young families, and to build upon and further explore areas of paucity in this field. These pursuits possibly include investigating insights that family members' lived experiences can offer us, the idiosyncratic nature of 'the family', and the nuanced social ecological systems in which they are located.

Many disciplines, multi-disciplinary teams, and fields of expertise are increasingly seeing value in researching with and about families, including insights into their affordances, home settings and environments, behaviours, values, and practices (Anandalalakshmy, Chaudhary, & Sharma, 2008; Bushin, 2009; Coe, Reynolds, Boehm, Meredith Hess, & Rae-Espinoza, 2011; Daly, 2007; Dockett et al., 2009; Harden et al., 2010). Many are also venturing beyond traditional boundaries and methods of research, recognising the importance of critically reflecting on issues such as agency, consent, power, rights, voice, and level of involvement of family members in research (Bermúdez et al., 2016; Greenstein & Davis, 2012; Hägglund, 2012; Hendricks & Mirka Koro-Ljungberg, 2015). In the end, a common goal that drives many of us is that our research contributes insight and findings that will help to create stronger, more resilient families and family practices.

Conclusion—Why Research 'with' Young Families in Ethical and Respectful Research?

So why invest time and money researching about, or with, young families? Why pursue the insights, narratives, and perspective of young families? It is appreciated that all qualitative research, to some degree, involves engaging 'with' participants in inquiry. However, researching 'with' others in inquiry varies greatly, dependent on interpretations of 'participant involvement', the degree to which involvement is embraced and valued, and the research methods and practices employed (Bergold & Thomas, 2012; Palaiologou, 2014). This text adopts the approach of researching 'with', and 'of', young families in ethical and respectful research, rather than 'researching on' young families. This reflects contemporary positioning and innovative approaches to research, as well as the body of literature that addresses aspects of interactional constraints (Roulston, 2014), and the interplay between power and powerlessness, which often emerge prior to and during all stages of the inquiry process (Greenstein & Davis, 2013; Vähäsantanen & Saarinen, 2013).

Consequently, rather than 'researching on' young families (where individuals are viewed as objects), this text reflects a more inclusive and respectful approach to 'researching with young families'. This approach adopts a perspective in which individuals are recognised as having the right to participate, individuals having agency, as well an appreciation of their significant contribution to meaning-making (Gray & Winter, 2011; Palaiologou, 2014; Sumsion & Goodfellow, 2012). Affording family members the opportunity to engage with us in inquiry, and to share their stories, reflects the value placed on their voices and insight. In doing so, we celebrate how their insights contribute to our understandings of their lives, behaviours, and nuanced worlds (Geia et al., 2013; Rinaldi, 2006).

Researching 'of' or 'with' young families acknowledges the intent and value placed on exploring the lifeworlds and meaning-making of others, sensitively and respectfully, and ensuring that the rights and well-being of each party are considered, and that the methods employed afford for ethical and humane practices, as well as respectful and meaningful relationships (Hammersley, 2015). Researching 'with' acknowledges the importance of participant involvement (Dockett et al., 2009; Gabb, 2010; Sumsion & Goodfellow, 2012). And, just like our image of the child will impact on the way we observe, engage with, and support children, considering the way that we position inquiry with young families will impact on the strategies and decision-making we employ, prior to and during our engagement and in conducting research. Furthermore, adopting practices that are ethical and respectful assists us in producing rich data, ensuring benefits for all stakeholders, and representing new possibilities in rendering our research with families respectfully, authentically, and dialogically.

References

Ajandi, J. (2011). "Single mothers by choices": Disrupting dominant discourses of the family through social justice alternatives. *International Journal of Child, Youth and Family Studies, 2*(3/4), 410–431.

Anandalalakshmy, S., Chaudhary, N., & Sharma, N. (Eds.). (2008). *Researching families and children*. Thousand Oaks, CA: Sage.

Arabena, K., Panozzo, S., & Ritte, R. (2016). 'What hope can look like': The first 1000 days – Aboriginal and Torres Strait Islander children and their families. *The Child, Youth and Family Work Journal, 44*, 25–36.

Australian Bureau of Statistics. (2016). *Family characteristics and transitions, Australia, 2012–2013*. Retrieved from http://www.abs.gov.au/ausstats/abs@.nsf/mf/4442.0

Australian Institute of Health and Welfare. (2012). *A picture of Australia's children 2012. Cat. no. PHE 167*. Retrieved from Canberra, ACT. https://www.aihw.gov.au/getmedia/31c0a364-dbac-4e88-8761-d9c87bc2dc29/14116.pdf.aspx

Bachraz, V., & Grace, R. (2009). Creating a different kind of normal: Parent and child perspectives on sibling relationships when one child in the family has autism spectrum disorder. *Contemporary Issues in Early Childhood, 10*(4), 317–330.

Baxter, J. (2016). *The modern Australian family*. Retrieved from Melbourne, VIC. https://aifs.gov.au/sites/default/files/families-week2016-final-20160517.pdf

Bergold, J., & Thomas, S. (2012). Participatory research methods: A methodological approach in motion. *Historical Social Research/Historische Sozialforschung, 37*, 191–222.

Bermúdez, J. M., Muruthi, B., & Jordan, L. (2016). Decolonizing research methods for family science: Creating space at the centre – Decolonizing research practices. *Journal of Family Theory & Review, 8*(2), 192–206.

Bratich, J. (2017). Observation in a surveilled world. In N. Denzin & N. Lincoln (Eds.), *The SAGE handbook of qualitative research*. Thousand Oaks, CA: Sage.

Bronfenbrenner, U. (1979). *The ecology of human development*. Cambridge, MA: Harvard University Press.

Bronfenbrenner, U. (1995). Developmental psychology through space and time. In P. Moen, G. Elder Jr., & K. Luscher (Eds.), *Examining lives in context* (pp. 619–647). Washington, DC: American Psychological Association Press.

Bronfenbrenner, U. (2004). *Making human beings human: Bioecological perspectives on human development*. Thousand Oaks, CA: Sage.

Bronfenbrenner, U., & Morris, P. (2006). The bioecological model of human development. In W. Damon & R. M. Lerner (Eds.), *Handbook of child psychology, volume 1, theoretical models of human development* (6th ed., pp. 793–828). New York: Wiley.

Brown, A. (2012). *The new frontier: A social ecological exploration of factors impacting on parental support for the active play of young children within the micro-environment of the family home*. PhD, University of Southern Queensland, Toowoomba, QLD.

Brown, A. (2013, October 3–November 2). *The parental and micro-environmental model (PMEM): A conceptual framework for exploring factors that impact on early adult/child relationships*. Paper presented at the Infant and early childhood social and emotional wellbeing conference, Canberra, ACT. http://www.iecsewc2013.net.au/presentations/Alice-Brown.pdf

Brown, A., & Reushle, S. (2010). People, pedagogy and the power of connection. *Studies in Learning, Evaluation, Innovation and Development, 7*(3), 37–48.

Brown, A., & Smolenaers, E. (2016). Parents' interpretations of screen time recommendations for children under two years. *Journal of Family Issues, 20*, 1–24.

Brown, A., Stokols, D., Sallis, J., Hiatt, R., & Orleans, T. (2013). *The possibilities and potential of social ecological frameworks to understand health behaviours and outcomes*. Paper presented at the proceeding of: Symposium (24) presented at the 34th annual conference of the Society of Behavioral Medicine, San Francisco. http://www.sbm.org/UserFiles/file/Symposium_24_Stokols.pdf

Bushin, N. (2009). Researching family migration decision making: A children-in-families approach. *Population, Space and Place, 15*(5), 429–443.

Byard, E., Kosciw, J., & Bartkiewicz, M. (2013). Schools and LGBT-parent families: Creating change through programming and advocacy. In A. E. Goldberg & K. R. Allen (Eds.), *LGBT-parent families: Innovations in research and implications for practice* (pp. 275–290). New York: Springer.

Center on the Developing Child at Harvard University. (2010a). *The foundations of lifelong health are built in early childhood*. Retrieved from http://www.developingchild.harvard.edu

Center on the Developing Child at Harvard University. (2010b). *The foundations of lifelong health are built in early childhood*. Retrieved from Cambridge, MA: http://www.developingchild.harvard.edu

Center on the Developing Child at Harvard University. (2016a). *Building core capabilities for life: The science behind the skills adults need to succeed in parenting and in the workplace*. http://www.ddcf.org/globalassets/child-well-being/16-0304-core-capabilities-for-life.pdf

Center on the Developing Child at Harvard University. (2016b). *From best practices to breakthrough impacts: A science-based approach to building a more promising future for young children and families*. Retrieved from http://46y5eh11fhgw3ve3ytpwxt9r.wpengine.netdna-cdn.com/wpcontent/uploads/2016/05/HCDC_From_Best_Practices_to_Breakthrough_Impacts.pdf

Centre for Social Research and Evaluation. (2011). *Parents as first teachers evaluation: Phase II report*. Retrieved from New Zealand, QLD. https://www.msd.govt.nz/documents/about-msd-and-our-work/publications-resources/evaluation/parents-as-firstteachers/parents-as-first-teachers-evaluation-phase-2-report1.pdf

Coe, C., Reynolds, R., Boehm, D., Meredith Hess, J., & Rae-Espinoza, H. (Eds.). (2011). *Everyday ruptures: Children, youth and migration in global perspective*. Nashville, TN: Vanderbilt.

Cowan, C., Callaghan, B., Kan, J., & Richardson, R. (2016). The lasting impact of early-life adversity on individuals and their descendants: Potential mechanisms and hope for intervention. *Genes, Brain and Behavior, 15*(1), 155–168.

Dahlberg, G., & Moss, P. (2005). *The ethics and politics of early childhood education.* New York: Routledge Falmer.

Daly, K. J. (2007). *Qualitative methods for family studies and human development.* Thousand Oaks, CA: Sage.

Davison, K., & Lawson, C. (2006). Do attributes in the physical environment influence children's physical activity? A review of the literature. *International Journal of Behavioural Nutrition and Physical Activity, 3*(19), 1–17.

Dockett, S., Perry, B., Kearney, E., Hamshire, A., Mason, J., & Schmied, V. (2009). Researching with families: Ethical issues and situations. *Contemporary Issues in Early Childhood, 10*(4), 353–365.

Eisenstadt, N. (2011). *Providing a Sure Start: How government discovered early childhood.* Bristol, UK: Policy Press.

Emerson, L., Fear, J., Fox, S., & Sanders, E. (2012). *Parental engagement in learning and schooling: Lessons from research. A report by the Australian Research Alliance for Children and Youth (ARACY) for the Family-School and Community Partnerships Bureau.* Retrieved from Canberra, ACT. https://www.aracy.org.au/publicationsresources/command/download_file/id/7/filename/Parental_engagement_in_learning_and_schooling_Lessons_from_research_BUREAU_ARACY_August_2012.pdf

Fiese, B. (2013). Family context in early childhood. In O. Saracho & B. Spodek (Eds.), *Handbook of research on the education of young children* (3rd ed., pp. 369–384). New York: Routledge.

Foucault, M. (1979). *Discipline and punish: The birth of the prison.* New York: Vintage/Random House.

Gabb, J. (2010). Home truths: Ethical issues in family research. *Qualitative Research, 10*(4), 461–478.

Geia, L. K., Hayes, B., & Usher, K. (2013). Yarning/Aboriginal storytelling: Towards an understanding of an Indigenous perspective and its implications for research practice. *Contemporary Nurse, 46*(1), 13–17.

Goldberg, A. E. (2014). Lesbian, gay, and heterosexual adoptive parents' experiences in preschool environments. *Early Childhood Research Quarterly, 29*(4), 669–681.

Grace, R., Cashmore, J., Scott, D., & Hayes, A. (2017). Effective policy to support children, families and communities. In R. Grace, K. Hodge, & C. McMahon (Eds.), *Children, families and communities* (pp. 358–375). South Melbourne, VIC: Oxford University Press.

Grace, R., Hayes, A., & Wise, S. (2017). Child development in context. In R. Grace, K. Hodge, & C. McMahon (Eds.), *Children, families and communities*. South Melbourne, VIC: Oxford University Press.

Grace, R., Hodge, K., & McMahon, C. (Eds.). (2017). *Children, families and communities* (5th ed.). South Melbourne, VIC: Oxford University Press.

Gray, C., & Winter, E. (2011). Hearing voices: participatory research with preschool children with and without disabilities. *European Early Childhood Education Research Journal, 19*(3), 309–320.

Greenstein, T. N., & Davis, S. N. (2012). *Methods of family research*. Thousand Oaks, CA: Sage.

Greenstein, T. N., & Davis, S. N. (2013). *Methods of family research* (3rd ed.). Thousand Oaks, CA/Los Angeles: Sage.

Hägglund, S. (2012). Forward. In J. Sarjeant & D. Harcourt (Eds.), *Doing ethical research with children*. Maidenhead, UK: Open University Press.

Hamilton, M., & Redmond, G. (2010). *Conceptualisation of social and emotional wellbeing for children and young people, and policy implications*. Retrieved from https://www.aracy.org.au/publicationsresources/command/download_file/id/91/filename/Conceptualisation_of_social_and_emotional_wellbeing_for_children_and_young_people,_and_policy_implications.pdf

Hammersley, M. (2015). On ethical principles for social research. *International Journal of Social Research Methodology, 128*(4), 433–449.

Harden, J., Backett-Milburn, K., Hill, M., & MacLean, A. (2010). Oh, what a tangled web we weave: Experiences of doing 'multiple perspectives' research in families. *International Journal of Social Research Methodology, 13*(5), 441–452.

Heckman, J. (2006, February 8–9). *The economics of investing in early childhood prevention: Invest now or pay later*. Paper presented at the NIFTeY National Conference, Sydney.

Heckman, J. (2008). Schools, skills, and synapses. *Economic Inquiry, 46*(3), 289–324.

Heckman, J., & Masterov, D. (2007). *The productivity argument for investing in young children*. Review of Agricultural Economics, *American Agricultural Economics Association*, 29(3), 446–493.

Heckman, J., Moon, S. H., Pinto, R., Savelyev, P. A., & Yavitz, A. Q. (2010). The rate of the return to the High/Scope Perry preschool program. *Journal of Public Economics, 94*(1–2), 114–128.

Hendricks, J., & Mirka Koro-Ljungberg, M. (2015). Inquiring through and with Deleuze: Disrupting theory and qualitative methods in family studies. *Journal of Family Theory & Review, 7*(3), 265–283.

Hertzman, C., & Williams, R. (2009). Making early childhood count. *Canadian Medical Association Journal, 180*(1), 68–71.

Jamner, M., & Stokols, D. (Eds.). (2000). *Promoting human wellness: New frontiers for research, practice, and policy*. Ewing, NJ: University of California Press.

Kiser, L. J. (2015). *Strengthening family coping resources: Intervention for families impacted by trauma*. New York: Routledge.

Knudsen, E., Heckman, J., Cameron, J., & Shonkoff, J. P. (2006). Economic, neurobiological, and behavioral perspectives on building America's future workforce. *Proceedings from the National Academy of Science of the United States of America, 103*(27), 10155–10162.

Koplan, J., Liverman, C., Vivica, K., & Wisham, S. (2007). *Progress in preventing childhood obesity: How do we measure up?* Washington, DC: The National Academies Press.

Lamanna, M. A., Riedmann, A., & Stewart, S. D. (2015). *Marriages, families, and relationships: Making choices in a diverse society* (12th ed.). Belmont, CA: Cengage Learning.

Lawlor, D., & Mishra, G. (2009). Why family matters. An introduction. In D. Lawlor & G. Mishra (Eds.), *Family matters: Designing, analysing and understanding family based studies in life course epidemiology*. Oxford, UK: Oxford University Press.

Lawrence, D., Johnson, S., Hafekost, J., Boterhoven De Haan, K., Sawyer, M., Ainley, J., & Zubrick, S. (2015). *The mental health children and adolescents. Report on the second Australian child and adolescent survey of mental health and wellbeing*. Retrieved from Canberra, ACT. https://www.health.gov.au/internet/main/publishing.nsf/Content/9DA8CA21306FE6EDCA257E2700016945/$File/child2.pdf

Lohoar, S., Butera, N., & Kennedy, E. (2014). *Strengths of Australian Aboriginal cultural practices in family life and child rearing*. Retrieved from https://aifs.gov.au/cfca/sites/default/files/publication-documents/cfca25.pdf

Mannion, K., & Walker, B. (2015). Families as first teachers: Engaging families, strengthening learning and successful transitions. *Every Child, 21*(2), 10.

Martorell, R. (2017). Improved nutrition in the first 1000 days and adult human capital and health. *American Journal of Human Biology, 29*(2).

McCarthy, J. R. (2012). Why family meanings? In J. R. McCarthy, M. Doolittle, & S. D. Schlater (Eds.), *Understanding family meanings: A reflective text* (pp. 1–21). Bristol, UK: The Open University.

McCarthy, J. R., Doolittle, M., & Schlater, S. D. (2012). *Understanding family meanings: A reflective text*. Bristol, UK: The Open University.

McCarthy, J. R., & Edwards, R. (2011). *Key concepts in family studies*. Thousand Oaks, CA: Sage.

McCubbin, L. D., McCubbin, H. I., Zhang, W., Kehl, L., & Strom, I. (2013). Relational well-being: An indigenous perspective and measure. *Family Relations, 62*(2), 354–365.

McMahon, C., & Camberis, A. (2017). Family as the primary context of children's development. In R. Grace, K. Hodge, & C. McMahon (Eds.), *Children, families and communities*. South Melbourne, VIC: Oxford University Press.

Melhuish, E., Phan, M., Sylva, K., Sammons, P., Siraj-Blatchford, I., & Taggart, B. (2008). Effects of the home learning environment and preschool centre experience upon literacy and numeracy development in early primary school. *Journal of Social Issues, 64*(1), 95–114.

Merlo, J. (2011). Contextual influences on the individual life course: Building a research framework for social epidemiology. *Psychosocial Intervention, 20*(1), 109–118.

Moloney, L., Weston, R., Qu, L., & Hayes, A. (2012). *Families, life events, and family service delivery. A literature review* (Research report No. 20). Retrieved from Melbourne, VIC. https://aifs.gov.au/sites/default/files/publication-documents/rr20_0.pdf

Montirosso, R., & Provenzi, L. (2015). Implications of epigenetics and stress regulation on research and developmental care of preterm infants. *Journal of Obstetric, Gynecologic, & Neonatal Nursing, 44*(2), 174–182.

Moore, T., Arefadib, N., Deery, A., Keyes, M., & West, S. (2017). *The first thousand days: An evidence paper – Summary*. Parkville, VIC: Centre for Community Child Health, Murdoch Children's Research Institute.

Moore, T., & McDonald, M. (2013). *Acting early, changing lives: How prevention and early action saves money and improves wellbeing. Prepared for The Benevolent Society*. Retrieved from Parkville, VIC: http://www.benevolent.org.au/~/media/Benevolent/Think/Actingearlychanginglives%20pdf.ashx

Moore, T., McDonald, M., McHugh-Dillon, H., & West, S. (2016). *Community engagement: A key strategy for improving outcomes for Australian families*. Retrieved from Melbourne, VIC.

Mori, S., Nakamoto, H., Mizuochi, H., Ikudome, S., & Gabbard, C. (2013). Influence of affordances in the home environment on motor development of young children in Japan. *Child Development Research*, 898406, 1–5. https://doi.org/10.1155/2013/898406.

Morin, M., Glickman, J., & Brooks-Gunn, J. (2015). Parenting and the home environment. In A. Farrell, S. Kagan, E. Tisdall, & M. Kay (Eds.), *The Sage handbook of early childhood research*. Thousand Oaks, CA: Sage.

Moss, P. (2015a). Time for more storytelling. *European Early Childhood Education Research Journal, 23*(1), 1–4.

Moss, P. (2015b). Where am I? Position and perspective in researching early childhood education. In A. Farrell, S. Kagan, E. Tisdall, & M. Kay (Eds.), *The Sage Handbook of Early Childhood Research*. Thousand Oaks, CA: Sage.

Mustard, F. (2008). *Investing in the early years: Closing the gap between what we know and what we do*. Retrieved from Adelaide, South Australia: http://www.thinkers.sa.gov.au/lib/pdf/Mustard_Final_Report.pdf

Nader, P., O'Brien, M., Houts, R., Bradley, R., Belsky, J., Crosnoe, R., et al. (2006). Identifying risk for obesity in early childhood. *Pediatrics, 118*(5), 594–601.

National Preventative Health Taskforce. (2009). *Australia: The healthiest country by 2020 – National Preventative Health Strategy – The roadmap for action*. Retrieved from http://www.afa.org.au/images/PressReleases/PHT_Report.pdf

Neal, J. W., & Neal, Z. (2013). Nested or networked? Future directions for ecological systems theory. *Social Development, 22*(4), 722–737.

Oers, V. (1997). From context to contextualizing. *Learning and Instruction, 8*(6), 473–488.

Organisation for Economic Co-operation and Development (OECD). (2015). *Starting Strong IV: Monitoring quality in early childhood education and care*. Retrieved from Paris: http://www.keepeek.com/Digital-Asset-Management/oecd/education/starting-strong-iv_9789264233515-en#.V-ITUvl97IU

Palaiologou, I. (2014). 'Do we hear what children want to say?' Ethical praxis when choosing research tools with children under five. *Early Child Development and Care, 184*(5), 689–705.

Paris, D., & Winn, M. (Eds.). (2014). *Humanizing research: Decolonizing qualitative inquiry with youth and communities*. London: Sage.

Pearce, P. (2009). Physical activity: Not just for quantitative researchers (comment). *Qualitative Health Research, 19*(7), 879–880.

Poulton, R., Moffitt, T. E., & Silva, P. A. (2015). The Dunedin Multidisciplinary Health and Development Study: Overview of the first 40 years, with an eye to the future. *Social Psychiatry and Psychiatric Epidemiology, 50*(5), 679–693.

Reupert, A., Maybery, D., & Kowalenko, N. (2012). Children whose parents have a mental illness: Prevalence, need and treatment. *Medical Journal of Australia, 1*(Supp 1), 7–9.

Rinaldi, C. (2006). *In dialogue with Reggio Emilia: Listening, researching, and learning*. London: Routledge Falmer.

Rogers, P. (2016). Family is NOT an institution: Distinguishing institutions from organisations in social science and social theory. *International Review of Sociology, 27*(1), 1–16.

Roulston, K. (2014). Interactional problems in research interviews. *Qualitative Research, 14*(3), 277–293.

Sallis, J., & Glanz, K. (2006). The role of built environments in physical activity, eating, and obesity in childhood. *Future of Children, 16*(1), 89–108.

Sallis, J., Prochaska, J., & Taylor, W. (2000). A review of correlates of physical activity of children and adolescents. *Medicine and Science in Sports and Exercise, 32*(5), 963–975.

Salmon, J., Timperio, A., Telford, A., Carver, A., & Crawford, D. (2005). Association of family environment with children's television viewing and with low level of physical activity. *Obesity Research, 13*(11), 1939–1951.

Sameroff, A. (2009). *The transactional model of development: How children and contexts shape each other.* Washington, DC: American Psychological Association.

Save The Children. (2009). *State of the worlds mothers 2009: Investing in the early years.* https://www.savethechildren.org/content/dam/usa/reports/advocacy/sowm/sowm-2009.pdf?WT.mc_id=0509_sowm_b_fullr

Schary, D., Cardinal, B., & Loprinzi, P. (2012). Parenting style associated with sedentary behaviour in preschool children. *Early Child Development and Care, 182*(8), 1015–1026.

Seigman, M. (2013). *Building the State of Wellbeing: A strategy for South Australia.* Retrieved from Adelaide, South Australia: http://www.thinkers.sa.gov.au/seligmanreport/

Shehan, C. L. (2016). *The Wiley Blackwell encyclopedia of family studies, 4 volume set* (Vol. 4). Chichester, UK: Wiley.

Shonkoff, J. P. (2012). Leveraging the biology of adversity to address the roots of disparities in health and development. *Proceedings from the National Academy of Science of the United States of America, 109*(Supp 2), 1–6.

Shonkoff, J. P. (2013). *Building adult capabilities to improve child outcomes: A theory of change.* Retrieved from http://developingchild.harvard.edu/resources/multimedia/videos/theory_of_change/

Shonkoff, J. P. (2017). Breakthrough impacts. What science tells us about supporting early childhood development. *Young Children, 72*(2), 8–16.

Shonkoff, J. P., & Fisher, P. (2013). Rethinking evidence-based practice and two-generation programs to create the future of early childhood policy. *Development and Psychopathology, 25*(4), 1635–1653.

Siegel, D. (2015). Interpersonal neurobiology as a lens into the development of wellbeing and resilience. *Children Australia, 40*(2), 160–164.

Stokols, D. (2000). The social ecological paradigm of wellness promotion. In M. Jamner & D. Stokols (Eds.), *Promoting human wellness: New frontiers for research, practice and policy* (pp. 21–37). Berkeley, CA: University of California Press.

Sumsion, J., & Goodfellow, J. (2012). 'Looking and listening-in': A methodological approach to generating insights into infants' experiences of early childhood education and care settings. *European Early Childhood Education Research Journal, 20*(3), 313–327.

Sweeny, K. (2014). *The influence of childhood circumstances on adult health: Report to the Mitchell Institute for Health and Education Policy.* Retrieved from Melbourne, VIC. http://vuir.vu.edu.au/31117/1/Influence-of-childhood-circumstances-on-adult-health.pdf

Trost, S., Sallis, J., Pate, R., Freedson, P., Taylor, W., & Dowda, M. (2003). Evaluating a model of parental influence on youth physical activity. *American Journal of Preventive Medicine, 25*(4), 277–282.

Vähäsantanen, K., & Saarinen, J. (2013). The power dance in the research interview: Manifesting power and powerlessness. *Qualitative Researcher, 13*(5), 493–510.

Veldhuis, L., van Grieken, A., Renders, C., HiraSing, R., & Raat, H. (2014). Parenting style, the home environment, and screen time of 5 year old children: The 'Be Active, Eat Right' study. *PLoS On, 9*(2). https://doi.org/10.1371/journal.pone.0088486.

Walker, S., & Berthelsen, D. (2010). Social inequalities and parent involvement in children's education in the early years of school. In V. Green & S. Cherrington (Eds.), *Delving into diversity: An international exploration of issues of diversity in education* (pp. 139–149). New York: Nova Science Publishers.

Wise, P. (2009). Confronting social disparities in child health: A critical appraisal of life-course science and research. *Pediatrics, 124*(3), 203–211.

Wise, S. (2003). *Family structure, child outcomes and environmental mediators: An overview of the development in Diverse Families study* (Research paper no. 30). Retrieved from http://www.aifs.org.au/institute/pubs/wise5.html

Zecevic, C., Tremblay, L., Lovsin, T., & Michel, L. (2010). Parental influence on young children's physical activity. *International Journal of Pediatrics, 468526*, 1–9. https://doi.org/10.1155/2010/468526.

Zubrick, S., Smith, G., Nicholson, J., Sanson, A., Jackiewicz, T., & LSAC Research Consortium. (2012). *Parenting and families in Australia.* Retrieved from Canberra, ACT. https://www.dss.gov.au/sites/default/files/documents/05_2012/sprp34.pdf

2

'An Audit on Self'—Positioning Ourselves for Researching with Young Families

Scenario 2: A Cup of Tea, and Time to Reflect on One's Positionality

Alice is preparing to embark on the data collection phase of her research project, a research journey that she has spent several years committed to now. Her goal being to explore active play within these environments, and the pervasive influence that multiple factors exert on parental practices, understandings, and values. Often times during these solitary days and months, she has felt like an explorer, journeying through unchartered territory, required to take risks, and track through ground that was often troubling. Like grappling with how she might engage in authentic, rigorous, and meaningful research about young families, yet go about it respectfully, conscious to create 'humanising spaces'. As she sits in her comfortable arm chair, a cup of tea in hand, and a computer balanced surreptitiously on her lap, she allows herself time to ponder and reflect on the task ahead of her. She considers how she might enter into the private lives of families to interview parents, scan the environment, attempt to walk in their shoes, and perhaps, rather naively, attempt to see these domestic spaces through their eyes in order to gain a contextual understanding of the idiosyncratic experiences and motivations of these families.

In the quiet of her lounge room, she reflects back on her early motivations to explore the topic of active play, thinking back to her frustration as a teacher

© The Author(s) 2019
A. Brown, *Respectful Research With and About Young Families*, Palgrave Studies in Education Research Methods, https://doi.org/10.1007/978-3-030-02716-2_2

at the overcrowded curriculum, and lack of priority given to physical activity. She remembers her concerns over 'adult-controlled', and 'sports-focussed' lessons, where competitive games were turning children away from the enjoyment of free play and the joy of creative exploration. She thinks back to her own childhood, and of being a free-ranged kid, where the days were one big long play, and the only care in the world was 'How long till the sun went down?' There weren't too many restrictions, limits, or boundaries, and most of the playing took place in trees, backyards a few blocks away, sidewalks, streets, vacant blocks, or any spare mud puddle to be found. She contemplates the childhood of many children today, who prefer to spend their leisure time stimulated by computers, televisions, and screens, rather than playing outside. Finally, she is reminded of her reading on the topic of the importance of active play and movement in the first three years of life, and the impact this has on all areas of long-term health and development.

While she recognises her inescapable subjectivity as a social researcher, she is still concerned about how her positionality, and the way that she views the world, might bias the 'shoes' that she wears into entering, and researching in the domestic spaces of young families. As she continues to think about this, she realises that her subjectivity is much more subsuming than that, and has already impacted on the decisions she has made regarding the focus of her research, the questions posed, and the methods she has chosen to employ to seek answers to the phenomenon she wishes to investigate. It becomes clear to her that she is overtly and actively shaped by her standpoint and position, and that this will frame and filter into all aspects of her research journey.

As time passes, she moves on to thinking about the other ways that she is positioned within this study, as a person, but also from the various epistemological, axiological, and ontological lenses that she views and makes sense of the world and others. Finally, she comes to the realisation that families and family members are also positioned. Each family located in a complex system, which impacts how they view the world, how they view themselves, their practices and behaviours, and how they view others. The cup of tea cold now, Alice appreciates that more time needs to be invested in giving further consideration to these issues, before entering the private lives of young families.

Note: This scenario draws from reflections of my doctoral journey (Brown, 2008, 2012).

Chapter Synopsis

The researcher and the researched are unavoidably situated in a complex mix of paradigms, and framed by discourse that shifts and morphs, depending on context and over time (Moss, 2015). This chapter illuminates considerations regarding our's and others' positionality. Later in the chapter, a number of valued axiological perspectives are profiled that researchers may wish to consider when engaging in family research. The intent is that these topics may provoke reflection, a raised sense of consciousness, and hopefully a sensitivity to one's inescapable subjectivity as a social researcher in entering the privileged space of the family home, or other environments where young children and families reside, and are embedded. In doing so, it is anticipated that these' endeavours will create more 'humanised spaces' for researching with members of young families (Paris & Winn, 2014).

What are your notions of parents, children, and 'the family'?

What perspectives, values, and lens do you bring to 'researching with families'?

How might your view of 'young families' and that of 'research participant' conflict? How can this be anticipated and proactively addressed?

How do our perspectives, beliefs, and the lens in which we view children and families impact on the way we enter 'domestic spaces', and interact with individuals in these environments?

How might our positionality impact on the research methods we choose to investigate in these settings and our interactions with individuals?

How can notions of positionality be addressed in researching with young families?

This chapter is set out a little differently from other chapters, as readers are guided through 'an audit of self', as a way of provoking thought regarding entering, and being invited into this very privileged space. This requires us to direct a critical lens at our subjectivity, and a closer inspection of our context, our acculturated assumptions, culture, and the discourses and theory that we privilege. It also provokes thought regarding how a collection of contextual factors may impact on our views, the views of others, and our 'sense-making' of the world around us (Darder, 2015).

Attention then shifts to encouraging the reader to 'tune in to' the positionality of others, and all that doing so entails.

Considering the positionality of ourselves, and others, including those being researched, means heightening our awareness of the bias and interpretations we carry with us into the social milieu and spaces of others, while at the same time being conscious that others also carry their own 'virtual suitcase'. When entering the space of the family home, or another community or environment where we engage with people that are diverse or marginalised, the researcher and the research participant each bring their own history, values, perspectives, and 'lived experiences'[1] in relation to notions, issues, and topics, in this case issues related to such topics as interpretations of what it means to be a family, its function, parenting, and the image of the child.

This chapter aims to illuminate considerations regarding positionality, and other associated topics, with the intent of provoking reflection for researchers entering the private lives and spaces of the families. In doing so, the intent is that the reader will develop an increased appreciation, a raised sense of consciousness, a sensitivity to one's inescapable subjectivity as a social researcher, while hopefully cognisant that participants are also engaged as social actors in research, and bring their own positionality to the research space (Milner, 2007; Moss, 2015). It is anticipated that armed with a greater attentiveness to our and others' positionality, we will be able to create more 'humanised spaces' for researching with young families (Paris & Winn, 2014). An awareness and consideration of positionality in entering these research spaces also supports ethical practice with the intent of building "relationships of care and dignity and dialogical consciousness raising for both researchers and participants" (Paris & Winn, 2014, p. xvi).

The second part of this chapter explores a number of perspectives and paradigms that researchers may wish to consider, in terms of framing, or perhaps even reframing (Lakoff, 2014) the axiological positioning of their research. Specific and practical suggestions are included within this

[1] 'Lived experiences' are defined as the way an individual interprets and describes experiences which occur within particular contexts of their everyday lives (Van Manen, 1990).

section to support the reader's reflection on, and engagement with each topic, while at the same time reinforcing how each of these perspectives are framed to support ethical and respectful research.

2.1   Perspectives and Positionality—So What?

Considerations of positionality, 'our standpoint', the way in which we frame ourselves, and others, and how these perspectives influence approaches to inquiry are definitely not new notions (Franklin, 2014; hooks, 1984; Lakoff, 2004, 2014; Paris & Winn, 2014; St Louis & Barton, 2002). There have been many over the years, including critical, post-colonial, post-structural, and critical feminist theorists, whose work in fields such as education and social science have challenged us to consider our positionality as a strategy for better understanding our place and 'situatedness' in research (Bhabha, 1994; Bourke, 2014; Few-Demo, 2014). This has included concepts such as researchers being embodied, embedded, or situated in a particular time and place, as well as exploring our positionality through a cultural, social, racial, or gendered lens.

Qualitative researchers also recognise that 'humanising research' (Paris, 2011), which includes our positionality, subjectivity, and how we see the world, as well as our biases, will come to bare, and strongly influence our motivations, and guide all aspects of our research (Walter, 2013b). As social researchers these sorts of sentiments reflect the words of Tudge (2008) who comments that "when the 'objects' of research are human beings, and therefore makers of meaning, the researcher is always present, always exerting an influence" (p. 61).

As interpretivist researchers, we are immersed in the role of being a primary instrument of data, where understanding our's and others' positionality and subjectivity are integral considerations within an inquiry (St Louis & Barton, 2002). We are framed by the lived experiences and contexts in which we are embedded. From deciding on the focus of our research, the questions posed, the methods employed to seek answers, to how research participants are viewed, the ways we translate and communicate our research findings, and how we represent our findings to others within the professional community. As such, we are overtly and actively shaped by our 'our standpoint' or position.

Critical reflection, reflexivity, and an awareness and understanding of our positionality are all important aspects of ethical co-construction with participants, and in addressing the trustworthiness of our research (Berger, 2015; Carolan, Forbat, & Smith, 2016). Efforts to articulate, and account for aspects of our 'selves', and our 'relational space' (including our interests, reactivity, prejudices, and assumptions), are usually addressed when outlining our axiology, epistemology, and ontology, as well as part of a "continuing mode of self-analysis" (Callaway, 1992, p. 33). A process of conducting a 'self-audit' and being self-critical of ourselves as researchers needs to be employed upfront, before entering, as well as throughout, the research journey. Moreover, once we as researchers are sensitive or 'hyper-aware' of our positionality, and that of others, it affords us entrance into a more 'intuned world', induces self-discovery, and, I would argue, affords for more rigorous research.

Positionality can be understood as identifying where one stands in relation to another. In some ways, our positionality, or our framing, is how we make sense of our realities, or make meaning of our world (Moss, 2015). Our positionality is influenced by the contents jammed into our metaphorical suitcase, or the baggage that we carry around with us as we travel within, amongst context, and through the social cultural milieu. This context can be defined by our values, the theoretical perspectives and paradigms we privilege, our culture, life experiences, identity, class, our language, and even the political positions we hold that frame significant social dimensions. Of course, we need to acknowledge that this suitcase of artefacts we bring with us to the research space is integrally embedded in who we are, our personality, individual characteristics, limitations, and unique history (Thayer-Bacon, 2000). As such, these elements we carry with us pervade and shape the research spaces we engage in, as well as all aspects of our research and methodological approaches, while also shaping our world view and subjectivity (Carolan et al., 2016; Walter, 2013a).

Lakoff (2014) talks about our world view as a complex set of ideas, or a 'conceptual framework', that determine how we think, and understand our world to operate, or what we understand as 'normal'. So, for example, we might have a picture, or 'frame' of a young family, as being a collection of individuals including a mum and dad and at least one child. Included in this frame might also be an image of a 'family' located in a particular community or domestic space (including home, contents, and outdoor spaces), having particular functions, and being of a particular race, and socio-economic status (Caiola, Docherty, Relf, & Barroso, 2014). Of course, this is only one person's frame, at one point in time.

As our positionality is largely invisible to us, we might also be unaware that we bring with us to our research, multiple roles, attributes, and identities, including being of a particular nationality, race, gender, and social status; to positions of power, privilege, or marginalisation (Caiola et al., 2014). Each of these aspects impact on how we enter, move, interpret, and engage in different contexts, and with others. Unfortunately, if we are oblivious to our own positionality, we might also be unaware of the consequences that our actions may have on others, including those being investigated (England, 1994). We might also miss how we are perceived by others in different contexts, or how they in fact position themselves, or are positioned. Certainly, I would argue that these are all legitimate aspects to consider when planning to conduct, engage with, and enter places of research.

Epistemologically, it is important to appreciate that we are continually colonising knowledge, and creating co-constructed knowledge, dynamically, reciprocally, and collaboratively. We do this as a collection of social actors, within a particular space and time (Berger, 2015). As part of the understandings and perspectives we hold, we also need to recognise that each of us, researchers included, hold particular understandings and notions of parents, parenting, childhood, childrearing, 'the family', as well as holding beliefs and values about families, and their role, composition, and even their function (Greenstein & Davis, 2012). McCarthy et al. (2012) notes "that 'family' is a notion that is suffused with values, desires and fears ... it is therefore very rare for people to discuss without making judgements" (p. 3).

In summary, as researchers, we need to be cognisant that many of the narratives around parents, children, and 'the family' may privilege a particular notion, or perspective of 'family', over another (McCarthy et al., 2012). There is also a risk that these paradigms and perspectives might cloud the way we view individuals within these environments, and the interpretations and judgements we make of their narratives, storying, and the insights of individuals within these spaces (Guenther, Osborne, Arnott, & McRae-Williams, 2017). Moreover, although we can be sensitive, and open to gaining insight into the perspectives of others, we can never truly see the world through their eyes. We now move forward to further interrogate issues pertaining to positionality, particularly with regard to entering the space of researching with young families.

Re-thinking Our Positionality and What's in Our Suitcase

Conducting a personal audit on and of ourselves, and the research context we are entering, through a lens of intersectionality, is an invaluable process. This process provides us with insight into where we are positioned. It is a way of palpating concepts, or feeling them out (Hendricks & Mirka Koro-Ljungberg, 2015). A way of engaging in this process offers us the opportunity for gaining a heightened sense of awareness of how these artefacts, our lived experiences, and our values can, and will, inform all aspects of our inquiry (Bermúdez, Muruthi, & Jordan, 2016). So, let's set aside a little time now to start this process by conducting an audit of, and on, ourselves.

Either on a sheet of paper, or by adopting a journaling approach, you might like to consider who you are in terms of the following points, and feel free to expand on these:

Audit 1

Gender	Occupation	The types of roles you adopt
Class	Ethnicity	Family history/type of family
Personality	Age	Values and theories that you privilege and support

You might also like to reflect, and make notes on the following:

• Does my positionality shift in different contexts? Or across time? When? How?
• Does my positionality shift with different people? If so, with whom? And how?
• Do I take aspects of my positionality foregranted? If so, which aspects?
• What assumptions, values, and perspectives do I bring to these research spaces? To researching with families?
• Does my positionality impact, or shift, the power differential with others in different research contexts?
• How might my reading and research related to 'families' influence my positionality? How might it impact on the inquiry process?
• How might my lived experience of 'family' impact on the lens I view other young families?
• How might young families view my role as researcher, or the other roles I bring with me to the research space?

As scholars, it is important that we are not only aware of our own standpoint, axiological perspectives (our value systems), and ontology, but are also transparent of who we are, and the goals and intent we have as researchers (Bermúdez et al., 2016; Walter, 2013b). For example, we may see our research as being the pursuit of more than just the production of knowledge, but also find importance in creating links, joining the dots, advancing understandings, or perhaps making visible the voices and experiences of others (Denzin & Lincoln, 2017). For others, their purpose might be "pedagogical, political, moral, and ethical, involving the enhancement of moral agency, the production of moral discernment, a commitment to praxis, justice, and ethic of resistance, and performative pedagogy that resists oppression" (Denzin, Lincoln, & Smith, 2008, p. 14).

Culturally responsive and humanising research ideally starts by reflecting upon, and clearly articulating to ourselves, and to the research participants, the intent of our research, and who will benefit from it. Consider reflecting on some of these questions in relation to this topic:

- What agenda do I bring with me to the research space of studying young families, and their views, values, and perspectives?
- What aspects of my axiology (my values) have impacted on the research topic I have chosen?
- What strategies can I employ in an attempt to even out the power differential?
- How can I revision, or reframe, the way that I am positioned, or others are positioned, when researching with young families?

2.2   Tuning into the Positionality of Others

"The qualitative researcher's perspective is perhaps a paradoxical one: it is to be acutely tuned-in to the experiences and meaning systems of others—to indwell—and at the same time to be aware of how one's own biases and preconceptions may be influencing what one is trying to understand" (Maykut & Morehouse, 1994, p. 114).

In the previous section of this chapter, we focussed attention on the rationale for an awareness of our positionality and standpoint as researchers, as well as the pervasiveness of our positionality in relation to all aspects of the research process, including our engagement with other social actors. However, as McCarthy et al. (2012) points out, in order to be truly open to listening to the storied lives of others, and to make sense of their contexts, researchers need to not only have a heightened sensitivity of their own positionality, but an acute awareness of how others might be positioned. They need to be prepared to set aside, as much as possible, their own assumptions and values, to be open to the possibilities and potentialities of what is unfolding around them, and truly reflect the reality of others in context (Guenther et al., 2017).

We now shift our lens to focus more closely on what Maykut and Morehouse (1994) refer to as "tuning in" to the "meaning systems of others" (p. 114). Moss (2015) talks about "the researched" being positioned "within a complex network of people, structures and relationships" (p. 90). He relates this back to an analogy similar to Bronfenbrenner's (1979) ecological systems theory, where, just like a child is understood to be located within numerous interconnected systems (micro, meso, chrono, and macro), so too are the families that engage with us in inquiry seen as influencing, and being influenced by environments and contexts.

This example reinforces that 'the other' is also framed, positioned, and located within a complex set of systems. Moss (2015) continues by writing that "if there are many positions and a multiplicity of perspectives, and if what we research is also positioned in very particular contexts, our knowledge, and that of others, is always situated and local, partial and provisional, conditional and contingent" (p. 90). Few-Demo (2014) builds on these sentiments, suggesting that "researchers are encouraged to examine the fluidity, variability, and temporality of interactive processes that occur between and within multiple social groups, institutions, and social practices" (p. 170).

Researchers in remote Aboriginal and Torres Strait Islander contexts within Australia, Guenther et al. (2017), highlight how researchers working in intercultural and diverse spaces are frequently challenged, particularly in spaces "where channels of communication are garbled with interference created by the complexities of misunderstood worldviews, languages, values and expectations" (p. 197). Guenther et al. (2017) make an important point that is worth considering in relation to researching about, or with, young families. They reinforce the importance of bringing with us to this research space a heightened sensitivity of the narratives and paradigms related to 'the other'. This is particularly important in terms of how 'the other' sees themselves, and how they may be positioned and perceived within the greater social cultural milieu, as well as through and across time (intersectionality).

This view recognises that 'others', as well as ourselves as researchers, are positioned as social actors that engage, and move within and amongst, multiple systems (Walter, 2013a). As such, some of these systems may silence, while others may privilege, particular paradigms and perspectives (Paris, 2011). Therefore, proactively paying careful attention to others' positionality, including feelings of marginalisation, current and past 'lived experiences', and the impact these have on their ways of knowing, seeing, and acting, will help us to be forearmed of any unforeseen issues, and, just as importantly, more sensitive to the perspectives of others.

While we may want to understand the perspectives of others, and to fully attend to the positionality and world view of others when conducting research, we must also be mindful that we will not remove the impact of how we see the world, how we make meaning, and our position as active agents in the inquiry process (Walter, 2013b). As Daly (2007) points out, we are "caught in our own existential practice of trying to fit that experience into our own schemes of relevancy and typification. We are always limited by our own schemes of relevancy and typification. The key is to be aware of these limitations, to reflect on them as we endeavour to understand the other, and to know when these are of such a radically different nature that they surpass our ability to understand or see clearly" (p. 7).

Interpretivist research is about gaining a context-specific understanding of the lifeworld of another (Warr, 2004). As such, it is important that we enter the research space with an appreciation of how the world is viewed from the perspective of 'the other'. Seeking to appreciate, or gain insight into, the 'positioning of others' is part of a methodological stance, or what some academics refer to as 'humanizing research' (Bermúdez et al., 2016; Paris, 2011). Researchers that seek to gain insight into lived experiences and perspectives of others help build reciprocal and authentic relationships, as it offers dignity and respect through providing opportunities for genuine dialogue. This will be further discussed in Chap. 3, as well as privileged at length in Chap. 6, 'Considering CHE (connectivity, humanness, and empathy): Principles for sustaining respectful, authentic, and dialogical research with young families'.

Audit 2

- What are some of the systems and networks that influence 'the others' positionality?
- How does an awareness of another's positionality enable more respectful and effective research?

- How can we incorporate the voices of 'others' "without colonising them in a manner that reinforces patterns of domination? Can these types of dilemmas be resolved, and if so, how?" (England, 1994, p. 242)

Perspectives and Positionality of Young Parents and the Family

Chapter 1 highlighted that there is no universal definition of how 'a family' is referred to, or an enduring form in which it is understood. That throughout time, as the world changes, sociocultural constructions of 'family' also change (Bushin, 2009). In considering the positioning of members of young families, it is therefore important to appreciate that individuals sitting within the micro-environment of the family home, as well others located within overlapping systems of the social cultural milieu (including across time and contexts), will have differing world views. Each with their own unique perspectives, and different inherent assumptions about themselves and others that are culturally and socially constructed (Baxter, 2015; Moore, McDonald, McHugh-Dillon, & West, 2016).

Therefore, in seeking to investigate the perspectives and lived experiences of individuals within young families, it is important to appreciate their positionality. It is important to be very aware of the dynamic, evolving, and developmental nature of the different roles that members of families adopt, such as the role of 'parent' and 'primary caregiver'; the role of the child or sibling; and the functions of family members, all of which may shift and vary over time. We also need to be aware that the roles and responsibilities of family members may differ, depending on culture and the contexts of significant caregivers and children within this space.

We could look at the perspectives that families have of themselves from the position of holding a particular identity, or several different identities, depending on the various social, political, institutional, and other environmental structures in which they are embedded. These perspectives and identities will impact on their level of perceived, or real, vulnerability. For example, Crenshaw (1991) noted that these perspectives, in this case located within families, may privilege some groups, while silencing the rights of others. This type of perspective is located in feminist sociological literature, which refers to the term 'intersectionality' as the study of "the relationships among multiple dimensions and modalities of social relationships and subject formations" (McCall, 2005, p. 1771).

A poignant example of differing world views in relation to families described as 'disadvantaged' is discussed in a paper by Docket and her team (2009). They point out, that in extensive literature, and broader community discourse, there are many definitions of terms such as 'risk', 'vulnerable' and 'disadvantage', and while many of the families in their study would fall under the banner as fitting within these categories, many of the families they were working with "did not characterise themselves in such ways" (p. 356). The authors continued by pointing out, that inherent in their project were "multiple definitions of 'complex support needs', each of which they observed to be socially and contextually constructed" (p. 356).

For example, they pointed out that DoCS (New South Wales Department of Community Services, n.d.), defined "families with complex support needs as experiencing at least one of the following characteristics: domestic violence; parental drug and alcohol misuse; parental mental health issues; a lack of extended family or social support; parents with significant learning difficulties or an intellectual disability; and/or child behaviour management problems" (p. 356). This example highlights the diversity of assumptions held by the individuals, in this case families, and the importance of being aware of assumptions that are held both within the dominant discourse, but also, and just as importantly, held by the families engaged in an inquiry.

In relation to entering the space of young families, it is also important that we consider the different identities through which this unique group are viewed, or whom others may discriminate against. From a decolonising perspective, Bermúdez et al. (2016) refer to families having a strong connection to "their ancestors and ancestral history, and their roots of both the past and present cultures" (p. 198), and of identity being integrally woven into the fabric of intergenerational tradition, history, relationships, and beliefs. Therefore, in valuing the positionality of young families, it is important that we acknowledge the collective ideals that exist, and are embedded in each micro-environment, and that endure and exist through and across time. However, we also need to be conscious that these values and perspectives exist, and intersect through multiple environments and social contexts (Uttal, 2009).

Intersectionality, which emerged and was adopted in the early 1990s by scholars to highlight white feminist discourse that silenced concerns of black women and families (Bowleg, 2012; Crenshaw, 1991), is now gaining traction, and being applied in a range of other disciplines and fields of study, such as the humanities and social sciences (Alexander-Floyd, 2012; Henne, 2013). Adopting such a lens, in relation to our thinking about families helps us focus our attention on the other intersects, or how an individual's location and environment connect to, and with, other intersecting systems (such as gender, race, and class). These systems impact, and are in turn impacting, and being impacted by power and relational experiences within these systems.

Further, intersectionality, deployed in the field with and of young families, offers researchers a counter-hegemonic response, or a tool for understanding the frames in which our participants, ourselves, and our inquiry are positioned. As such, an increased awareness of 'intersectionality' helps us to develop a raised consciousness, and critical perspective regarding our own, and others' intersection. This could include the intersections of the young families engaged in inquiry with us, related to aspects such as gender, roles, and race, and the impact these types of intersections have on 'familied life' (Few-Demo, 2014).

Another aspect that is worth considering in the examination and critical reflection of the positionality of young families is the pervasiveness of colonising narratives regarding families, evidenced in the literature and embedded in the dominant discourse of the social cultural milieu. These multiple narratives will directly, and indirectly, influence how we perceive families, including our relationships with families, as we enter and engage within the research space (Bermúdez et al., 2016). These narratives are reinforced at the ecological level, and filter through the ecosystem and chronosystem (through time) to reinforce, or perhaps conflict with, particular values and expectations of how our society positions and views families, and in turn how family members see themselves.

Feminist family researchers such as Milner (2007) and Bermúdez et al. (2016) have paid close attention to this topic. They point out that for many years there has been a grand narrative, reinforced by white male researchers, and that this myopia has "created a single view of function and dysfunction in families, especially families that did not look like those of the researchers. A normative definition of family (e.g., nuclear family, two-parent household) dominated academic scholarship produced by men", and Western ideologies (Bermúdez et al., 2016, p. 193).

Although we as scholars appreciate that there are many interpretations and forms of constructions of 'the family', we still see evidence in the literature, as well as at a broader societal level, normative interpretations of 'the family'. These include notions of 'the family' as nuclear, biological, and patriarchal, "even though as scholars we acknowledge adopted families, single-parent families, foster families, and fictive kin, to name a few" (Bermúdez et al., 2016, p. 197). These types of perpetuating narratives, shaped by dominant ideology, position all nonconforming families as 'othered', and perpetuates a cycle that then impacts on the way that 'the other' sees themselves.

As such, the challenge we have as researchers of, and with, young families is to heighten our awareness, and be sensitive to the grand narratives that are evident within the social cultural milieu, as we move through and engage in this research space, and frame. In adopting this practice we make efforts to take care not to perpetuate these dominant frameworks. Adopting a lens such as feminist, post-structuralism (Allen, Lloyd, & Few, 2009) helps us to challenge and 'think otherwise' regarding these dominant narratives. It also helps us to deconstruct, and reflect, on how these notions of 'family' impact on our own positionality, and our work as researchers, as well as the positionality of those being researched.

Bermúdez et al. (2016) go so far as to point out that "this normative yardstick delineating family structures and members of families who carry out normative family functions has constrained our research and understanding of families" (p. 197). Kaestle (2016) continues by commenting that one way to challenge 'othering', and counteract marginalisation, is "through representation without comparison" and "pursuing research with nonconforming families that are underrepresented in the literature" (p. 72). This may mean rejecting traditional research paradigms, and methodological approach that privileges 'othering', instead seeking to ensure that our efforts explore the lived experiences of the diversity of young contemporary families.

There are a range of other pervasive narratives, and 'regimes of truth', that you may be aware of that also exist in relation to young families, and individuals within these domestic spaces. These examples of decontextualised views have become 'normalised' over time and place, perpetuating a particular view of individuals, or groups (Ferfolja, Díaz, & Ullman, 2015). Examples include a particular role of the mother as the primary attachment figure, the discourse of which has been perpetuated by scholars such as John Bowlby (1990; van der Horst, 2011).

No matter what the construct, it is important that in our endeavours as researchers we are sensitive of how young families and family members may be, or are, positioned. Furthermore, it is important to be cognisant that this positioning changes through and across time, and context. From a post-structuralist, or a reconceptualist perspective, we need to recognise these changing contexts, and if necessary challenge these norms. If necessary, we may even need to be prepared to challenge, or to reframe our own perspectives, or positioning (Lakoff, 2014; Yelland, 2010). Bermúdez et al. (2016) comment that the extent of this influence can be seen in the types of questions asked, "who is asking them, and which types of methods and studies are deemed legitimate, valuable, rigorous, and fundable" (p. 197).

From a decolonialising, as well as a social ecological perspective, the positionality of young families is understood to be inherently connected and interwoven through and with intergenerational systems, values, traditions, and practices (McGregor, Morelli, Matsuoka, & Minerbi, 2003). Each family member is embedded, and relationally linked to their context and family, as part of a kinship network or tribe. This includes a range of collective ideals, experiences, behaviours, and ways of making meaning. It is important that as researchers entering communities, and domestic spaces, that we approach these contexts humbly and respectfully, honouring these communities, their aspirations and positioning, in our actions and methodological approaches (Hart, 2010) (further details on this will be addressed in Chaps. 4, 5, 6, and 7).

Hopefully, the rationale and reasons outlined in the first section of this chapter, for considering our own and 'others' positionality have hopefully provoked reflection, and that these considerations will assist and empower you in the ethical and respectful "process, production and outcomes of inquiry, and hold researchers more accountable to the communities and people with whom they conduct research" (Milner, 2007, p. 389). The final set of questions are included to guide researchers towards a deeper awareness and consciousness of the positionality of young families:

- What are my notions of parents, children, and 'family'?
- In entering a research space with young families, what grand narratives and dominant discourses are evident within this context?
- Where am I positioned in relation to those being researched, and their communities?
- What strategies can I employ to increase my awareness of the cultural knowledge, and of the positioning of young families, and communities being investigated?
- How do these discourses impact marginalisation and perceptions of power, or powerlessness?
- How can my methodological approaches attempt to do justice to those being researched?
- How can the positionality of young families be considered in my research?
- In what ways will research participants' racial and cultural backgrounds influence their meaning-making?
- How might the multiple roles, identities, and positions I hold impact, or change, during the inquiry process with young families?

2.3   The Consideration of Perspectives

The qualitative researcher's perspective is perhaps a paradoxical one: it is to be acutely tuned-in to the experiences and meaning systems of others—to indwell—and at the same time to be aware of how one's own biases and preconceptions may be influencing what one is trying to understand. (Maykut & Morehouse, 1994, p. 114)

In Chap. 1 of this text the important role that parents and primary carers play in the health, development, and well-being of children and young people was discussed. The micro-environment of the family home was identified as a significant site of inquiry, investigation, and intervention. However, within the context of the family home, or more broadly in other sociocultural contexts, there is also evidence of families being positioned from a deficit perspective, and understood as needing advice and capacity building or intervention from experts. Therefore, an important component of conceptualising any inquiry and associated methodologies, including that of researching with and of young families is exploring our standpoint and positionality in terms of how we view and understand young families. This will include our understanding of knowledge and theory ('ways of knowing', our epistemology), our understanding and theory of what constitutes reality, as well as how we view the world (our ontology), and the values we hold (our axiological considerations) (Walter, 2013b).

Critically reflecting on our axiology is important as a way of heightening our awareness of the paradigms, positions, and perspectives that we value, and that underpin our approach, or the lens(es) in which we view research and our work with young families. The filters in which we see the world, and the paradigms in which we choose to work within, and perhaps even constrain us, will impact on all aspects of our research. Early career researchers, or those entering the space of researching with young families, may initially find it challenging to reflect on the values they hold, or their axiological perspectives, at the outset of project. What is important is that we are open to reflecting on the possibilities of what these might look like, and be prepared to make efforts to challenge our existing paradigms and dominant discourse in order to appreciate the impact these perspectives will have on the methodological approaches we adopt, and the relationships we have with individuals within families.

The next section of this chapter will explore a particular axiological position, referred to as a 'strengths-based' perspective and how adopting this particular axiological perspective can potentially impact and frame all aspects of an inquiry, including the lens in which we view our interactions with research participants (Daly, 2007; Walter, 2013b). As you engage with these themes you may like to reflect on how adopting such a perspective might impact on your positionality, how participants are positioned, and the values and practices associated with this perspective. A number of questions are integrated throughout this section of this chapter to encourage reflection.

Working Within a Strengths-Based Perspective

Theoretical Constructs For several decades professionals and scholars from a range of disciplines, such as early childhood education and care, psychology, social work, and family support workers, have adopted what is referred to as a strengths-based approach. This perspective has been adopted as a theoretical, methodological, and practical framework (Fenton, Walsh, Wong, & Cumming, 2015; Saleebey, 2012) for their work and research with individuals in community, including work with families (Brownlee, Rawana, MacArthur, & Probizanski, 2010; Gardner & Toope, 2011; Seligman, Ernst, Gillham, Reivich, & Linkins, 2009). This perspective has emerged from professional practice, and involves working and engaging with others framed within a positive paradigm. This framing is linked to valuing the rights, dignity, and the capacity of others. These types of practices often emerge from, and are evidenced with, professionals and researchers working as part of transdisciplinary teams, or integrated services.

Characteristics of a Strengths-Based Perspective Although various fields and disciplines may adopt slightly different interpretations of what is understood as a 'strengths-based approach', most emphasise a view of embracing opportunities to mobilise the existing strengths (McCashen, 2005;

Saleebey, 2012), resources, capacities, talents, motivations, and various types of capital of individuals, families, or communities. As such, a strengths-based perspective is framed within a paradigm of potentiality and possibility, with an understanding that individuals have the power to make a difference. Those who choose to adopt a strengths-based approach recognise the strengths of others, but just as importantly see the importance to helping others to recognise and appreciate their own strengths, and the capital they have access to, as opportunities to build and extend upon (Fenton et al., 2015; Weick, 1992).

Professionals that adopt a strengths-based approach look upon these interactions, and experiences, with others as collaborative opportunities for empowerment, and as opportunities to mobilise others to build capacity, self-esteem, self-determinism, dignity, and self-efficacy (McCashen, 2005). Adopting such an approach enables researchers and professionals the opportunity to create environments where others are afforded time to share their stories and narratives as 'knowledge', "and acts according to the belief that the teller (the individual, family or community) is the expert in their own life" (Wong & Cumming, 2008, p. 17).

Adopting a 'Strengths-Based Perspective' with Young Families

As a consequence of a range of normative family discourse, reinforced within the social cultural milieu, parents and members of young families may experience the effects of their 'familied lives' being judged, or viewed through a range of lenses by others (Harding, 2006; Uttal, 2009). This is particularly the case in marginalised or disenfranchised families, whose life experiences may be perceived as different to what is understood, or viewed as normal, or acceptable by 'the other'. As our lives and worlds become more transparent and scrutinised in the public arena, even the most contemporary of young families may experience feelings of being judged, 'viewed as deficient', 'needing to be fixed (a pathologised lens)', or through a deficit lens (Bermúdez et al., 2016). Perhaps even experiencing what Milner (2007) describes as "kidnapped into believing that they are inferior" as others concentrate on the negative attributes of individuals within these domestic spaces (p. 388).

Those who choose to work within a strengths-based paradigm embrace a counter-narrative in an effort to reframe or disrupt a dominant perspective, such as that of a deficit paradigm. A strengths-based perspective shifts attention from reinforcing inadequacies, limitations, and problems of a situation, behaviour, or practice, instead focussing attention and energy on the resources and potentiality of individuals, groups, communities, and circumstance (McNeil, 2010; Rinaldi, 2006). This approach embraces the diversity and strengths that exist within families, in terms of how these can be harnessed as assets in relation to an issue, practice, behaviour, or aspect relevant to their lived experiences (Fenton, MacDonald, & McFarland, 2016).

Working or researching with young families, by adopting a strengths-based approach, means recognising the important role that significant adults play in the lives of young children (Fenton & McFarland-Piazza, 2014), particularly in the formative stages of a young child's development, learning, health, and well-being (the first 1000 days) (Arabena, Panozzo, & Ritte, 2015; Thurow, 2016). Further, this view sees significant adults in the lives of young children as 'the experts' in the relationship forming, social emotional development, and loving of young children, as well as the first-hand experience they have as 'parents as first teachers'. This perspective would view parents, no matter how disadvantaged, as having at their disposal an idiosyncratic set of enablers and potential resources (Center on the Developing Child at Harvard University, 2010; McNeil, 2010).

However, those adopting such a perspective are not naïve in recognising the existence of contexts and circumstances, where families and parents may experience difficulty, adversity, or be in a position of vulnerability. These factors may challenge parents, and their ability to best support their children (Morton et al., 2015; Thurow, 2016). In circumstances such as these, it is recognised that survival and basic needs will take priority (see Maslow's Hierarchy of Needs) (Berk, 2015). However, even in these circumstances there is an underpinning belief in the capacity of parents and significant caregivers being motivated and driven by an endearing love and desire to want the best for their children (Kana'iaupuni, 2005).

In overlooking the potentiality of families, we miss the opportunity to view families as experts, instead looking at 'outside experts' to always step in, to mediate, to resolve, or to fix (Kana'iaupuni, 2005). Adopting a strengths-based approach means working with parents and significant carers to overcome barriers. This is accomplished by harnessing implicit and explicit resources, and drawing upon their 'life experiences', and various sources of capital, in efforts to support their practices, behaviours, and decision-making in relation to providing quality early experiences for young children (Sanders & Munford, 2009; Ziersch, 2005).

Working within a strengths-based paradigm also means adopting a philosophical and practical perspective of recognising the potentiality of children. This perspective sees children as competent and capable, and significant social actors in spaces in which they are engaged, live, and play (discussion around this topic and affording dialogic opportunities for children is addressed in Chaps. 3 and 7). Note also that a range of topics addressed in Chap. 1 contribute to the theory underpinning the value and importance of adults and families of young children, and therefore supporting a strengths-based perspective.

Strengths-Based Perspectives—Implications to Inquiry

Ways of Working As like the pervasive impact of a researcher's positionality, working within an axiology that values a strengths-based perspective will have implications for all aspects of an inquiry, including the methodological approaches, and analytic frameworks that researchers choose to adopt (Fenton & McFarland-Piazza, 2014; McCashen, 2005). These practices and considerations will be addressed and expanded upon in later chapters; however, for now, it is important to reinforce that adopting a strengths-based approach to inquiry will have implications to the way that we approach, view, and work with families (see Fig. 2.1).

Ways of working…..Strengths-based methodological approaches

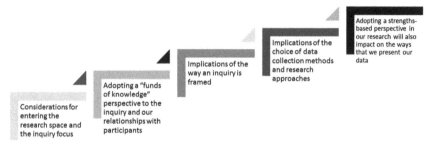

Adopting a 'strengths-based perspective' with young families and Australian show families – a way of disrupting existing paradigms

Fig. 2.1 Adopting a strengths-based perspective with young families

Adopting a strengths-based approach from the very beginning of an inquiry will mean that researchers are cognisant of how they 'enter' the research space, and the lens in which they view young families. This will require the employment of a degree of skills aligned with emotional intelligence (Brown & Danaher, 2017). This approach shifts the inquiry focus, and our relationship with parents and children, away from one of interrogation, to one where researchers are much more in tune with developing enduring relationships with participants, which in turn acknowledges and values their stories, and positions.

Those who choose to work within a strengths-based perspective in researching with young families might also see many parallels and value in aligning their approach with 'funds of knowledge' (González, Moll, & Amanti, 2005). Funds of knowledge is based on the premise that children, family members, and communities are a valuable social and intellectual asset, and a source in which to draw knowledge and insight, with respect to the issues, places, and spaces in which they are integrally connected. Further, this axiological perspective builds upon an approach, or philosophy, adopted by researchers and practitioners in a range of disciplines, including education and health, that recognises what individuals and groups, particularly families, 'bring to the table', such as the skills, strategies, and knowledge that contribute to their ability to engage in household functioning, and support children's well-being, health, and development.

This view recognises that communities, families, parents, significant carers, and children contribute to social change through the experiences, knowledge, resources, and expertise they possess and share with others (Munford & Sanders, 2003; Sanders & Munford, 2009). Thus, the concept of 'funds of knowledge' positions individuals (more specifically members of young families) as having first-hand experience. As such, due to the intuitive and dynamic knowledge that families possess, we have the potential to collectively harness this knowledge, culture, and skills as a resource (González et al., 2005). The dynamic potentiality of embracing funds of knowledge affords individuals within communities a voice to proactively inform issues that involve them, and others, including strategies to overcome adversity, and difficulties families may experience.

As a researcher in context, adopting a strengths-based/funds of knowledge perspective means being open to the possibilities of learning from, and with, parents and children. It also means being sensitive and open to the different types of capital that families have access to, and the possibilities and potentialities our interactions with families offer in terms of being in a privileged position to gain insight from their knowledge and expertise. As such, those adopting such a paradigm enter the research space humbly, with a view that we can learn so much from young families, as they provide insight into phenomena. The methods we choose to adopt will therefore afford those being researched the opportunity to share their stories, issues, and experiences. It will also mean being guided by approaches that harness, and are open to gathering, the implicit and explicit resources and strategies that young families have at their disposal, and within their own contexts (Campbell et al., 2008; Ziersch, 2005).

Adopting a strengths-based perspective will also have implications to how an inquiry, and its associated research questions are framed, as well as the type of questions posed to participants. As such, rather than an inquiry adopting a deficit lens for seeking to understand a phenomenon, or exploring why a phenomenon doesn't exist; or concerned with investigating factors which impact on a behaviour not evidenced; or why practices don't occur, researchers working within a strengths-based paradigm may choose to adopt a more balanced approach to their inquiry, an approach which includes exploring the positive side of a phenomenon, and family behaviours, views, and perspectives.

The following example from my doctoral research shares the adoption of a strengths-based approach to inquiry. A funds of knowledge lens framed my inquiry, where I sought to investigate parents' insights, behaviours, practices, and environments that afforded opportunities for young children's' active play within the home context (Brown, 2009). Adopting such an approach was reflected in the type of questions that were asked, and the way in which the phenomenon was framed and explored. An example of the research questions then became the following:

Question 1: How do parents 'support' the active play experiences and environments of their children (birth to four)? (Aligned with Goal 1);

Question 2: How do multiple environments and social ecological factors influence parental behaviours, values, and practices for supporting active play with their young children? (Aligned with Goal 2); and finally

Question 3: How do ecological factors influence the way that determinants are skewed to become barriers or enablers of parental support for active play experiences and environments? (Aligned with Goal 3). Note that the final question did explore the barriers as well as the enablers, as both negative and positive determinants were important to explore and gain insight into.

Another example of a research project underpinned by a strengths-based approach was one I engaged in, in partnership with a government health organisation (Brown, 2009). The project team recognised the significant contribution families, and key agencies in contact with families, had in disseminating information. This included their efforts and strategies to provide routines, experiences, and environments for young children which supported bonding and attachment, and stimulated early brain development (including physical activity strategies). The study invited key agencies (early childhood services, playgroups, schools, community health agencies, support networks, and other organisations that support families and protect children), and parents of young children, to share their insights and stories. And, rather than focussing on what wasn't happening in families and communities, attention focussed on gaining a contextual understanding of how parents and key agencies and services acquired and used information (in particular in relation to bonding, attachment, and active play); and their preferred avenues for information dissemination.

At this point it would be of value to pause, to regroup, and to consider the following questions in order to help tease out your own position related to adopting a 'strengths-based perspective' to inquiry:

- What capacity do I see individuals within families as having?
- How can these strengths and capacity be incorporated, and harnessed, in terms of ways in which my inquiry is framed?
- Do the data methods employed for this study enable families to share their insights and resources?
- In what ways is there evidence of research being underpinned by a strengths-based paradigm?
- How does my approach to research respect and value families' ways of knowing?
- What practices do I adopt in my inquiry that are sensitive and open to the different types of capital, or funds of knowledge, that families have access to?
- How might adopting a strengths-based perspective be reflected in the type of questions posed in research?
- How is a strengths-based approach evidenced within my research practices?
- How might adopting a strengths-based perspective be reflected in the type of questions asked of those being researched?
- How might adopting a strengths-based perspective impact on my relationships with the researched, and on my sensitivity in entering these research spaces?
- How might a strengths-based perspective guide my interpretations, recommendations, and implications for future practice and research?

Finally, adopting an axiology that supports a strengths-based perspective will also impact on the way data is presented, and the ways stories of others are retold. This will be addressed in detail in Chap. 7 of this text;

however to conclude this section of the chapter, an example from my doctoral research is included which reflects the value placed on the stories, capacity, and contexts of families with young children. The example reflects the impact a significant micro-environment had on the practices and perspectives of 'the Calmings' (parents Patricia and Matthew, and their two children, Tiffany and Jeffery) that existed beyond the domestic space of the family home. By far, the greatest resource, or asset, identified by the Calmings was that of friends and extended family, or 'The Clan'. Field (2003) sums this up succinctly when he comments that "relationships matter" (p. 2).

This valuable asset, often referred to in my thesis as an aspect of the Calmings' 'social capital' (Stone, 2003), was an aggregate which combined the love, care, and support parents Patricia and Matthew provided for their children, as well as the resources and environments afforded for active play. Patricia (the mother) reinforced this when she remarked, "my aunties and uncles as well as our parents' love buying things for the kids. If they just see something, and they think that it looks good for a kid, then they just buy it and we end up with it". The 'heartfelt moment below', titled 'Support from the Clan', attempts to capture my reflections of the richness of social capital to which the Calming family sourced, and had access to:

Support from the Clan

Patricia: *My aunty just lives up the road and she always used to look after Tiffany Tuesdays and Thursdays when I was working. Even now that I'm at home, she looks after Jeffery for me on Tuesdays, and when Tiffany finishes Prep I go and pick her up and drop her up there. Before dinner, they walk them back down here and they have dinner with us. On Wednesday night, every week, they go to their grandmas, my mum, she lives up the road as well. Every Sunday, the children and I visit my grandma out of town, and there are another couple of my aunties and uncles out there that often drop in and enjoy having breakfast with us. While we're out there, Tiffany and Jeffery get the opportunity to play with their cousins and run around out in the big backyard.*

The Calmings shared a number of stories of being surrounded by 'their Clan' of extended family, comprising of their parents, brothers and sisters, aunts, uncles and their children. In reflecting on how this close-knit group of people played an integral role in the care and socialisation of the members of the Calming family, it reminded me of how similar this was to traditional cultures where it was 'the clan', rather than the immediate family, that was responsible for nurturing young children. Hence the reference to 'it takes a village to raise a child'.

At these intersections of family life, there appeared to be a blurring of the boundaries between what was understood as the micro-environment of the family home, and that of the greater microsystem. These cultural fronts, wrapped in traditions and customs, where the Calmings spent a great deal of their time, offered not only moral and emotional support, but also a strong sense of belonging. These environments, and the people located within them, would often model, support, and share their understandings of, and values for, the health and the physical activity of young children.

Patricia and Matthew's family would often provide a range of equipment and resources to support Tiffany and Jeffery's play, and were always giving the family toys for the children to play with at home. However, just as importantly, time spent with extended family would often include walks to the local park, errands to the post office and shops, and their involvement in daily routines. All of these practices offered opportunities for supporting play, some of which were active play opportunities.

Perhaps one of the most significant methodological contributions that adopting a strengths-based approach makes to researching with young families is its ability to enhance the potential for connectedness, empathy, and relationships with participants. It does this by moving the focus way from one of interrogation and impersonal data collection, to one where researchers are mindful and open to the scene that unfolds in front of us. This approach opens a lens to the valuing of participant history, where lived experiences and views are acknowledged and celebrated—an approach that shifts the researcher from one of 'being the expert', to one where there is a 'shared learning' platform (this will be elaborated further in Chap. 4 of this text) (Dockett et al., 2009).

Although exploring any further perspectives goes beyond the scope of this chapter, brief mention is made of adopting a social ecological perspective. This is important to share at this point, as 'context' is reinforced as such an important consideration that continues to arise as a critical consideration when researching with children and young families. Finally, whether researchers do adopt a strengths-based perspective, or view the world through a social ecological lens, the perspectives we adopt as researchers will have significant implications to multiple aspects of an inquiry, including the framing of young families, the framing of our inquiry, and the framing of our relationships and the ways we engage with young families.

The Situatedness of Families in Context—A Social Ecological Perspective

Chapter 1 highlighted that families are uniquely embedded in context—understood to be "a set of conditions or circumstances that operate on or are embedded in the life of an individual, a group, a situation or an event, which gives meaning to its interpretation" (Brown & Reushle, 2010, p. 37; Oers, 1997). Chapter 1 identified the idiosyncratic nature of young families, and that families are located, move within, and are impacted by dynamic and multiple systems (Fiese, 2013; Zubrick et al., 2012). Reference was also made to Bronfenbrenner's (1979; Bronfenbrenner & Morris, 2006) ecological systems theory as a way of helping to make sense of the many factors that impact on family relationships, behaviours, practices, and perspectives, in turn having a flow-on effect on child behaviours, outcomes and development.

The current popularity of understanding the power of context appears to be grounded in social practices, beliefs, and values that interconnect and move within and amongst the immediate microsystem, and the broader milieu of people's everyday lives. Those who embrace the valuing and pervasiveness of context have a desire to, or seek to understand individuals within places and spaces (Stokols, 2018). This includes the role the environment directly or indirectly plays in influencing the behaviour, and the beliefs of others. The premise behind this being that it is only when we truly appreciate the power of context and the multiple layers of influence, that we can gain a deeper understanding of a phenomenon (Brown, 2009; Stokols, Grzywacz, McMahan, & Phillips, 2003). The valuing of context locates us in a space that embraces the complexity of peoples' lives, the interplay between the individual and their immediate environment, and the impact that these environments have on individual actions, decisions, and outcomes.

Further, those motivated to explore phenomenon located in context, and who choose to adopt a social ecological perspective, will have a keen focus on the perceived realities, social worlds, and meaning-making of others, and are more than likely to position themselves within an interpretivist paradigm. They will also value the importance of context, and the role social ecological factors play in human behaviour. They will acknowledge that behaviour does not occur in a vacuum, and will be cognisant that individuals are located in a series of ecological niches (Belsky, 2014; Brown, 2012).

Researchers who choose to work within this frame will therefore be adept in asking a particular set of questions, with the intent being to elucidate how individuals make sense of their surroundings, and the role that intrapersonal, interpersonal, physical, environmental, and sociocultural factors have on human behaviour, attitudes, and practices (Berg, 2016; Gubrium, Holstein, Marvasti, & McKinney, 2012). Finally, those that seek to investigate the understandings and behaviours of others, or how individuals make meaning of their lives, will usually locate research in natural settings (such as significant micro-environments), and recognise the social-constructedness of knowledge (Bryman, 2015; Daly, 2007). (Note that the 'valuing of context' is privileged in Chap. 3, with a focus on interpretivistism.)

Those who contributed to the conceptualisation of the ecological paradigm, such as the ecological model proposed by Bronfenbrenner (1977, 1979), acknowledge the synergistic or reciprocal causation that exists between the individual and the environment, in both creating and exerting a combined impact on each other (Moos, 1979; Stokols, 1988; Warren & Warren, 1977). Often divided into various systems of influence, the popularity of these models is partly due to their capacity to comprehensively understand and analyse behaviours, in order to better inform and guide approaches for intervention. Ecological and social ecological models have continued to morph, and be adapted to suit a range of research goals and purposes. However those who adopt such models have found them of value to analyse and help make sense of the direct or indirect levels of influence of intrapersonal, interpersonal, physical, environmental, and sociocultural factors and their impact on human behaviour (Kolar & Soriano, 2000).

2.4   Conclusion—Creating More Humanising Research by Reframing and Repositioning

As interpretivist researchers, we acknowledge that both the researcher and the researched are unavoidably positioned and framed (Moss, 2015). In efforts to create more humanising (Paris & Winn, 2014) and respectful spaces for researching with and of young families, researchers are encouraged to consider engaging in 'an audit of self'. Such a process offers researchers an opportunity to point a critical lens at our own subjectivity, while also pushing the pause button before entering the domestic space of the family home, or other spaces in which young families are engaged. Hopefully, in doing so we are able to pay closer attention to the contexts and positioning of others (Darder, 2015).

Armed with these insights, rather than adopting a position of ambivalence, we are hopefully better able to engage in ethical and respectful inquiry. This process will surely entail adopting an axiological perspective that challenges, and works 'against the grain' of established regimes of truths or dominant discourse which may marginalise or silence the voice of others, in turn adopting an approach to inquiry that reframes participants in a more positive and empowering light. This type of approach to inquiry has the potential to generate more productive and transformative relationships with young families who choose to engage in inquiry with us.

References

Alexander-Floyd, N. G. (2012). Disappearing acts: Reclaiming intersectionality in the social sciences in a post-black feminist era. *Feminist Formations, 24*(1), 1–25.

Allen, K. R., Lloyd, S. A., & Few, A. L. (2009). Reclaiming feminist theory, method, and praxis for family studies. In S. A. Lloyd, A. L. Few, & K. R. Allen (Eds.), *Handbook of feminist family studies* (pp. 3–17). Thousand Oaks, CA: Sage.

Arabena, K., Panozzo, S., & Ritte, R. (2015). *The first 1000 days researchers' forum report.* Retrieved from Onemda VicHealth Group, University of Melbourne, VIC: http://www.onemda.unimelb.edu.au/sites/default/files/2%20%20The%20First%201000%20Days%20Researchers%27%20Forum%20Report.pdf

Baxter, J. (2015). *The modern Australian family.* Retrieved from Melbourne, VIC. https://aifs.gov.au/publications/modern-australian-family

Belsky, J. (2014). Social- contextual determinants of parenting. In R. F. Tremblay, M. Boivin, & R. D. Peters (Eds.), *Encyclopedia on early childhood development [online]* (3rd ed., pp. 1–7). Montreal, Quebec: Centre of Excellence for Early Childhood Development and Strategic Knowledge Cluster on Early Child Development.

Berg, B. (2016). *Qualitative research methods for the social sciences* (9th ed.). Boston: Pearson.

Berger, R. (2015). Now I see it, now I don't: Researcher's position and reflexivity in qualitative research. *Qualitative Research, 15*(2), 219–234.

Berk, L. (2015). *Infants and children: Prenatal through middle childhood* (8th ed.). Boston: Pearson Education.

Bermúdez, J. M., Muruthi, B., & Jordan, L. (2016). Decolonizing research methods for family science: Creating space at the centre – Decolonizing research practices. *Journal of Family Theory & Review, 8*(2), 192–206.

Bhabha, H. (1994). A commitment to theory. In H. Bhabha (Ed.), *The location of culture* (p. 29). London: Routledge.

Bourke, B. (2014). Positionality: Reflecting on the research process. *The Qualitative Report, 19*, 1–9.

Bowlby, J. (1990). *A secure base parent-child attachment and healthy human development.* New York: Basic Books.

Bowleg, L. (2012). The problem with the phrase women and minorities: Intersectionality—An important theoretical framework for public health. *American Journal of Public Health, 102*(7), 1267–1273.

Bronfenbrenner, U. (1977). Toward an experimental ecology of human development. *American Psychologist, 32*(7), 513–531.

Bronfenbrenner, U. (1979). *The ecology of human development.* Cambridge, MA: Harvard University Press.

Bronfenbrenner, U., & Morris, P. (2006). The bioecological model of human development. In W. Damon & R. M. Lerner (Eds.), *Handbook of child psychology, volume 1, theoretical models of human development* (6th ed., pp. 793–828). New York: Wiley.

Brown, A. (2008). Towards a new frontier in understanding the contextual influences on paediatric inactivity. In R. Henderson & P. A. Danaher (Eds.), *Troubling terrains: Tactics for traversing and transforming contemporary educational research* (pp. 149–168). Teneriffe, QLD. Post Pressed.

Brown, A. (2009). *South Burnett early movement and stimulation project.* Retrieved from Toowoomba, QLD. https://eprints.usq.edu.au/7703/1/Brown_Project_Report_2009_AV.pdf

Brown, A. (2012). *The new frontier: A social ecological exploration of factors impacting on parental support for the active play of young children within the micro-environment of the family home.* PhD, University of Southern Queensland, Toowoomba, QLD.

Brown, A., & Danaher, P. A. (2017). CHE Principles: Facilitating authentic and dialogical semi-structured interviews in educational research. *International Journal of Research & Method in Education*, 1–15. https://doi.org/10.1080/1743727X.2017.13799.

Brown, A., & Reushle, S. (2010). People, pedagogy and the power of connection. *Studies in Learning, Evaluation, Innovation and Development, 7*(3), 37–48.

Brownlee, K., Rawana, E., MacArthur, J., & Probizanski, M. (2010). The culture of strengths makes them valued and competent: Aboriginal children, child welfare, and a school strengths intervention. *First Peoples Child & Family Review, 5*(1), 96–103.

Bryman, A. (2015). *Social research methods.* Oxford, UK: Oxford University Press.

Bushin, N. (2009). Researching family migration decision making: A children-in-families approach. *Population, Space and Place, 15*(5), 429–443.

Caiola, C., Docherty, S., Relf, M., & Barroso, J. (2014). Using an intersectional approach to study the impact of social determinants of health for African-American mothers living with HIV. *ANS. Advances in Nursing Science, 37*(4), 287.

Callaway, H. (1992). Ethnography and experience: Gender implications in fieldwork and texts. In J. Okely & H. Callway (Eds.), *Anthropology and autobiography* (pp. 29–49). New York: Routledge.

Campbell, K., Hesketh, K., Crawford, D., Salmon, J., Ball, K., & McCallum, Z. (2008). The infant feeding activity and nutrition trial (INFANT) an early intervention to prevent childhood obesity: Cluster-randomised controlled trial. *BMC Public Health, 8*(103), 1–9.

Carolan, C. M., Forbat, L., & Smith, A. (2016). Developing the DESCARTE model: The design of case study research in health care. *Qualitative Health Research, 26*(5), 626–639.

Center on the Developing Child at Harvard University. (2010). *The foundations of lifelong health are build in early childhood*. Retrieved from http://www.developingchild.harvard.edu

Crenshaw, K. (1991). Mapping the margins: Intersectionality, identity politics, and violence against women of color. *Stanford Law Review, 43*(6), 1241–1299.

Daly, K. J. (2007). *Qualitative methods for family studies and human development*. Thousand Oaks, CA: Sage.

Darder, A. (2015). Decolonizing interpretive research: A critical bicultural methodology for social change. *The International Education Journal: Comparative Perspectives, 14*(2), 63–77.

Denzin, N., & Lincoln, N. (2017). *The Sage handbook of qualitative research* (5th ed.). Thousand Oaks, CA: Sage.

Denzin, N. K., Lincoln, Y. S., & Smith, L. T. (Eds.). (2008). *Handbook of critical and indigenous methodologies*. Thousand Oaks, CA: Sage.

Dockett, S., Perry, B., Kearney, E., Hamshire, A., Mason, J., & Schmied, V. (2009). Researching with families: Ethical issues and situations. *Contemporary Issues in Early Childhood, 10*(4), 353–365.

England, K. (1994). Getting personal: Reflexivity, positionality, and feminist research. *The Professional Geographer, 46*(1), 80–89.

Fenton, A., MacDonald, A., & McFarland, L. (2016). A strengths approach to supporting early mathematics learning in family contexts. *Australasian Journal of Early Childhood, 41*(1), 45.

Fenton, A., & McFarland-Piazza, L. (2014). Supporting early childhood preservice teachers in their work with children and families with complex needs: A strengths approach. *Journal of Early Childhood Teacher Education, 35*(1), 22–38.

Fenton, A., Walsh, K., Wong, S., & Cumming, T. (2015). Using strengths-based approaches in early years practice and research. *International Journal of Early Childhood, 47*(1), 27–52.

Ferfolja, T., Díaz, C. J., & Ullman, J. (2015). *Understanding sociological theory for educational practices.* Port Melbourne, VIC: Cambridge University Press.

Few-Demo, A. (2014). Intersectionality as the "new" critical approach in feminist family studies: Evolving racial/ethnic feminisms and critical race theories. *Journal of Family Theory & Review, 6*(2), 169–183.

Field, J. (2003). *Social capital.* London: Routledge.

Fiese, B. (2013). Family context in early childhood. In O. Saracho & B. Spodek (Eds.), *Handbook of research on the education of young children* (3rd ed., pp. 369–384). New York: Routledge.

Franklin, Y. (2014). Virtually unpacking your backpack: Educational philosophy and pedagogical praxis. *Educational Studies, 50*(1), 65–86.

Gardner, M., & Toope, D. (2011). A social justice perspective on strengths-based approaches: Exploring educators' perspectives and practices. *Canadian Journal of Education, 34*(3), 86–102.

González, N., Moll, L. C., & Amanti, C. (Eds.). (2005). *Funds of knowledge: Theorizing practices in households, communities, and classrooms.* Mahwah, NJ: Routledge.

Greenstein, T. N., & Davis, S. N. (2012). *Methods of family research.* Thousand Oaks, CA: Sage.

Gubrium, J., Holstein, J., Marvasti, A., & McKinney, K. (2012). *The Sage handbook of interview research: The complexity of craft.* Thousand Oaks, CA: Sage.

Guenther, J., Osborne, S., Arnott, A., & McRae-Williams, E. (2017). Hearing the voice of remote Aboriginal and Torres Strait Islander training stakeholders using research methodologies and theoretical frames of reference. *Race Ethnicity and Education, 20*(2), 197–208.

Harding, S. (2006). *Science and social inequality: Feminist and postcolonial issues.* Champaign, IL: University of Illinois Press.

Hart, M. A. (2010). Indigenous worldviews, knowledge, and research: The development of an indigenous research paradigm. *Journal of Indigenous Voices in Social Work, 1*(1), 1–16.

Hendricks, J., & Mirka Koro-Ljungberg, M. (2015). Inquiring through and with Deleuze: Disrupting theory and qualitative methods in family studies. *Journal of Family Theory & Review, 7*(3), 265–283.

Henne, K. (2013). From the academic to the UN and back again: The travelling politics of intersectionality. *Intersections: Gender and Sexuality in Asia and the Pacific, 33.* Retrieved from http://intersections.anu.edu.au/issue33/henne.htm

hooks, b. (1984). *From margin to center.* Boston: South End Press.

Kaestle, C. (2016). Feminist perspectives advance four challenges to transform family studies. *Sex Roles, 75*(1), 71–77.

Kana'iaupuni, S. M. (2005). Ka'akālai Kū Kanaka: A call for strengths-based approaches from a Native Hawaiian perspective. *Educational Researcher, 34,* 32–38.

Kolar, V., & Soriano, G. (2000). *Parenting in Australian families: A comparative study of Anglo, Torres Strait Islander, and Vietnamese communities.* Retrieved from Melbourne, VIC. https://aifs.gov.au/publications/parenting-australian-families

Lakoff, G. (2004). *Don't think of an elephant! Know your values and frame the debate: The essential guide for progressives.* New York: Recorded Books.

Lakoff, G. (2014). *The all new don't think of an elephant!: Know your values and frame the debate.* White River Junction, VT: Chelsea Green Publishing.

Maykut, P., & Morehouse, R. (1994). *Beginning qualitative researchers: A philosophical and practical guide.* Washington, DC: Falmer.

McCall, L. (2005). The complexity of intersectionality. *Journal of Women in Culture and Society, 30*(3), 1771–1800.

McCarthy, J. R., Doolittle, M., & Schlater, S. D. (2012). *Understanding family meanings: A reflective text.* Bristol, UK: The Open University.

McCashen, W. (2005). *The strengths approach.* Bendigo, VIC: St. Luke's Innovative Resources.

McGregor, D., Morelli, P., Matsuoka, J., & Minerbi, L. (2003). An ecological model of well-being. In *The international handbook of social impact assessment: Conceptual and methodological advances* (pp. 109–126). Northampton, MA: Elgar.

McNeil, T. (2010). Family as a social determinant of health: Implications for governments and institutions to promote the health and well-being of families. *Healthcare Quarterly, 14*(Special Issue, Child Health Canada), 60–67.

Milner, H. R. (2007). Race, culture, and researcher positionality: Working through dangers seen, unseen, and unforeseen. *Educational Researcher, 36*(7), 388–400.

Moore T., McDonald, M., McHugh-Dillon, H., & West, S. et al. (2016). *Community engagement: A key strategy for improving outcomes for Australian families.* Retrieved from Melbourne, VIC. https://aifs.gov.au/cfca/publications/community-engagement

Moos, R. (1979). Social ecological perspectives on health. In G. Stone, F. Cohen, & N. Adler (Eds.), *Health psychology: A handbook* (pp. 523–547). San Francisco: Jossey Bass.

Morton, S. M., Atatoa Carr, P. E., Grant, C. C., Berry, S. D., Mohal, J., & Pillai, A. (2015). *Growing up in New Zealand: A longitudinal study of New Zealand children and their families. Vulnerability Report 2: Transitions in exposure to vulnerability in the first 1000 days of life.* Retrieved from Auckland, New Zealand: http://ebooks.fmhs.auckland.ac.nz/growing_up_-_vulnerability_report_2/files/assets/common/downloads/publication.pdf

Moss, P. (2015). Where am I? Position and perspective in researching early childhood education. In A. Farrell, S. Kagan, E. Tisdall, & M. Kay (Eds.), *The Sage handbook of early childhood research*. Thousand Oaks, CA: Sage.

Munford, R., & Sanders, J. (2003). *Making a difference in families: Research that creates change*. Sydney, NSW: Allen & Unwin.

Oers, V. (1997). From context to contextualizing. *Learning and Instruction, 8*(6), 473–488.

Paris, D. (2011). 'A friend who understand fully': Notes on humanizing research in a multiethnic youth community. *International Journal of Qualitative Studies in Education, 24*(2), 137–149.

Paris, D., & Winn, M. (Eds.). (2014). *Humanizing research: Decolonizing qualitative inquiry with youth and communities*. London: Sage.

Rinaldi, C. (2006). *In dialogue with Reggio Emilia: Listening, researching, and learning*. London: Routledge Falmer.

Saleebey, D. (2012). *The strengths perspective in social work practice* (6th ed.). Boston: Pearson.

Sanders, J., & Munford, R. (2009). *Working with families: Strength-based approaches*. Wellington, New Zealand: Dunmore publishing.

Seligman, M. E., Ernst, R. M., Gillham, J., Reivich, K., & Linkins, M. (2009). Positive education: Positive psychology and classroom intervention. *Oxford Review of Education, 35*(3), 393–311.

St Louis, K., & Barton, A. (2002). Tales from the science education crypt: A critical reflection of positionality, subjectivity, and reflexivity in research. *Forum: Qualitative Social Research, 3*(3), 249–264.

Stokols, D. (1988). Transformational processes in people-environment relations. In J. E. McGrath (Ed.), *The social psychology of time: New perspectives* (pp. 233–252). Newbury Park, CA: Sage.

Stokols, D. (2018). *Social ecology in the digital age: Solving problems in a globalised world*. San Diego, CA: Academic.

Stokols, D., Grzywacz, J., McMahan, S., & Phillips, K. (2003). Increasing the health promotive capacity of human environments. *American Journal of Health Promotion, 18*(1), 4–13.

Stone, W. (2003). Bonding, bridging and linking with social capital. *Stronger Families Learning Exchange Bulletin, 4*(Spring/Summer), 13–16.

Thayer-Bacon, B. (2000). *Transforming critical thinking: Thinking constructively.* New York: Teachers College Press.

Thurow, R. (2016). *The first 1000 days – A crucial time for mothers and children.* New York: Public Affairs.

Tudge, J. (2008). *The everyday lives of young children: Culture, class, and child rearing in diverse societies.* Cambridge, UK: Cambridge University Press.

Uttal, L. (2009). (Re)visioning family ties to communities and contexts. In S. A. Lloyd, A. L. Few, & K. R. Allen (Eds.), *Handbook of feminist studies* (pp. 134–146). Thousand Oaks, CA: Sage.

van der Horst, F. C. (2011). *John Bowlby from psychoanalysis to ethology: Unravelling the roots of attachment theory.* West Sussex, UK: Wiley-Blackwell.

Van Manen, M. (1990). *Researching lived experience: Human science for an action sensitive pedagogy.* New York: State University of New York Press.

Walter, M. (2013a). The nature of social science research. In M. Walter (Ed.), *Social research methods* (pp. 3–23). Melbourne, VIC: Oxford University Press.

Walter, M. (Ed.). (2013b). *Social research methods* (3rd ed.). Melbourne, VIC: Oxford University Press.

Warr, D. (2004). Stories in the flesh and voices in the head: Reflections on the context and impact of research with disadvantaged populations. *Qualitative Health Research, 14*(4), 578–587.

Warren, A., & Warren, S. (1977). Ecological perspectives in behavior analysis. In R. Catalano's (Ed.), *Health, behavior, and the community: An ecological perspective.* New York: Pergamon Press.

Weick, A. (1992). Building a strength based perspective for social work. In D. Saleebey (Ed.), *The strength based perspective in social work practice.* New York: Longman.

Wong, S. M., & Cumming, T. (2008). *Practice grounded in theory: The theoretical and philosophical underpinnings of SDN's Child, Family and Children's Services Programs. The second of eight reports investigating SDN's Child, Family and Children's Services Program.* Retrieved from Sydney, NSW. https://www.researchgate.net/publication/265347796_Practice_Grounded_in_Theory

Yelland, N. (Ed.). (2010). *Contemporary perspectives on early childhood education.* New York: McGraw Hill/Open University Press.

Ziersch, A. (2005). Health implications of access to social capital: Findings from an Australian study. *Social Science & Medicine, 61*(10), 2119–2131.

Zubrick, S., Smith, G., Nicholson, J., Sanson, A., Jackiewicz, T., & LSAC Research Consortium. (2012). *Parenting and families in Australia.* Retrieved from Canberra, ACT. https://www.dss.gov.au/about-the-department/publications-articles/research-publications/social-policy-researchpaper-series/number-34-parenting-and-families-in-australia?HTML

3

Interpretivism—Valuing the Unfolding Lives and Stories of Young Families

Scenario 3: The Power of 'Oral Storying'

'Oh, not me! I never went to any of that! (Referring to prenatal and antenatal classes). It was most often the case that I got information from my aunties, my mum, or my grandmother about breastfeeding and connecting with my kid. My sista' was visited by the Blue Nurses when she had her kids, and they taught her all about preparing for the birth, and ways to play with her baby, and she shared that stuff with me. It's kind of like Chinese Whispers!' (Jenny, a playgroup mum with a daughter aged 2.5 years).

In a corner of the park grounds in a small town, north west of Hervey Bay, Queensland, Australia, Dr Mandy Johnson (an academic from the local university), and her two research assistants, Joshua and Tanya, sit laughing with a group of Murri mums at another one of their research playgroup catch-ups. There's a whole lot of yarning going on amongst the group, made up of three generations of indigenous mums, as several bubs crawl over their legs and play amongst them. At opportune moments, Mandy or one of the other researchers, tries to steer the conversation back to their groups' understandings of 'connecting with kids' (a term adopted when referring to bonding and attachment), and active play, and how they had acquired their knowledge and information.

© The Author(s) 2019

A. Brown, *Respectful Research With and About Young Families*, Palgrave Studies in Education Research Methods, https://doi.org/10.1007/978-3-030-02716-2_3

Mandy's team are engaged with local health services on a project titled The Wide Bay Early Stimulation and Movement, a research project which sets out to continue well-established partnerships with Murri families and local support networks in the region, in efforts to build collective understandings and knowledge of context. The current part of the project, collaboratively designed by Murri parents, involves narrative story work, seeking the insights and perspectives of parents (elders, grandparents, and new parents) involved in a local playgroup, along with other key agencies, early childhood services, playgroups, schools, community health agencies, support networks, and other organisations that support families and protect children.

Typically, reports and discourse of Aboriginal parenting and Aboriginal families and children are positioned within a deficit paradigm. However, their project is underpinned by a strengths-based perspective, which recognises the affordance of Aboriginal culture, including celebrating the collective community approach to child-rearing and parenting (Lohoar, Butera, and Kennedy, 2014), *The goal of the project is to engage in storying 'with' Murri parents, about their early parenting experiences, and understandings of 'connecting with kids'. The employment of storywork was seen of value, as it honoured oral traditions, and helped to give voice to the lived experiences of others, but was also attempted to reframe the research-participant dynamics, and relationships, in terms of research practices that support a more equal distribution of power and agency. The naturalistic design of the project meant that storying occurred on their 'own turf', where participants as co-researcher felt more comfortable, with the added benefit of their narratives contributing to authentic, rich, and in-depth data.*

Note: This scenario is loosely based on research conducted as part of the South Burnett project (Brown, 2009), *as well as inspired by the research and words of* Robyn Sandri (2013).

Chapter Synopsis

Storytelling and oral history are embedded in, and a notable part of the practices and culture of many tribes and families across generations and through time (Hodge, Pasqua, Marquez, & Geishirt-Cantrell, 2002). Stories serve a range of purposes, including passing on practices, history, values, and the meanings and interpretations of life events (Hampton & Toombs, 2013; Kiser, Baumgardner, & Dorado, 2010). Valuing the storied lives of young families opens up new research spaces, where the focus becomes one of gaining insights into how families make sense of their social worlds, while also giving voice and honouring the personal experiences, practices, and environments of others (Fiese, 2013). When families are offered the opportunity to recount and provide narratives about their domestic lives, they draw from an interpretivist frame that reflects their understandings of their contexts and the contexts of others.

What aspects of an interpretivist paradigm align with your beliefs, ways of viewing the world, or philosophical assumptions?

How does an interpretivist perspective impact on the types of research questions you pose, and the types of data you gather?

Why are the storied lives of families of value to researchers?

How will your relationships and interactions with family members impact on them sharing their stories?

How does your image of children and childhood impact on how you see their engagement in research?

How does your perspectives, beliefs, and the lens in which you view children and families impact on the way you enter 'domestic spaces' and interact with individuals in these environments?

What does it mean to 'listen' to children and adults in family research? What would it look like?

In this chapter, we focus more specifically on the value of interpretivism as a lens that affords us the opportunity to understand young families, why people do what they do (their motives), their behaviours, and their perceived realities. Interpretivism affords us the opportunity to explore a particular context, to investigate 'lived experiences', and to gain the perspectives and insights of others (Denzin & Lincoln, 2008; Merriam & Tisdall, 2016). Adopting such a perspective means seeing the world as being socially constructed and perceived. As such, interpretivists are interested in investigating the meaning-making that people ascribe to phenomenon within particular contexts and environments (Creswell, 2013).

Interpretivists appreciate the contextual insights, nuances, idiosyncrasies, and interpretations that research can reveal about individuals and groups in natural settings (Berg, 2016). Interpretivists do so through an adeptness in asking a particular set of questions, and by creating dialogical opportunities for others to share their stories (Gubrium & Holstein, 2003; Harden, Backett-Milburn, Hill, & MacLean, 2010). This chapter moves readers into a heightened awareness of 'what is' an interpretivist paradigm and its distinguishing features. The chapter provides a rationale for adopting such a paradigm, and illuminates key considerations for those considering employing this approach for engaging in research with, of, or about young families.

The second part of this chapter then explores a rationale for the important act of storying. In particular, we focus on the possibilities and potentiality that these dialogic opportunities offer to researchers, as mechanisms for better understanding everyday lives and perspectives. Such an approach requires a paradigmatic repositioning of the valuing of storying, and adopting a strengths-based perspective that celebrates the potentiality of others, and the insights into storied lives so generously shared (Fenton, Walsh, Wong, & Cumming, 2015; Saleebey, 2012). Working within an interpretivist paradigm requires researchers to reframe their methodological techniques, and theoretical orientations in ways that are sensitive, authentic, relevant, and rigorous (Palaiologou, 2014). In doing so we are better able to illuminate effectively and respectfully the lived experiences of family members (Mannion, 2007).

Finally, this chapter addresses the mechanics of listening, particularly in relation to the inclusion of 'child voice' within family. Attention is directed to the process of ethical co-construction of research with family members and what this might entail. This includes recognising the role of both researcher and the researched as active agents, co-constructors, and meaning-makers. The chapter concludes by reflecting on the important role that researchers play in the storying and meaning-making of others, and the responsibility we have as 'custodians of these stories'.

3.1   Interpretivism as a Method of Inquiry

Interpretivism and positivism are two dominant ontological and episte-mological ideologies which researchers choose to work within. These beliefs and values guide the actions and choices of the researcher in rela-tion to approaching and engaging in inquiry, including the relationships we engage in with participants (Creswell, 2013). Distinctly different paradigms from one another, interpretivists believe that there are multi-ple interpretations (multiple realities) and ways of viewing the world. Each situation and experience dependent on individual 'lived experi-ences', ways of knowing, and systems of meaning (Lincoln & Guba, 1988; Merriam & Tisdall, 2016).

Moreover, just like other scientific endeavours, those who choose to work within an interpretivist paradigm position themselves, and 'the other', in a particular way, adopting a distinct discourse, and a particu-lar set of terms and associated concepts. For interpretivists, this dis-course is descriptive, and supports the framing of inquiry strongly linked to the multiple realities and social worlds of others, and how these worlds are co-constructed and integrally linked (Merriam & Tisdall, 2016). For example, the term 'social actors' is often adopted as part of the discourse of interpretivism. This metaphor aptly describes the part that individuals play, and 'the stage' in which 'the play' unfolds and takes place, as well as the actors who are positioned in the 'theatre of life'.

Interpretivists believe that as individuals we act out multiple roles, and have multiple parts to play, in accordance to our own interpretations. Other terms such as 'explore' and 'investigation' are also popular words associated with interpretivist research, based on a mode a or goal of inquiry, that being, to elucidate and gain an in-depth understandings of a phenomenon. Further, this intent is linked to an interpretivists' desire to illuminate the world of the other, their stories, and their human expe-riences, therefore often employing the term 'lived experiences' (Van Manen, 1990).

Distinguishing Qualities of an Interpretivist Paradigm

Just as there are distinctive discourses, terms, and concepts associated with the humanistic virtues of an interpretivist paradigm, there are also a number of distinguishing qualities and features for engaging in this type of inquiry. One of the most important distinguishing qualities of this paradigm is the value for investigating how individuals give meaning to their experiences and context (Bryman, 2015). As such, interpretivists seek to reveal the buried meaning of the human experience, and have an genuine interest in the perspectives, and different ways that others interpret their world (Creswell, 2013).

Those who work within an interpretivist paradigm understand that knowledge and ones' experiences as being socially constructed, rather than objective. Those who choose to view the world through such a lens see individual experiences as being inextricably connected to, and taking place within the social worlds, social systems, and constructed in context with others (Daly, 2007). Interpretive processes are deeply embedded in shared meaning where inquiry is about, of, and with individuals situated in, and inextricably linked to, social systems, rather than viewing individuals in isolation, or removed from context (Denzin & Lincoln, 2011; Walter, 2013).

While the interpretivist researcher usually enters the field with an understanding and contextual appreciation of 'the other', he also recognises the idiosyncratic, complex, and nuanced nature of individuals. Therefore, interpretivists don't presume to know the position or perspective of 'the other', or the position 'the other' is coming from (note that Chap. 2 addresses the rationale for a heightened appreciation of the positionality of the researcher and the participant). An interpretivist's mission being not to extract one truth, but to seek out multiple realities and interpretations of meaning, based on individual values, standpoints, and perspectives (Clark & Moss, 2011).

Interpretivists focus on investigating participant experiences by adopting humanistic research methods that are primarily qualitative in nature. Interpretivists place value on research structures that elucidate factors that influence behaviour, and help capture the meaning, perceived and multiple realities, and the interactions of others. Underpinning this axiological perspective is the value interpretivists hold for creating dialogic opportunities with others, which in turn afford individuals and groups the ability to share accounts of their lived experiences (Warr, 2004). Critical to the success of this approach is building rapport and interpersonal relationships with participants (this topic will be addressed in Chap. 6 of this text).

Discovering the meaning that people attribute to their experiences requires a dedicated research framework, one designed to be flexible, fluid, and organic, rather than rigid and prescriptive. In this way, an interpretivist approach to inquiry is one that is not fixed, but adopts the type of approach that allows for methods and research practices to evolve, and emerge, dependent on the agency of the individuals involved, and the direction of the research. Such an approach requires interpretivists to employ research methods that will afford for gathering rich data that helps unravel a phenomenon (Stake, 2010; Walter, 2013). This position recognises the need for collecting data in the context in which participants are situated, as well as recognising the importance and uniqueness of each context. Finally, this perspective acknowledges the place of the researcher, in the dynamic facilitation and co-construction of meaning (Clark & Moss, 2011).

Interpretivist research activities would centre around modes of communication, and mediums that discern the lived experiences and stories of others. These methodological approaches could include interviews, focus groups, and the observation and photo-documentation of others, or a combination of these and other methods (see Chaps. 5 and 6 for further details on research methods and data collection strategies). Interpretivists come to understand the reality of the other through interaction, and by engaging in social processes and contexts where meaning is created (Daly, 2007). In relation to researching with young families, these contexts might include various environments within the domestic space such as the kitchen, the backyard, local neighbourhood, local community, or other places where families eat, share meals, engage in leisure and social activities, or related to education. Each of these, and many other potential contexts, offer an opportunity to better understand and appreciate the reality of families, and of how individuals make sense of and experience their surroundings, daily lives, and phenomena (Berg, 2016).

Time for Some Personal Reflection
How would adopting an interpretivist paradigm be reflected in the inquiry questions adopted, or the interview questions employed for a study?

What approaches, practices, and discourse would distinguish an interpretivist approach to research, from that of a positivist approach?

3.2   A Rationale for Adopting an Interpretivist Approach for Researching with Young Families

The lives and perspectives of real people in real situations has so much to offer educational and social researchers, in terms of the rich accounts, sense-making, and insights gained. With increased attention now focussed on venturing beyond traditional boundaries and contexts for research, parents as first educators, family members, and the domestic space of the family home are increasingly recognised not only as significant sites of intervention but as important ecological niches and sites worthy of inquiry, in all their complexity and richness. Further, the voices of members of families, including those of young children, are increasingly being acknowledged as having the right to be heard, and their insights acted on regarding issues that affect them.

One could argue that adopting an interpretivist approach to research with, of, or about young families is therefore highly appropriate, as it provides an opportunity for members of young families to recount their lived experiences, values, perspectives, and the lens in which they see the world and others (McHale, Booth, & Amato, 2014). Warr (2004) reinforces this, commenting that "the illuminative power of people's own life stories gives researchers valuable access to context-dependent accounts of people's lives and the values and practicalities that frame them" (p. 580).

As such, adopting an interpretivist approach to research affords family members the right to communicate through multiple modes their insights, thoughts, and experiences regarding issues in their social world, and places in which they are connected (Daly, 2007). Such an approach privileges the perspectives of individuals, particularly those who have to date been historically marginalised, disenfranchised, or whose voices have been silenced (Fiese, 2013).

In many ways, interpretivist research has the potential to be emancipatory in terms of seeking input from, and recognising the perspectives, and voice of the other. The intent of these efforts being the gathering of perspectives, data, and findings that together will inform decision-making, insights into a phenomenon, and may even contribute to leading to action, and the perspectives of others being acted upon (Miles, Chapman, & Francis, 2015). As such, working within an interpretivist paradigm offers a mode of inquiry that engages members of young families in a dialogical and reciprocal process, with the potential that this process may contribute to educational, social change, or reform.

From a social ecological perspective, it can be appreciated that the contexts and systems in which members of young families are positioned are complex and idiosyncratic. Adopting an interpretivist paradigm in research with young families opens up a type of inquiry that enables one to peel back some of this complexity, and layers of context, and in doing so affords for multiple meaning to be exposed (Miles et al., 2015). Interpretivism helps frame a mode of inquiry, where there is significant value placed on the multiple lifeworlds and experiences of individuals. As such, the challenge for researchers is to employ a range of methods which will support the pursuit of in-depth insight into the lives of families with young children, and the opportunity for their commonly held assumptions to be explored (Creswell, 2013; Merriam & Tisdall, 2016). Adopting these types of strategies affords researchers the opportunity to capture the details, richness of context, accounts, nuances, and social situations of others in an ever-changing world (Daly, 2007).

The excerpt below shares my reflection of engaging in research with the Mason family, one of the three families that formed part of case study in my doctoral research. The Masons are a very active and busy family comprising of parents Sarah (45) and Tom (40) and their 4.5-year-old daughter Helen. They also have two chickens (Beauty and Bell) and two dogs named Millie and Maxie (who form an integral part of their family). The journal entry captures the interpretivist paradigm in which I was positioned, and the value I placed on gathering context-dependent knowledge about parents' decision-making, and the practices they adopted for supporting active play with their children in the home context. Within the domestic space of the Masons' family home, and broader micro-environment, I spent many hours over several visits talking to the Masons, and watching Helen engaged in active play and documenting/scanning the home environment.

Sarah: "Helen's so excited. She's been saying, 'I can't wait to tell Alice about all the things I love to do!'"

Journal Entry: Getting to Know the Masons

I was welcomed into the Masons' home by Sarah and her daughter, Helen. I popped my things down, and informally chatted with them both. Within a few minutes of arriving, Helen invited me into her room to show me her toys. We chatted there for quite a while as she enthusiastically pointed out the favourite toys she loved to play with. I asked her for permission to photograph these items and invited her to do the same. As we did this, Helen chatted about which were her favourites and how she played with them. Sarah was occupied in the kitchen. She called out as we were finishing up in Helen's room and invited us to join her for a cup of tea and some nibbles.

As we were sitting down, Tom arrived home. This was rare, as Tom works long hours as co-owner of a local gym. It was a bonus for him to be able to join us for tea and a bite to eat. The interview process became quite busy, and a little bit overwhelming for me, as at times, several conversations occurred at once, and I was trying to spread my time between Sarah, Tom, and Helen, while remembering what sorts of questions I needed to ask. We all sat around the table drinking tea out of a Japanese pot and little cups and snacking, while Tom ate his lunch.

During these visits, I used prompts to evoke responses, and encourage participants to share their story of their context and experiences. These included questions such as: 'Can you share your routine, or how you spend time with your child each day?', or 'Where have you acquired your knowledge and understandings of active play from?' These types of questions helped elicit the contextual details of their unfolding stories. Each visit afforded opportunities to observe their 'household happenings', offering insight into the reality of family routines, the spaces where children played, and the busyness of a young family. I achieved this through the employment of a range of data collection techniques including: semi-structured interviews (which involved the active listening of participant stories), and conducting an environmental scan (using observations and photo-documentation). The combination of these techniques helped to capture individual perspectives, build an idiographic body of knowledge, and construct a more accurate portrayal of the multiple layers of meaning in each context (Cohen, Manion, & Morrison, 2007; Stark & Torrance, 2005). These understandings of situated meaning were based in a particular temporal moment, and the context of participants being interviewed (adapted from Brown, 2012).

As the 'Mason family' example highlights, researching within an interpretivist frame means appreciating the presence of the researcher in the research process. Stake (1995) reminds us that as researchers "we enter the scene with a sincere interest in learning how they function in their ordinary pursuits and milieus and with a willingness to put aside many presumptions while we learn" (p. 1). High on the agendas of interpretivist researchers is the goal of eliciting a version of participants' lived experiences and constructions of reality. However, we are also conscious of the fact that by virtue of locating ourselves within an interpretivist paradigm we are in fact co-constructors in the creation of meaning, and integrally embedded in framing the meaning-making of others. As such, interpretivists are transparent in the fact that our interests and bias frame all aspects of the research project, including the ways we make sense of and scrutinise participant stories, and the way in which another's reality is constructed and represented.

Interpretivist methods continue to evolve, and are also becoming increasingly innovative. For example, researchers Geia, Hayes, and Ushe (2013), located in the field of health, employed a method of inquiry that developed "a deeper understanding of the Aboriginal and Torres Strait Island perspective", by the privileging of voice (p. 16). Their approach was one that valued engaging with participants in a relaxed and informal mode of inquiry, where family members engaged in storytelling, or yarning, and were able to talk freely about their lived experiences (Bessarab & Ng'andu, 2010). The type of approach employed by Geia et al. (2013) is now gaining traction not only for research in Australian Aboriginal and Torres Strait Island studies and health, but also in education and social sciences (Kovach, 2009; Kovacha, 2010; Yunkaporta & Kirby, 2011).

An Interpretivist Paradigm with a Naturalistic Perspective

Observing the unfolding 'household happenings' often occurred while I was present with families during meal times. Where almost invariably, as I sat and conversed with parents and children around a table, or in the kitchen, family members would talk to one another and move off task, or into 'routines of parenting'. In these cases, it was important to just "go with the flow", and observe the natural unfolding of domestic events. This approach providing insight into the reality of family routines, the spaces where children played, the busyness of a young family, and the benefit of collecting authentic data. (Excerpt adapted from Brown, 2012, p. 124)

Adopting an interpretivist paradigm, with a naturalistic frame, is excellent for those whose intent is to investigate the storied lives and lived experiences of young families. It enables researchers to focus on processes such as active listening, and the sharing of dialogue, by being 'situated' or positioned within the lived environment. By observing families within their micro-context, or another context of relevance, people's stories can be fleshed out (Denzin & Lincoln, 2017). This is particularly the case where participants are on 'their turf' or in an environment where they feel comfortable, and not threatened.

Being present on a family's 'own turf' enables researchers to elicit participants' views, and gather rich details of their taken-for-granted contexts, and experiences (Berg, 2016). Researchers achieve this by drawing on a range of data collection methods, such as observations, interviews, and photo-documentation. Although often busy and even chaotic, the situated nature of these encounters offers a 'researcher in context' with an invaluable opportunity to observe environments, uncover behaviours, and develop a context-dependent understanding of a phenomenon. This is in line with two assumptions of a naturalistic perspective where it is understood that:

- Meaning-making occurs only in the context of the natural environment where individuals are influenced by the interplay of multiple systems and environments (Stokols, 1987); and
- An individual's interpretation as well as her or his experiences and knowledge is unique to a situation and a given set of circumstances.

Adopting a naturalistic approach to research supports Connelly and Clandinin's (1990) view that participants are storied people, "who individually and socially lead storied lives" (p. 2). Employing a naturalistic perspective for research with young families supports the pursuit of methods that are able to account for the complexity in the lives of parents of young children, and the composite of their realities. The primary focus of adopting an interpretivist paradigm with a naturalistic focus for engaging in inquiry with young families is to gain a great appreciation of the interrelated factors that influence the unique micro-context of the family home, and human behaviour, perspectives, and values within this domestic space, or other contexts in which families are located and engage in (Denzin & Lincoln, 2017).

This approach supports inquiry where the realities of individuals are socially constructed, and emerge from the ways in which individuals engage with, and make meaning of, their world and everyday realities. Daly (2007) points out that within this paradigm, there is recognition that "reality is changing and subject to interpretation by the participants themselves. As a result, there is less concern here with what 'really happened' and more concern with how people are making sense of events at this point in time" (p. 34).

3.3 Valuing the 'Storied Lives of Others'

The world, the human world, is bound together not by protons and electrons, but by stories. Nothing has meaning in itself: all the objects in the world would be shards of bare mute blankness, spinning wildly out of orbit, if we didn't bind them together with stories (Brian Morton, from "Starting out in the evening", as cited in Schoemperlen 2000, p. 141).

The Act of Storying

The act of storytelling and oral history are part of the fabric of what makes up and sustains human cultures. It is how we have sought to understand ourselves, and others, and pass these understandings and experiences on through time and place (Geia et al., 2013; Hancox, 2011). The act of storying communicates meaning, similar to that of messages passed on by fire sticks—from person to person, tribe to tribe, and generation to generation (Brown, 2012). 'Storying' includes the sharing of our own and others' stories. 'Storying', understood in its broadest form, includes oral storying, or stories communicated through dance, song, body languages, and even through imagery and image making. As such, storying is a way of making "sense of life" (Daiute & Lightfoot, 2004, p. ix), a vehicle for communicating a message, but also opens up the possibility of new constructions of reality, and new ways of thinking (Bruner, 1986, 1996).

Stories can empower, educate, guide, and support people as they navigate through social territory. Stories help to reveal what stands at the heart of an individual, their context, values, thoughts, fears, and beliefs (Perrino, 2011). Stories can function as a powerful tool of self-expression (Hancox, 2011). The act of storytelling serves to create shared understandings of events, or what Kansteiner (2002) calls our "collectively shared representations of the past" (p. 182). Storying is a fundamental approach, and one which we have used over the centuries to illuminate the meaning of our lived experiences and events (Kiser, 2015).

The Richness of Family Stories

The strong oral tradition of stories and storytelling has been, and continues to be, embraced as an integral element of the daily life in many cultures, including that of Indigenous cultures (Geia et al., 2013; Kovach, 2009). The telling and sharing of stories in many families occurs routinely, as an ordinary part of everyday interactions and family life. Storying is often a feast of "moving dialogue interspersed with interjections, interpretations, and addition" (Geia et al., 2013, p. 15). Stories, and storytelling, form part of the ongoing narrative and information exchange between family members—a practice integrally linked to family meals, leisure time, and times of, nurturing, interaction, and bonding.

The act of storytelling takes many forms, and supports many functions. These range from informal banter and brief conversations, to storytelling functioning as endearing moments of bonding, to "providing emotional nourishment" and support (Williams & Fraga, 2011, p. 179). More formal, oral storying can weave together and communicate shared lived experiences, feelings, thoughts, and life lessons, as well as recall threads of shared history (Fiese & Wamboldt, 2003; Kiser et al., 2010).

In this text, 'storying' is viewed through an interpretivist lens, and understood as a dualistic process, which involves the researcher intentionally illuminating the subtleties and richness of the 'lived experiences' of research participants, as part of an inquiry. 'Lived experiences' are understood to be those experiences which occur within particular contexts, temporality, or part of the everyday lives of an individual, or group (Grbich, 2007; Van Manen, 1990). Storying refers to an individual's expression of their experiences and views of the world. It is a process which captures the 'lived experiences' of parents, children, and other significant social actors. Storying takes place, and is generously conveyed and shared, within domestic spaces, or other environments in individuals move and live, through various medium, particularly verbally, through song, or in a written form.

The emergence of storytelling, or 'yarning', employed as a legitimate data collection method, is gaining momentum, particularly in Indigenous (Geia et al., 2013; Lohoar, Butera, & Kennedy, 2014), education, and social science research (Bessarab & Ng'andu, 2010; Kovach, 2009; Rinaldi, 2006). Whether it be about family beliefs, relationships, rules around conduct, roles and responsibilities, or views around issues such as education, storying provides insight into the nuanced worlds of others. Indeed, storying can be said to serve as a 'panopticon', strategically focussing 'the gaze', and offering increased visibility and illumination into the lives, behaviours, and meaning-making of family members (Gubrium et al., 2012; Harden et al., 2010). (Note that Chap. 7 continues to explore storytelling in terms of researchers being 'Custodians of the story'.)

While not necessarily intending to do so, affording individuals within families the opportunity to share their rich accounts, and insights of their social world and domestic spaces, storying has the potential to legitimise their theories, perspectives, experiences, and practices (Rinaldi, 2006). For those living within context, storying can serve as a vehicle of expression, offering individuals an opportunity to share their lived experiences with others (including their feelings, values, perceptions, and beliefs), or to tell their story in their own way (Kiser et al., 2010; Thomas, 2014). This dual process moves from the 'storyteller' sharing their 'lived experiences', understandings, and insights of lived events, feelings, perceptions, and expectations, providing an interpretive frame not afforded by any other avenue. 'Storying' then shifts to the researcher's role as 'storyteller', and the process of 'restorying'. This is understood as a very privileged task and comes with the responsibility of giving shape to an individual's thoughts, actions, and understandings, in all their complexity and subtlety (Clandinin, 2007).

3.4   Methodological Considerations for Creating Dialogic Opportunities

Researchers that wish to maximise respectful dialogic opportunities with young families, and to ensure their voices are privileged, and stories are heard, need to be attuned to interpersonal dynamics. Researchers need to be prepared to adopt particular theoretical, methodological, and practical frames for their work (Brown & Danaher, 2017; Fenton et al., 2015). A necessary part of this process is researchers being attentive to the ways in which participants present their stories, and how these stories may be positioned within, or outside existing or dominant discourse (Daly, 2007).

Adopting a paradigmatic positioning which supports the storying of others will in turn frame the questions we ask, and the conversations we have with individuals, as ones based on potentiality and possibility. The processes and methods we employ will need to afford opportunities for others to share their stories in ways that acknowledge their history, experience, values, and views (Dickson-Swift, James, Kippen, & Liamputtong, 2007). This approach also helps to maximise the authenticity, relevance, and rigour of the data collected, and the inquiry processes employed (Palaiologou, 2014). The next section of this chapter attends to some of these considerations, including extending on an earlier discussion on the value of adopting a strengths-based perspective in our research with family members (see Chap. 2 for more attention given to this topic).

Adopting a 'Strengths-Based' Approach to Dialogic Opportunities

In entering the space of the family home, or other spaces where we research with young families, it is important to appreciate that family members may come from a position of vulnerability, particularly those families who have experienced, or are experiencing, oppression, or marginalisation (Brown & Danaher, 2012; Paris, 2011), due to the discourse and values situated within the broader social cultural milieu (Mannion, 2007). Adopting a genuine 'strengths-based' approach to dialogic opportunities with young families, through our thoughts and actions, helps to reposition this discourse and set individuals at ease. This includes validating that the stories and narratives of others are legitimate and employing strategies that value, attend to, and recognise participant voice (Dreher, 2012). Such an approach sees participants as not only having rights, 'but insights', and that "the teller (the individual, family or community) is the expert in their own life" (Wong & Cumming, 2008, p. 17).

A critical aspect of adopting a strengths-based perspective for our inquiry is recognising that children are an integral part of young families, and in their own right can teach us a great deal about their everyday lives and contexts (Clark, 2001; Clark & Moss, 2011). Children, being children, offer us a unique insight into a range of phenomenon, that by their very nature they are embedded, and have a vested interest in. Entering the research space with the mindset of children being effective communicators changes the methodological approaches we adopt to capture and listen to their views and experiences. This include framing the types of conversations we have, the questions we ask, as well as ensuring that we set up conditions that afford for children to feel comfortable in sharing their insights and stories (Harden et al., 2010).

Engaging in the Act of Attentiveness, Listening, and Hearing

"The respondent is someone who can provide amazingly detailed descriptions of his or her thoughts, feelings, and activities—presumably better than anyone else—if one asks and listens carefully" (Gubrium, Holstein, Marvasti, & McKinney, 2012, p. 29).

If we value the perspectives and stories of 'the other', then an important task in creating dialogical opportunities is the act of listening and validating the stories of individuals. The act of listening enables researchers to better understand experiences, perspectives, and multiple interpretations of meaning in context, while at the same time seeking to gain greater insight into another's world. The act of listening enables researchers an avenue for extending on narratives, through prompts, as well as opportunities to elicit more details with additional questions (McCashen, 2005).

Although the act of listening takes up a significant part of our day, and so should come quite naturally, unfortunately, this is not always the case. As such, in order for this form of communication and the co-construction of shared meaning to be effective, it requires a certain level of experience, expertise, and the employment of a range of interpersonal skills (Fedesco, 2015). The act of listening is a skill, as well as a disposition. It includes breaking down communication barriers by establishing a bond and a sense of trust and respect with another (Daly, 2007). The act of listening goes beyond just the mechanics of listening. It requires a degree of authentic connectivity and openness with the participant (Geia et al., 2013). (Note that this topic will be expanded upon further in Chap. 6.)

The act of listening involves a heightened sense of awareness of 'the other'. It requires focussing attention on processes such as receptivity, recognition, and response. Listening in this context goes beyond a generic concept (Alasuutari, 2013), or simply viewed as "aurality, but rather as a powerful metaphor for analysing 'the other side' of voice – that is, the importance of attention and response, openness and recognition to complete the circuits of democratic communication" (Dreher, 2012, p. 161). This attentiveness, or attunement to others, includes the use of physical gestures (such as body language, making eye contact, and tone of voice), and the use of 'backchannels' or auditory responses such as 'yes', 'mmm', 'uh huh' and 'ok' (Fedesco, 2015; Geia et al., 2013; Macnamara, 2015).

If we support the thinking that the act of listening is not only with the end goal being one of knowledge extraction, but also for knowledge creation, then viewing children, as active agents, is an integral part of the process of the co-construction of meaning, and data generation (Palaiologou, 2014). This position recognises that children offer their own thoughts and insights that are situated, and different to those of adults (Harcourt, Perry, & Waller, 2011). However, Palaiologou (2014) points out that there is also a risk of research "losing its rigour in the name of participation" or to the tokenistic approach of the inclusion of children in research (p. 692). Therefore, due to the complexity of researching with young children, and the valuing of their perspectives and voice, experts advise the importance of reconsidering, rethinking, and even reframing our approaches and methods (Dockett & Perry, 2011; Harcourt et al., 2011).

For example, our thinking needs to critically consider the interpretation of the term 'voice' (Dockett & Perry, 2011), the complexity of listening to young children, and the contextual nature of phenomenon located within these research spaces (Palaiologou, 2014). We also need to account for and recognise the power differential that exists between the researcher and the researched (in this case the young child). Further, we need to be mindful of the multifaceted, relational, and socio-spatial dimensions "around children's voice and participation", ensuring that attention is given to the socialness of human behaviour (Gergen, 2009; Mannion,

2007, p. 405). This includes accounting for children's spaces being co-constructed by the actions of significant adults (Palaiologou, 2014).

Palaiologou (2014), also cautions that our methodological approaches support "plurality, difference and diversity" (p. 690). This includes appreciating that young children's communication occurs in multiple forms, and, as such, requires researchers to think carefully about how 'voice' may be interpreted or comprised. This debate emphasises that researchers need to be open to "alternative ways of 'listening' to children", which includes going beyond the spoken word, to employing tools such as children's drawing, photographs, and observation (Clark & Moss, 2011; Dockett & Perry, 2011; Palaiologou, 2014, p. 701).

In her book *In dialogue with Reggio Emilia: Listening, researching, and learning*, Rinaldi (2006) refers to "a pedagogy of relationships and listening" (p. 64). The approach addressed in her text is underpinned by a strengths-based perspective, and positioned within a lens of deep respect for children, adults, family, and community. Rinaldi (2006) refers to listening as "a metaphor for having the openness and sensitivity to listen and be listened to, listening not just with our ears, but with all our senses (sight, touch, smell, taste, orientation)" (p. 65).

As researchers, there is much that we can take away from the work of academics, such as Rinaldi, in terms of methodological considerations for creating dialogical opportunities with members of young families. These include:

- Listening being a sensitive act;
- Listening meaning an awareness of the various modes in which others communicate;
- Listening taking time, "a time full of silences, of long pauses" (Rinaldi, 2006, p. 65);
- Listening requiring deep awareness and suspension of judgement; and
- Listening being a process of legitimation that enriches those who listen and those who share their storying.

We can also draw from other disciplines for insights into approaches to listening, including those from public communications expert Macnamara (2015). He identifies seven 'canons of listening', and shares some key

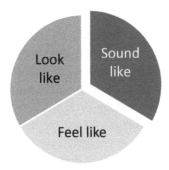

Fig. 3.1 Looks like, sounds like, feels like

ideas that are worthwhile considering in terms of researching with young families. These include the recognition of 'the other' having legitimate rights; acknowledging the stories and perspectives of others; being attentive to others; being open and ethical about interpreting what others have to say; and listening not to only to reply or respond, but to understand (Covey, 1989).

Time for Some Personal Reflection

- What would it 'look like', 'sound like', or 'feel like', to engage with others in research where listening is respectful, active, and open (see Fig. 3.1)?
- How would active listening be evidenced in practice?
- What are the qualities and practices of a good listener?
- What are the distinctions between listening and hearing in research?
- What impact might our body language have on the act of listening to others?

Ethical Co-construction—Recognising All Family Members as Active Agents

When we research with family members, we engage in a process of the co-construction of meaning, rather than just focussing on knowledge extraction (Clark & Moss, 2011; Kellett, 2010). This approach supports an interpretivist paradigm, and a social learning process, rooted in human relationships. Both of these recognise the involvement of the researcher and research participants (family members), with each adopting the role of 'active agent', and meaning-maker (see Chap. 4 for further details on this topic, and the role of participants in inquiry). As such, the level of engagement and involvement by each party, which could include children, parents, significant caregivers, and extended family, is positioned in ways that value and prioritise perspectives, experiences, and knowledge, while cognisant that our storying is dynamic, and transformed as part of being embedded in socio-cultural contexts (Bermúdez, Muruthi, & Jordan, 2016; Bushin, 2009).

Humanizing research, and adopting decolonising epistemologies and methodologies, privilege the voices of others, particularly those often silenced, ignored, or marginalised. Seeking to investigate individuals in context helps create rich pictures of participants' lived experiences and understanding of their micro-environments, and supports the ethical co-construction, and prioritising of 'participant voice' (Kellett, 2010). It is a process of inquiry that is underpinned by "relationships of care and dignity and dialogic consciousness raising", by both the researcher and participant (Paris & Winn, 2014, p. xvi).

This approach also recognises the richness of local wisdom, context, and experience, and the contribution this in turn has on knowledge production. Working within such a framework opens up opportunities for researchers to "decenter the dominant discourse of knowledge production, and loosen the grip of neocolonial paradigms" (Bermúdez et al., 2016, p. 192). This responsive approach to research lends itself to methodological and data collection methods with young families that are ethical and respectful (see Chaps. 5 and 6 of this text where these topics are addressed further).

Adopting such an ontological and epistemological perspective is underpinned by the premise that meaning-making occurs, and is embedded in context, and dependent upon ongoing collaboration with others. This approach supports a process of sharing ideas and negotiating new meaning, where constructions of new understandings of reality are created (Pring, 2000). Within the social spaces of people's everyday lives (including social, cultural, historical, geographical, and political realms), it is also appreciated that multiple contextual factors will impact on individual and group behaviours.

Privileging the Narratives and Perspectives of Children

Young families exist within complex social, political, and cultural settings, where children form part of the family ecology (Clark, 2001; Grace, Hodge, & McMahon, 2017; James & Prout, 1997). Within this ecological framework there exists a duality of relationships and bi-directional forces between the child, family members, and the greater social world. Within these spaces, children actively influence the environments and lives of others around them. At the same time their perspectives, experiences, and behaviours are constructed by individuals within the micro-environment, and more broadly from the socio-cultural milieu in which they are embedded (Bronfenbrenner & Morris, 2006).

In privileging the storied lives of young families, it is important to not forget about children as active agents, important social actors, and skilled communicators (Clark & Moss, 2005; Kellett, 2010). We need to view children as actively engaging in, and with, their environment. Viewing children through an ecological lens positions children as offering a distinct insight into their own lives, and a nuanced and inclusive picture of their familied life, and other social spaces they inhabit (Bushin, 2009; Podesta, 2013). Yet, while children may be understood as social actors in the construction of their own lives, their agency needs to be understood as being located in context, and strongly linked to the agency and power of adults (Dockett & Perry, 2011; Morrow, 2011).

From a very early age, developmentally and experientially, storytelling is part of the fabric of family life in many contexts and cultures. Hence, the act of storytelling and shared narratives offers a form of communication that comes naturally to young children. Fiese (2013) points out that "children as young as 3 years of age will actively engage in conversations with their parents about personal experiences that later remain as autobiographical memories" (p. 374). Therefore, children have much to offer regarding the insights into the domestic spaces, practices, and behaviours of young families, and important actors in storytelling.

Although children may increasingly be seen as legitimate participants in family research, traditionally their participation, their voice, their position and experiences have often been overlooked, and unheeded in social and educational research (Bushin, 2009; Levy, Murphy, & Lee, 2008). McKendrick (2001) refers to this phenomenon as an 'absent presence', where limited consideration has been given to dialogical opportunities that privilege the narratives of children, or value their stories. This can be tracked back to broader debates, discourse, and constructions of childhood, and a legacy of children being viewed as incompetent, needy, and vulnerable objects that required protection (Morrow & Richards, 1996; Moss & Petre, 2005; Woodhead, 2006). Within this paradigm, adults traditionally felt inclined to speak and choose for children, rather than involve them in decision-making. In many cases this practice has flowed through to traditional inquiry methods, and is still evidenced, where researchers employ practices of researching 'on children', rather than 'with young children' (Christensen & James, 2008; Palaiologou, 2014).

Encouragingly, over recent times, there has been a distinct paradigmatic shift and subversion of deficit images of childhood, influenced by the conceptual thinking of the sociology of children (James & Prout, 1997, 2015; Pole, Mizen, & Bolton, 1999). Further, post-foundational perspectives and understandings of childhood have led to more respectful methodological approaches for involving children, and honouring their perspectives and voices (Dockett & Perry, 2011; Palaiologou, 2014; Woodhead & Faulkner, 2008). This ideological shift has helped to position children as active citizens, and capable decision-makers aligned with a strengths-based approach discussed in the previous chapter (Palaiologou, 2014). This perspective also recognises children as competent social agents with expertise, valued opinions, and worthy of their contribution (James & Prout, 1997; MacNaughton, 2005; Malaguzzi, 1993; Moss & Petrie, 2002).

This change, or ideological repositioning, mirrors discourse foregrounded by Section 7 of the UN's Convention on the Rights of the Child (United Nations, 1989), where guiding principles have resulted in an uptake of a 'rights-based' approach, and adopting a participatory rights perspective in research (Kellett, 2010; Prout, 2000). This position recognises children as citizens of the present (rather than the future), who actively engage in, and are decision-makers in, and of, their social worlds (Rinaldi, 2013). Bushin (2009) refers to a 'child's rights' framework, where consideration is given to children being consulted in matters in which they are actively a part of and involved in, including not only the right to share their thoughts, but also the right to be heard, and taken seriously. This position also acknowledges a young child's choice to participate in research, where their perceptions, conceptions, and understandings of their world are foregrounded, and where they play an active part in the inquiry process, including the right to express their views regarding issues which affect them (Article 12).

Consequently, those seeking to embed and employ rights-based practices, and adopt humanistic approaches, have appreciated that there is great complexity associated with this task. This has included taking great lengths to ensure these approaches are inclusive, and account for the agentic nature of children. This focus adopts an approach concerned with 'researching with' children as active subjects, rather than 'researching on' children (as objects) (Alderson & Morrow, 2011; Gray & Winter, 2011; Sumsion & Goodfellow, 2012). This approach also includes a repositioning of children, with increased attention focussed on the recognition of 'child voice', and child participation (Lansdown, 2005), and is appreciative of the ways that children can shape and influence the research process and findings (Farrelly, Stewart-Withers, & Kelly Dombrowski, 2014; Lunn & Moscuazz, 2014).

In recent years, efforts have been made by many scholars to rethink and more carefully consider the research methods they choose to employ, and how these might best reflect child-inclusive practice and participative inquiry (McTavish, Streelasky, & Coles, 2012). Further, cognisant of the rights and agency of children to share their insights on everyday experiences, researchers are moving from predetermined methodological approaches, to ones which better afford for opportunities to research alongside children (Bushin, 2009; Fargas-Malet, McSherry, Larkin, & Robinson, 2010). This includes employing methods that elicit the perspectives of children, as well as adults, by engaging in conversations and the collection and sharing of artefacts such as photographs, and children's drawings. (See Chap. 6 for further information on research methods that support these practices, e.g. the Mosaic approach.) Research approaches have also demonstrated efforts to provide children with opportunities to express themselves and be involved with the direction of the research project (McTavish et al., 2012; Palaiologou, 2014).

For example, Hawkins (2010, p. 15) employed participatory action research to engage in a line of inquiry that examined strategies to support the teaching of social justice in early year's education. Influenced by the sociology of childhood, and a post-modernist view of children and childhood, Hawkins acknowledged children's capacity, their expert knowledge and ability to be self-reflective, and the value of children's voices and "young children's thoughts and understandings of social diversity" (p. 15). Others, such as Bushin (2009), have employed in-depth, semi-structured interviews, and 'child-inclusive methods', referred to as a 'children in families approach', to investigate children's experiences of family migration to the English countryside. In her case, adopting a 'children in families approach' afforded Bushin opportunities to explore experiences and understandings of both children, and adults in families. "It also illustrated how parents and children negotiate family migration decision-making and the ways in which this sometimes reproduces broader power relations between adults and children" (Bushin, 2009, p. 439).

A longitudinal study, conducted by Clark and Moss (2011), is another example of a research project where young children, and adults from a range of disciplines (including practitioners, architects, and health and social welfare professions), were involved in a project and invited to share their insights in the design of two early childhood environments in England. The researchers in this study utilised a Mosaic approach that "played to the strengths of young children" and their meaning-making (Clark, 2011, p. 324). They also utilised a range of documentation tools for gathering the perspectives of others, and provocations for further dialogue, such as observations, drawings, map-making, participant-generated images, photographs, and semi-and informal interviews.

Each of the projects mentioned and many other innovative examples (Harcourt et al., 2011; Pascal & Bertram, 2009) offer evidence of researchers' strong commitment to employ methods of inquiry that are participant-centred (Clark, 2011), respectful, and that recognise and value the voice and stories of children, whilst also seeking to support the participation of children in the research process. A common theme across these examples of inquiry is the value placed on collaborative meaning-making with children, and providing spaces in which children's theorising is taken seriously in efforts to seek to understand their 'storied lives' (Clark, Kjorholt, & Moss, 2005; McTavish et al., 2012). The combined approaches in many cases seek out research tools that run parallel with 'the hundred languages of children' that Malaguzzi (Edwards, Gandini, & Forman, 1998) refers to, in terms of recognising that there are many, many ways for individuals to express their perspectives and experiences, and be active agents in the inquiry process.

3.5   The Role of the Researcher in the Storying of Family Members

As research with young families continues to open up dialogical opportunities for meaning-making, which includes privileging the voices and stories of children as well as those of adults, there are opportunities to embrace innovative methods, to ask new ethical questions, and to reconsider the role of the researcher in these encounters. In our efforts to plan for and conduct research that embraces inclusive research practices, whilst being conscious of the power differential that exists between the researcher and participants, there is still much to learn. (Note that these types of considerations, particularly regarding participant involvement and ethical considerations, will be explored in the next chapter of this text.) This necessitates a research role that is no longer one of omnipotence and neutrality, but one where engagement with individuals is humanistic, is conscious of the relational of socio-spatial dimensions of the others, communicated through stories, and is built on a foundation of relationships based on trust, dignity, and respect (Clark et al., 2005; Gergen, 2009; Harcourt & Einarsdóttir, 2011; Mannion, 2007). (Note that Chap. 6 is dedicated to unpacking themes on building rapport, trust, and respect with research participants.)

Thus, in appropriating the voices and stories of others, the researcher is embedded, visible, and an integral part of the dialogic space. Our role is one which involves explicitly acknowledging the interest we have in meaning-making about the everyday lives of others, and "exposing the partiality of our perspective" (England, 1994, p. 86). We can achieve this by being open about our intentions, and honest about the limitations and scope of the study. As noted earlier in this chapter, this role also requires the researcher to draw upon a range of skills that go beyond purely mechanisms of 'aurality', including interpersonal skills, physical gestures that communicate openness, attentiveness, and acceptance to others, and auditory responses (Daly, 2007).

Finally, due to the complexity of research with and of young families, and valuing their perspective and voice, it is important that one of the roles of the researcher is a self-reflector. This necessitates engaging in ongoing introspection and self-scrutiny, which includes thinking carefully about the methods and approaches adopted. This process of self-reflection enables us to learn from our past research experiences, to reevaluate, to reframe, and to reconsider. At times, this may require the researcher to be more flexible, be more organic, and be willing to shift the direction of an inquiry, depending on the input and interactions of others involved in this process (Harcourt et al., 2011; Mannion, 2007). This process also involves an interplay between the goal of the research, the research participants, the paradigmatic positioning of the research, the contextual nature of the research, and the methods that afford constructed dialogue with others (Kovacha, 2010; Palaiologou, 2014).

3.6   Interpretivism—Engaging in the Storying with, and of, Young Families

This chapter has highlighted foundational thinking related to interpretivism, its features, as well as what it means to be an interpretivist. Hopefully, the reader might also come away from engaging with this chapter with a greater appreciation for the value of storying in the lives of young families, and the insights these narratives can provide to understandings of phenomenon related to young families, and their membership. Finally, the intent of this chapter was that the reader might gain a greater appreciation of their responsibility in creating respectful dialogic opportunities with family members, which might require greater consideration given to reframing methodological techniques and theoretical orientations to engage in inquiry that is authentic, ethical, and respectful.

As researchers, we may find ourselves in the privileged position of engaging in inquiry with young families, to explore their lifeworlds and lived experiences. However, with this task come responsibilities. As such, the role of the 'collector of stories' is not a task that should not be taken lightly, but one which we might refer to as being 'custodians of the storied lives of others'.

References

Alasuutari, M. (2013). Voicing the child? A case study in Finnish early childhood education. *Childhood, 21*(2), 1–8.

Alderson, P., & Morrow, V. (2011). *The ethics of research with children and young people: A practical handbook*. London: Sage.

Berg, B. (2016). *Qualitative research methods for the social sciences* (9th ed.). Boston: Pearson.

Bermúdez, J. M., Muruthi, B., & Jordan, L. (2016). Decolonizing research methods for family science: Creating space at the centre – Decolonizing research practices. *Journal of Family Theory & Review, 8*(2), 192–206.

Bessarab, D., & Ng'andu, B. (2010). Yarning about yarning as a legitimate method in indigenous research. *Journal of Critical Indigenous Studies, 3*(1), 37–50.

Bronfenbrenner, U., & Morris, P. (2006). The bioecological model of human development. In W. Damon & R. M. Lerner (Eds.), *Handbook of child psychology, volume 1, theoretical models of human development* (6th ed., pp. 793–828). New York: Wiley.

Brown, A. (2009). *South Burnett early movement and stimulation project*. Retrieved from Toowoomba, QLD. https://eprints.usq.edu.au/7703/1/Brown_Project_Report_2009_AV.pdf

Brown, A. (2012). *The new frontier: A social ecological exploration of factors impacting on parental support for the active play of young children within the micro-environment of the family home*. PhD, University of Southern Queensland, Toowoomba, QLD.

Brown, A., & Danaher, P. A. (2012, December 2–6). *Respectful, responsible and reciprocal ruralities research: Approaching and positioning educational research differently within Australian rural communities.* Paper presented at the Joint International Conference of the Australian Association for Research in Education and the Asia Pacific Educational Research Association (AARE 2012): Regional and Global Cooperation in Educational Research, Sydney, NSW.

Brown, A., & Danaher, P. A. (2017). CHE Principles: Facilitating authentic and dialogical semi-structured interviews in educational research. *International Journal of Research & Method in Education*, 1–15. https://doi.org/10.1080/1 743727X.2017.13799.

Bruner, J. (1986). *Actual minds, possible worlds.* Cambridge, MA: Harvard University Press.

Bruner, J. (1996). *The culture of education.* Cambridge, MA: Harvard University Press.

Bryman, A. (2015). *Social research methods.* Oxford, UK: Oxford University Press.

Bushin, N. (2009). Researching family migration decision making: A children-in-families approach. *Population, Space and Place, 15*(5), 429–443.

Christensen, P., & James, A. (Eds.). (2008). *Research with children: Perspectives and practices* (2nd ed.). Milton Park, Oxon: Falmer Press.

Clandinin, J. (2007). *Handbook of narrative inquiry: Mapping a methodology.* Thousand Oaks, CA: Sage.

Clark, A. (2001). How to listen to very young children: The Mosaic approach. *Child Care in Practice, 7*(4), 333–341.

Clark, A. (2011). Breaking methodological boundaries? Exploring visual, participatory methods with adults and young children. *European Early Childhood Education Research Journal, 19*(3), 321–330.

Clark, A., Kjorholt, A. T., & Moss, P. (2005). *Beyond listening: Children's perspectives on early childhood services.* Bristol, UK, Policy Press.

Clark, A., & Moss, P. (2005). *Spaces to play: More listening to young children using the Mosaic approach.* London: Jessica Kingsley Publishers.

Clark, A., & Moss, P. (2011). *Listening to young children: The Mosaic approach* (2nd ed.). London: National Children's Bureau and Joseph Rowntree Foundation.

Cohen, L., Manion, L., & Morrison, K. (2007). *Research methods in education.* New York: Routledge.

Connelly, M., & Clandinin, D. (1990). Stories of experience and narrative inquiry. *Educational Researcher, 19*(5), 2–14.

Covey, S. (1989). *He seven habits of highly effective people: Powerful lessons in person change.* New York: Free Press.

Creswell, J. (2013). *Qualitative inquiry and research design: Choosing among five approaches.* Thousand Oaks, CA: Sage.

Daiute, C., & Lightfoot, C. (2004). Theory and craft in narrative inquiry. In C. Daiute & C. Lightfoot (Eds.), *Narrative analysis: Studying the development of individuals in society* (pp. vii–xviii). Thousand Oaks, CA: Sage.

Daly, K. J. (2007). *Qualitative methods for family studies and human development.* Thousand Oaks, CA: Sage.

Denzin, N., & Lincoln, N. (2008). *The landscape of qualitative research: Theories and issues* (3rd ed.). London: Sage.

Denzin, N., & Lincoln, N. (Eds.). (2011). *The Sage handbook of qualitative research* (4th ed.). Thousand Oaks, CA: Sage.

Denzin, N., & Lincoln, N. (2017). *The Sage handbook of qualitative research* (5th ed.). Thousand Oaks, CA: Sage.

Dickson-Swift, V., James, E., Kippen, S., & Liamputtong, P. (2007). Doing sensitive research: What challenges do qualitative researchers face? *Qualitative Research, 7*(3), 327–353.

Dockett, S., & Perry, B. (2011). Researching with young children: Seeking assent. *Child Indicators Research, 4*(2), 231–247.

Dreher, T. (2012). A partial promise of voice: Digital Storytelling and the limits of listening. *Media International Australia Incorporating Culture and Policy: Quarterly journal of media research and resources, 42*, 157–166.

Edwards, C., Gandini, L., & Forman, G. (1998). *The hundred languages of children: The Reggio Emilia approach advanced reflections* (2nd ed.). Norwood, NJ: Ablex Publishing.

England, K. (1994). Getting personal: Reflexivity, positionality, and feminist research. *The Professional Geographer, 46*(1), 80–89.

Fargas-Malet, M., McSherry, D., Larkin, E., & Robinson, C. (2010). Research with children: Methodological issues and innovative techniques. *Journal of Early Childhood Research, 8*(2), 175–192.

Farrelly, T., Stewart-Withers, R., & Kelly Dombrowski, K. (2014). Being there: Mothering and absence/presence in the field. *Sites: A Journal of Social Anthropology and Cultural Studies, 11*(2), 1–32.

Fedesco, H. N. (2015). The impact of (In)effective listening on interpersonal interactions. *The International Journal of Listening, 29*(2), 103–106.

Fenton, A., Walsh, K., Wong, S., & Cumming, T. (2015). Using strengths-based approaches in early years practice and research. *International Journal of Early Childhood, 47*(1), 27–52.

Fiese, B. (2013). Family context in early childhood. In O. Saracho & B. Spodek (Eds.), *Handbook of research on the education of young children* (3rd ed., pp. 369–384). New York: Routledge.

Fiese, B., & Wamboldt, F. S. (2003). Coherent accounts of coping with a chronic illness: Convergences and divergences in family measurement using a narrative analysis. *Family Process, 42*(4), 439–451.

Geia, L. K., Hayes, B., & Usher, K. (2013). Yarning/Aboriginal storytelling: Towards an understanding of an Indigenous perspective and its implications for research practice. *Contemporary Nurse, 46*(1), 13–17.

Gergen, K. J. (2009). *Relational being: Beyond self and community.* Oxford, UK: Oxford University Press.

Grace, R., Hodge, K., & McMahon, C. (Eds.). (2017). *Children, families and communities* (5th ed.). South Melbourne, VIC: Oxford University Press.

Gray, C., & Winter, E. (2011). Hearing voices: Participatory research with pre-school children with and without disabilities. *European Early Childhood Education Research Journal, 19*(3), 309–320.

Grbich, C. (2007). *Qualitative data analysis: An Introduction.* London: Sage.

Gubrium, J., & Holstein, J. (2003). Analysing interpretive practice. In N. Denzin & N. Lincoln (Eds.), *Strategies of qualitative inquiry* (2nd ed., pp. 214–248). Thousand Oaks, CA: Sage.

Gubrium, J., Holstein, J., Marvasti, A., & McKinney, K. (2012). *The Sage handbook of interview research: The complexity of craft.* Thousand Oaks, CA: Sage.

Hampton, R., & Toombs, M. (2013). Culture, identity and indigenous Australian people. In R. Hampton & M. Toombs (Eds.), *Indigenous Australians and health: The wombat in the room* (pp. 3–23). South Melbourne, VIC: Oxford University Press.

Hancox, D. (2011). Stories with impact: The potential of storytelling to contribute to cultural research and social inclusion. *The Journal of Media and Culture, 14*(6). http://journal.media-culture.org.au/index.php/mcjournal/article/view/439

Harcourt, D., & Einarsdóttir, J. (2011). Introducing children's perspectives and participation in research. *European Early Childhood Education Research Journal, 19*(3), 301–307.

Harcourt, D., Perry, B., & Waller, T. (2011). *Researching young children's perspectives: Debating the ethics and dilemmas of educational research with children.* London: Taylor & Francis.

Harden, J., Backett-Milburn, K., Hill, M., & MacLean, A. (2010). Oh, what a tangled web we weave: Experiences of doing 'multiple perspectives' research in families. *International Journal of Social Research Methodology, 13*(5), 441–452.

Hawkins, K. (2010). *A cry to teach for social justice: Linking early childhood education, participatory action research and children's literature.* Toowoomba, QLD: University of Southern Queensland.

Hodge, F. S., Pasqua, A., Marquez, C. A., & Geishirt-Cantrell, B. (2002). Utilizing traditional storytelling to promote wellness in American Indian communities. *Journal of Transcultural Nursing, 13*(1), 6–11.

James, A., & Prout, A. (Eds.). (1997). *Constructing and reconstructing childhood.* London: Falmer.

James, A., & Prout, A. (2015). *Constructing and reconstructing childhood: Contemporary issues in the sociological study of childhood.* New York: Routledge.

Kansteiner, K. (2002). Finding meaning in memory: A methodological critique of collective memory studies. *History & Theory, 41*(2), 179–197.

Kellett, M. (2010). *Rethinking children and research: Attitudes in contemporary society.* London: Continuum International Publishing.

Kiser, L. J. (2015). *Strengthening family coping resources: Intervention for families impacted by trauma.* New York: Routledge.

Kiser, L. J., Baumgardner, B., & Dorado, J. (2010). Who are we, but for the stories we tell: Family stories and healing. *Psychological Trauma: Theory, Research, Practice, and Policy, 2*(3), 243–249.

Kovach, M. (2009). *Indigenous methodologies: Characteristics, conversations, and contexts.* Toronto, ON: University of Toronto Press.

Kovacha, M. (2010). Conversational method in indigenous research. *First Peoples Child and Family Review, 5*(1), 40–48.

Lansdown, G. (2005). *Can you hear me? The right of young children to participate in decisions affecting them* (Working papers in early childhood development, no. 36). ERIC.

Levy, D., Murphy, L., & Lee, C. K. (2008). Influences and emotions: Exploring family decision-making processes when buying a house. *Housing Studies, 23*(2), 271–289.

Lincoln, Y., & Guba, E. (1988). *Criteria for assessing naturalistic inquiries as reports.* Paper presented at the American Educational Research Association, April 5–9, New Orleans, LA.

Lohoar, S., Butera, N., & Kennedy, E. (2014). *Strengths of Australian Aboriginal cultural practices in family life and child rearing.* Retrieved from https://aifs.gov.au/cfca/sites/default/files/publication-documents/cfca25.pdf

Lunn, J., & Moscuazz, A. (2014). Doing it together: Ethical dimensions of accompanied fieldwork In J. Lunn (Ed.), *Fieldwork in the global south: Ethical challenges and dilemmas* (pp. 69–82). London: Routledge.

Macnamara, J. (2015). *Creating an 'architecture of listening' in organizations: The basis of engagement, trust, healthy democracy, social equity, and business sustainability.* Retrieved from Sydney, NSW. https://www.uts.edu.au/sites/default/files/fass-organizational-listening-report.pdf

MacNaughton, G. (2005). *Doing Foucault in early childhood studies: Applying post-structural ideas.* New York: RoutledgeFalmer.

Malaguzzi, L. (1993). History, ideas, and basic philosophy: An interview with Lella Gandini. In C. Edwards, L. Gandini, & G. Forman (Eds.), *The hundred languages of children: The Reggio Emilia approach – Advanced reflections* (2nd ed.). Greenwich, CT: Ablex Publishing.

Mannion, G. (2007). Going spatial, going relational: Why "listening to children" and children's participation needs reframing. *Discourse: Studies in the Cultural Politics of Education, 28*(3), 405–420.

McCashen, W. (2005). *The strengths approach.* Bendigo, VIC: St. Luke's Innovative Resources.

McHale, S., Booth, A., & Amato, P. (Eds.). (2014). *Emerging methods in family research.* London: Springer.

McKendrick, J. H. (2001). Coming of age: Rethinking the role of children in population studies. *International Journal of Population Geography, 7*(6), 461–472.

McTavish, M., Streelasky, J., & Coles, L. (2012). Listening to children's voices: Children as participants in research. *International Journal of Early Childhood, 44*(3), 249–267.

Merriam, S., & Tisdall, E. (2016). *Qualitative research: A guide to design and implementation* (4th ed.). San Francisco: Jossey-Bass.

Miles, M., Chapman, Y., & Francis, K. (2015). Peeling the onion: Understanding others' lived experience. *Contemporary Nurse, 50*(2–3), 286–295.

Morrow, V. (2011). *Understanding children and childhood* (Centre for Children and Young People background briefing series, no. 1). Retrieved from Lismore: https://studylib.net/doc/8773920/understanding-children-and-childhood

Morrow, V., & Richards, M. (1996). The ethics of social research with children: An overview. *Children and Society, 10*(2), 90–105.

Moss, P., & Petre, P. (2005). *From children's services to children's spaces: Public policy, children and childhood.* New York: Routledge Falmer.

Moss, P., & Petrie, P. (2002). *From children's services to children's spaces*. London: Routledge Falmer.

Palaiologou, I. (2014). 'Do we hear what children want to say?' Ethical praxis when choosing research tools with children under five. *Early Child Development and Care, 184*(5), 689–705.

Paris, D. (2011). 'A friend who understand fully': Notes on humanizing research in a multiethnic youth community. *International Journal of Qualitative Studies in Education, 24*(2), 137–149.

Paris, D., & Winn, M. (Eds.). (2014). *Humanizing research: Decolonizing qualitative inquiry with youth and communities*. London: Sage.

Pascal, C., & Bertram, T. (2009). Listening to young citizens: The struggle to make real a participatory paradigm in research with young children. *European Early Childhood Education Research Journal, 17*(2), 249–262.

Perrino, S. (2011). Chronotopes of story and storytelling event in interviews. *Language in Society, 40*(1), 91–103.

Podesta, J. (2013). *Listening to children's voices: Child-centred participatory research tools for sociologists*. Retrieved from https://www.tasa.org.au/wp-content/uploads/2013/11/Podesta.pdf

Pole, C., Mizen, P., & Bolton, A. (1999). Realising children's agency in research: Partners and participants? *International Journal of Social Research Methodology, 2*(1), 39–54.

Pring, R. (2000). *Philosophy of educational research*. London: Continuum.

Prout, A. (2000). Children's participation: control and self-realisation in British late modernity. *Children and Society, 14*(4), 304–315.

Rinaldi, C. (2006). *In dialogue with Reggio Emilia: Listening, researching, and learning*. London: Routledge Falmer.

Rinaldi, C. (2013). Carla Rinaldi: Re-imagining childhood. *Adelaide thinker in residence series*. Retrieved from http://www.decd.sa.gov.au/aboutdept/files/links/reimagining_childhood.pdf

Saleebey, D. (2012). *The strengths perspective in social work practice* (6th ed.). Boston: Pearson.

Sandri, R. A. (2013). *Weaving the past into the present: Indigenous stories of education across generations*. Doctor of Philosophy PhD, Queensland University of Technology, Brisbane, QLD.

Schoemperlen, D. (2000). *Our lady of the lost and found*. New York: Penguin Books.

Stake, R. (1995). *The art of case study research*. Thousand Oaks: Sage.

Stake, R. (2010). *Qualitative research: Studying how things work*. New York: Guilford Press.

Stark, S., & Torrance, H. (2005). Case study. In B. Somekh & C. Lewin (Eds.), *Research methods in the social sciences* (pp. 33–40). London: Sage.

Stokols, D. (1987). Conceptual strategies of environmental psychology. In D. Stokols & I. Altman (Eds.), *Handbook of environmental psychology* (pp. 41–70). New York: Wiley.

Sumsion, J., & Goodfellow, J. (2012). 'Looking and listening-in': A methodological approach to generating insights into infants' experiences of early childhood education and care settings. *European Early Childhood Education Research Journal, 20*(3), 313–327.

Thomas, R. (2014). Honouring the oral traditions of my ancestors through storytelling. In S. Strega & L. Brown (Eds.), *Research as resistance: Revisiting critical, indigenous and anti-oppressive approaches to research* (2nd ed., pp. 177–198). Toronto, ON: Canadian Scholars Press.

United Nations. (1989). *Convention on the rights of the child*. Retrieved from New York. https://www.ohchr.org/Documents/ProfessionalInterest/crc.pdf

Van Manen, M. (1990). *Researching lived experience: Human science for an action sensitive pedagogy*. New York: State University of New York Press.

Walter, M. (Ed.). (2013). *Social research methods* (3rd ed.). Melbourne, VIC: Oxford University Press.

Warr, D. (2004). Stories in the flesh and voices in the head: Reflections on the context and impact of research with disadvantaged populations. *Qualitative Health Research, 14*(4), 578–587.

Williams, D., & Fraga, L. (2011). Coming together around military families. In D. Osofsky (Ed.), *Clinical work with traumatized young children* (pp. 172–197). New York: The Guilford Press.

Wong, S. M., & Cumming, T. (2008). *Practice grounded in theory: The theoretical and philosophical underpinnings of SDN's Child, Family and Children's Services Programs. The second of eight reports investigating SDN's Child, Family and Children's Services Program*. Retrieved from Sydney, NSW. http://www.academia.edu/836851/Practice_Grounded_in_Theory

Woodhead, M. (2006). *Changing perspectives on early childhood: Theory, research and policy: A background paper the Education for All Global Monitoring Report 2007: Strong foundations: Early childhood care and education – Changing perspectives*. Retrieved from http://unesdoc.unesco.org/images/0014/001474/147499e.pdf

Woodhead, M., & Faulkner, D. (2008). Subjects, objects or participants? Dilemmas on psychological research with children. In P. Christensen & A. James (Eds.), *Research with children: Perspectives and practices* (2nd ed., pp. 10–39). Milton Park, Oxon: Falmer Press.

Yunkaporta, T., & Kirby, M. (2011). Yarning up Aboriginal pedagogies: A dialogue about eight Aboriginal ways of learning. In N. Purdie, G. Milgate, & H. R. Bell (Eds.), *Two way teaching and learning: Toward culturally reflective and relevant education* (pp. 205–213). Camberwell, VIC: ACER Press.

4

Knock, Knock! Who's There? Opening the Door to Creating Ethical, Respectful, and Participatory Research Spaces with Young Families

Scenario 4: The eKindy Program—Affording, or Unintentionally Silencing Participant Voices

Anthony and his research team from the 'eKindy Putting Family and Children first project' have been tasked with collecting data on the programmatic effectiveness of eKindy. This will include exploring families' experiences, stories, and insights of their involvement in the 'at home' kindergarten program (a program designed specifically for children living in rural and remote areas, travelling or medically unable to physically attend an early childhood service for kindergarten—the year before Prep). The eKindy program has been running as a new initiative in Queensland for several years now, and the intent of the current project is to research across the North and Central Queensland region of Australia with 18 families in total, who have at least one child attending and engaged in the eKindy program. (Note that the make-up, socio-economic and cultural backgrounds, includes several indigenous families, several families with a child having a medical issue, a number of single-parent families, and one family having three generations and extended family members living under the same roof.)

The project team feel very privileged and excited to have the opportunity of being 'invited' into the domestic spaces of rural and remote young families, and

© The Author(s) 2019
A. Brown, *Respectful Research With and About Young Families*, Palgrave Studies in Education Research Methods, https://doi.org/10.1007/978-3-030-02716-2_4

engaging 'with them' (rather than on them) in ethical, respectful, and meaningful research. They are keen to explore the lifeworlds and family meaning-making of the eKindy program in sensitive and respectful ways as part of their early planning for the project, including the process of seeking ethics approval. They have deliberated over the notion of 'participation', and the degree to which family members might be, or might want to be involved in the various stages of the project. The team are conscious that they don't want families to feel as if their role is just an opportunity to provide researchers with data, and they are also aware of the generosity of family members to disclose their personal views and experiences. They know that working with families will require a great deal of trust, and so the team have been reflecting deeply over issues such as the level of intrusion into the private lives of families, and questioning the degree to which the inquiry might violate the rights, dignity, and privacy of family members, including young children.

The team intend to employ a range of research methods. However at this point, they are still thinking about which methods may best afford children and families opportunities to share their stories. Their plan is that rather than physically visit each family (that would involve travelling great distances), they intend to connect, and build rapport with families, via an online platform (such as Skype). They will then use the platform as the main process for gathering data. However, they are concerned about how this method would afford, or unintentionally silence participant voices (and their perspectives). Other issues the team have been deliberating over is the degree to which the methods they are thinking of employing will consider the rights, dignity, and agency of participants, particularly family members who may have historically, through multiple generations, experienced marginalisation, including through their involvement in the educational system. They still have a lot to consider before the project gets underway.

Chapter Synopsis

Raising children is a collective undertaking, yet families and the domestic spaces in which they are located are still at the heart of these endeavours (Baxter, 2016). Researching with family members offers an unprecedented opportunity for family scholars to explore new understandings of lived experiences, and a range of other phenomenon associated with young children, parents, and significant carers (Gabb, 2010). However, due to the busy and very private nature of family life, being invited into these domestic spaces, and entering into dialogical relationships with others, is a privilege. It comes with an appreciation that families are opening their doors, entrusting us with their stories, and sharing a rare insight into the intimacy of their lifeworlds. It also comes with a responsibility of how we choose to act, engage with participants, and to use and communicate this data and their stories with others.

What does it mean for family members to authentically participate in research?

What factors need to be considered when seeking to conduct ethical and respectful research with members of young families?

In what way does the 'degree of participant involvement' impact on the rights and agency of 'the other' in an inquiry?

How can we rebalance the power differential between the researcher and the 'other', when researching with young families?

While planning to research with young families as participants may appear to be deceptively simple to the neophyte researcher, those more experienced appreciate that there are unexpected complexities and broader research and ethical dilemmas, including interactional constraints (Daly, 2007; Roulston, 2014), and the interplay between power and powerlessness, which often emerge prior to and during all stages of the inquiry process (Vähäsantanen & Saarinen, 2013). These include factors such as the degree of participant involvement, and intrusion into the private lives of others, the sensitivity of the subject being investigated, the age of participants, and the data methods employed. As such, interactions have the potential to place the researcher and research participants in positions of vulnerability and powerlessness, particularly those who have experienced marginalisation, or disadvantage. Therefore, engaging in inquiry, with the intent of exploring the lifeworlds and meaning-making of others, sensitively and respectfully, requires critical decision-making by the researcher. This process needs to start from the onset of a project, in order to ensure that the rights and well-being of each party are considered, and that the methods employed afford for ethical practices, and respectful and meaningful relationships (Hammersley, 2015; Palaiologou, 2014).

This chapter contributes to this topic by drawing upon the author's empirical research, her collaborative research with colleagues (Brown & Danaher, 2012, 2017; Brown et al., 2016), as well as from the extensive authoritative literature and contemporary studies that evidence reflexive practice, and consideration for the ethics of care, and participant involvement (Bergold & Thomas, 2012; Cook, 2012; Dockett, Perry, et al., 2009b; Gabb, 2010; Guillemin & Heggen, 2009; Harcourt & Einarsdóttir, 2011; Palaiologou, 2014; Sumsion & Goodfellow, 2012). The intent is that by addressing such topics, readers are afforded opportunities to more deeply consider the meaning of 'participation' in qualitative research, and to critically consider how these practices and strategies translate to ethical, respectful, and meaningful research with young families. It is also anticipated that by engaging in these associated themes, researchers will be motivated to critique their current perspectives on, and practices of, 'participant involvement', and be challenged to consider alternative and innovative approaches that reflect respectful and ethical praxis.

Throughout this chapter, reflective questions are included to provoke thought and guide decision-making, prior to and during engaging in inquiry with young families. While these topics and evidence-informed resources are certainly not proposed to be a panacea for research dilemmas, they are asserted to be valuable inclusions in a researcher's armoury, or toolkit of methodological resources, that may guide and facilitate data-gathering strategies, in turn maximising opportunities for authentic, ethical interactional encounters (De Fina & Perrino, 2011). Later, Chap. 6 builds upon and complements themes outlined in this chapter, by shifting attention more directly to considerations for building trust and rapport with participants, including outlining key strategies for building humanising and respectful relationships.

4.1   An Ethical Commitment of Engaging with Others in Inquiry

All qualitative research, to some extent involves engaging with others in inquiry. However, there is great diversity in the degree to which 'the other' will participate in the research process, or be involved in sharing their interpretations, meaning-making, and lived experiences of everyday life (Cook, 2012). Consequently, there may be the merging of the science of inquiry, with practice that includes varying forms of interactions and relationships. Palaiologou (2014) refers to this process as 'the complex union between methodology and ethical practices' with this union reflecting "an ethical commitment to creating conditions for engagement" (p. 691). As such, the level or degree to which 'the science' and 'the practice' converge is dependent on a range of factors, in turn affecting fundamental aspects with which an inquiry is designed, enacted, and in turn impacts on all those involved (Bergold & Thomas, 2012; Von Unger, 2012).

Levels of participation, decisions regarding who participates, and the capacity and the extent to which participants are involved in research inquiry, are just some of the considerations that will influence participatory processes, and the type of ethical commitment, as well as the emphasis placed on respectful research spaces and practices with others (Bergold & Thomas, 2012; Palaiologou, 2014). Other critical factors that will influence researcher decision-making will be the importance placed on the valuing of participant voice (and their perspectives), and the degree of agency and positioning of the participant in decision-making within an inquiry. Degrees of participant involvement will also be determined by the research questions posed, the priorities of funding bodies and their expectations regarding expected outcomes, and finally the context in which participants are situated (including their values, levels of trust, the physical environment, politics, social connectedness, age, and economics), and the extent to which these factors impact on individuals.

As researchers, our underlying axiological perspective, our positionality, the way we see the world (see Chap. 2), and the paradigms we adopt all too some extent impact and have a flow-on effect on the inquiry process. This includes the role we see participants playing, and the contribution we see them making to inquiry (Palaiologou, 2014). Our positionality regarding the way we view research participants, will most likely raise debate, challenge us, and cause a certain amount of consciousness-raising. Particularly in terms of thinking about the participatory methods and strategies we may adopt for engaging with others in inquiry in ways which are respectful, ethical, and meaningful (Brown & Danaher, 2017; Harcourt & Sargeant, 2012). And, while we may have the best intentions at heart, embedding research practices that recognise and value the perspectives, and privilege the voices of others, is often fraught with a range of ethical dilemmas, and embedded in a great deal of complexity.

As such, being forewarned is to be forearmed. This means being cognisant of the fact that our inquiry and the methods we plan to employ are not merely tokenistic efforts to jump on a particular paradigmatic bandwagon (Cook, 2012), but are intentionally ethical, authentic, and respectful. Efforts to capture their work, and the key considerations they offer for engaging in a more respectful, ethical and consultative inquiry with research participants, will now be more fully explored. This is particularly important so as not to perpetuate a dominant discourse that has the possibility of negatively impacting on those whose voices have been traditionally silenced, or who have experienced marginalisation and disenfranchisement historically, as a ramification of engaging in social research (Paris, 2011).

Although still in its infancy, there is an emerging body of innovative approaches and evidence of creative efforts by researchers, which reflect efforts to problematise ethical and respectful inquiry. These efforts often lead to reconsidering and reframing inquiry approaches, with the intent being to authentically embed ethical and respectful research strategies, and relationships with participants (Bergold & Thomas, 2012; Cook, 2012; Daly, 2007; Gabb, 2010; Harcourt & Einarsdóttir, 2011; Miller, Birch, Mauthner, & Jessop, 2012; Palaiologou, 2014).

Time for Some Personal Reflection

Palaiologou (2014) sets the bar high in this respect, by pointing out that "instead of examining methods as parts of participation, research should prioritise the structure of the complex union between methodology and ethical practices" (p. 691). The reflective questions outlined below are provided to challenge researchers to think about some of the fundamental considerations that may be faced when planning to engage with, and enter the space of engaging with young families in participatory research in ways which are ethical and respectful.

How can participatory research be achieved with young families?
How are children's engagement and their right to be heard considered in this process?
How can we achieve ethical research with young families?
How are the rights of families protected, and voices privileged?
How can environments be created where all family members are afforded autonomy and responsibility in the research process?
Does this inquiry and the inquiry process and spaces reflect ethical and respectful practice?
How is power negotiated, shaped, and considered throughout a research project?

4.2   Engaging in Respectful, Ethical, and Meaningful Research with Young Families

If the intent of our research is to 'research with', rather than research on young families, then a cornerstone of our approach would entail engaging in a continuous cycle of reflexivity that causes us to examine our perspectives and the frames in which we are positioned, as well as those of 'the other'. Careful reflection will also need to consider the research agendas we adopt, and whether these approaches and methods are respectful, ethical, and foregrounded by concern and consideration for the well-being of young families. There is great complexity in the notion of participation and an ethical commitment to engage with others in inquiry. These factors are embedded in all aspects of an inquiry, and track beyond simply procedural ethics employed at the outset of an inquiry (Cook, 2012). And, while a significant part of this process will require us to address, respond to, and meet critical principles of human ethics (i.e. informed consent, voluntary participation and the right to withdraw without sanction, and the confidentiality of participants and records) (Mohan, 2001; National Health and Medical Research Council Australian Research Council, 2007), there is much more that needs to be considered (Daly, 2007).

An ethical participatory methodology and research approach would include a holistic orientation to inquiry that affords for respectful relationships with others, and a synchronised approach that attempts to embed ethical praxis into all elements of an inquiry (Palaiologou, 2014). This process entails challenging traditional approaches to research with others, as well as reflecting on 'how' and 'why' questions, the result of which may lead to embedding these perspectives into our practice, and relationships with others, and in the construction and reconstruction of knowledge and meaning-making (Palaiologou, 2012b).

Ethical Conduct and Degrees of Participant Involvement

A first and essential hurdle in conducting any research with human participants is to reflect on and identify how an inquiry aims to address ethical values, principles, and practices (National Health and Medical Research Council Australian Research Council, 2007). These procedural ethical hurdles have become increasingly commonplace (Guillemin & Gillam, 2004; Miller et al., 2012). They reflect principles of justice and respect for the individuals engaged in an inquiry (Morrow, 2009), and require researchers to identify how a project will ensure no harm is experienced by the research participants (including emotional, physical, or psychological). This means adhering to agreed universal standards, with most universities now requiring academic research projects to move through the application process of ethical clearance, including obtaining approval from the relevant Human Research Ethics Committee, before conducting research on humans, or commencing their project (Gabb, 2010).

However, there are many nuances and subtleties associated with these standards in terms of balancing out the interests and goals of an inquiry, with the interests of the individuals, groups, and communities involved (Morrow, 2009). The intent of asking researchers to reflect on ethical and epistemological issues, as part of engaging and responding to the ethics clearance process regarding issues of 'ethical conduct', is underpinned by an ethos that these practices should permeate all aspects of engaging in human research. Considerations and responses to issues of ethics need to extend beyond just the 'front-loading' of a research project, and ensuring that ethics clearance is completed and the 'seeking of consent' addressed. Rather, ethical processes and practices need to be evidenced, as being reflected, enacted, and taking place across the trajectory of an inquiry (Palaiologou, 2012a, 2014). The Australian National Health and Medical Research Council (2007) reinforces this position, highlighting that consideration should be given to 'acting in the right spirit, out of an abiding respect and concern for ones' fellow creatures' (Preamble).

Many researchers over recent years have grappled with ethical considerations, and the implications this has to practice, including the degree of participant involvement that will be adopted for an inquiry, and what this may mean to the project being undertaken, and methodologies employed. As such, efforts have been made to capture participant involvement in research, through reference to visual representations which reflect the degree, or levels of participant involvement. These have included the development of hierarchical frameworks (Kirby, Lanyon, Cronin, & Sinclair, 2003) (see also Hart, 1992, Shier, 2001), non-hierarchical positions such as viewing 'involvement' along a continuum (Cornwall, 2008), and 'layers of ethical praxis' of participation in researching with young families. Each of these approaches adopts a particular lens for critically examining 'participant involvement', and associated ethical practice (Palaiologou, 2012a).

4.3   Layers of Participant Involvement and Ethical Praxis

The 'layers of ethical praxis and participant involvement' model (See Fig. 4.1, which outlines the LEPPI model) attempts to synthesise and build upon the fundamental principles and different levels of participation addressed and outlined in earlier studies, including the seminal works, conceptual models, writings, and numerous efforts of others (Arnstein, 1969; Chung & Lounsbury, 2006; Hart, 1992, 2008), as well as efforts of others to develop models of participant involvement and methodological approaches to ethical practice in research projects (Bergold & Thomas, 2012; Cornwall, 2008; Harcourt & Sargeant, 2012; Hart, 1992; Kirby, Lanyon, Cronin, & Sinclair, 2003; Palaiologou, 2014; Tuck, 2016). The LEPPI model includes four layers to represent varying degrees of participant involvement: Ethics isolated involvement, surface-level involvement, systematic-level involvement, and holistic paradigmatic model involvement. Consideration is given to defining the levels of involvement, as well as how each layer of involvement then translates, or might be reflected, in the ethical and respectful research processes and practice. The LEPPI involvement model moves from an inner layer, where participant involvement in inquiry is at a minimal level, and all decisions and power sits with the researcher whose primary focus is on

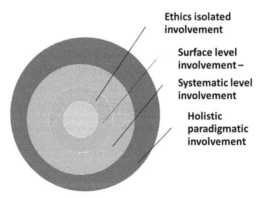

Fig. 4.1 The 'Layers of ethical praxis and participant involvement' model

ensuring ethical practices and 'doing no harm', to outer layers of the circle where participant involvement in research and embedding ethical and respectful practice increases and where the approach to ethics is more embedded and holistic. The outer layers of the model also place a greater emphasis on collaboration, input, and evidence of a more even distribution of power between the researcher and participants. While there may be distinguishable layers within the LEPPI model, these may not necessarily be demarcated, or linear; rather the model reflects practices of researchers which may start by being positioned in one layer of the model, and then move to being intermingled, or morph to another during the course of an inquiry (Palaiologou, 2014). This shifting of perspectives and practices may be dependent on a range of factors, such as contextual influences and situations experienced by participants, and the changing positioning that the researcher may have in relation to the role and input of participants within an inquiry. For example, a researcher may start with a strong focus specifically on the ethics process, which may include engaging in addressing a range of ethical hurdles, such as applying for ethical clearance and addressing how a project will ensure that no harm is experienced by the research participant. The researcher may then move to locating themselves in another layer of the model, dependent upon their perspective of participant involvement and a range of factors, including the type of Phenomenon being investigated. Finally, within unpacking each of the layers of the LEPPI model, consideration is given to two other important aspects that heavily impact on ethical and respectful research with young families; these are consideration for participant rights and agency; and consideration for power differentials.

However, there are many nuances and subtleties associated with these standards in terms of balancing out the interests and goals of an inquiry, with the interests of the individuals, groups, and communities involved (Morrow, 2009). The intent of asking researchers to reflect on ethical and epistemological issues, as part of engaging and responding to the ethics clearance process regarding issues of 'ethical conduct', is underpinned by an ethos that these practices should permeate all aspects of engaging in human research. Considerations and responses to issues of ethics need to extend beyond just the 'front-loading' of a research project, and ensuring that ethics clearance is completed and the 'seeking of consent' addressed. Rather, ethical processes and practices need to be evidenced, as being reflected, enacted, and taking place across the trajectory of an inquiry (Palaiologou, 2012a, 2014). The Australian National Health and Medical Research Council (2007) reinforces this position, highlighting that consideration should be given to 'acting in the right spirit, out of an abiding respect and concern for ones' fellow creatures' (Preamble).

Many researchers over recent years have grappled with ethical considerations, and the implications this has to practice, including the 'degree of participant involvement' that will be adopted for an inquiry, and what this may mean to the project being undertaken, and methodologies employed. As such, efforts have been made to capture 'participant involvement' in research, through reference to visual representations which reflect the degree, or levels of participant involvement. These have included the development of hierarchical frameworks (Kirby et al., 2003) (see also Hart, 1992; Shier, 2001), non-hierarchical positions such as viewing 'involvement' along a continuum (Cornwall, 2008), and 'layers of ethical praxis' of participation in researching with young families. Each of these approaches adopts a particular lens for critically examining 'participant involvement', and associated ethical practice (Palaiologou, 2012a).

Ethics Isolated Involvement

Levels, or dimensions of participant involvement, start with considerations related to ethical procedures and processes, primarily related to convincing the gatekeepers of research that we are doing no harm, as well as addressing issues of informed consent (Gabb, 2010, p. 10). With the intensification of ethical regulation associated with social research, or what Miller et al. (2012, p. 3) refer to as "ethics creep", particularly related to children, young people, and those identified as vulnerable or marginalised, researchers are under increased pressure and scrutiny to respond to the requirements related to the ethical clearance process (Miller et al., 2012). While the ethics approval process is observed widely, and is seen from a modernist perspective as a necessary part of the research process and reducible to a 'codified sets of principles', unfortunately, in doing so, there is a risk of compartmentalising participant involvement. Further, there is a risk of overlooking the sensitive nature, and nuances of researching the everyday lives of others (Gabb, 2009; Gallagher, 2009, p. 12). This approach may potentially restrict the fluidity of inquiry, which may not always be predictable, or certain up front (Palaiologou, 2014, p. 2944). The 'LEPPI' (layers of ethical praxis and participant involvement) model refers to this approach, or level of participant involvement, as *Ethics isolated involvement.*

A first and important hurdle in conducting any research with human participants is to consider, and identify, how an inquiry aims to address ethical values, principles, and practices (National Health and Medical Research Council Australian Research Council, 2007). These ethical hurdles reflect principles of justice, and respect for individuals engaged in an inquiry (Morrow, 2009). The difficulty with this process is that it requires researchers to delineate and anticipate all aspects of the inquiry up front, including how they will ensure that research participants are aware of what the project is about, potential risks, and the benefits of the study to themselves and others (Mapedzahama & Dune, 2017). It is also expected that researchers will identify: how the rights of participants will be protected, including how it is anticipated that no harm is experienced (including emotional, physical, or psychological); that informed consent is sought and communicated, and that the researcher maintains confidentiality and anonymity (Miller et al., 2012). This means adhering to agreed standards, and in most cases includes applying for ethical clearance in order to obtain approval from the relevant Human Research Ethics Committee to conduct research on humans.

Ethics isolated involvement can be understood as a compartmental approach to ethics, where there is a specific focus on applying for ethical clearance and adhering to the associated ethical practices, such as ensuring no harm. This involves a dedicated effort to tick the related boxes and fill out the associated ethics paper work, before moving onto engaging in the process of an inquiry. This focus will include a researcher addressing important ethical issues such as: ensuring transparency and clarity in communicating and overview and the intent of project to research participants; (including reference to ethical guidelines) (National

Health and Medical Research Council Australian Research Council, 2007); and the ethical seeking of participant consent[1] (Harcourt, Perry, & Waller, 2011). However, with 'ethics isolated involvement', participant involvement is usually limited to these types of aforementioned considerations.

Adopting an ethics isolated approach to involvement could be referred to as a top-down approach to the ethical processes. In this approach, researchers see themselves as the primary decision-maker, with little to no input by participants, other than seeking their permission to participate. The distribution of power in this case primarily sits with the researcher. For example, in seeking informed consent from young families, adopting an *ethics isolated involvement* approach would include ensuring that participants were aware, and understood the expectations and commitment of a research project, such as time commitments, and the voluntary nature of participant involvement (e.g. their right to withdraw at any time) (Dockett, Perry, et al., 2009b). The process would also involve clearly outlining the purpose of the research, the concept of anonymity, the expectations of individuals involved in the research, and what the data will be used for (Morrow, 2009). However, this approach provides limited or no opportunity for participants to provide feedback on the direction of the inquiry, or decision-making regarding aspects of the inquiry process.

Surface-Level Involvement

The nature of *surface-level participant involvement* can be understood as a deterministic approach to research, again positioned and primarily driven by the researcher. Surface-level participant involvement includes the

---

[1] Note that it is beyond the scope of this text to address in-depth ethical considerations and associated details regarding research with young children. I would argue that there are many excellent books and papers that already address this topic with great expertise and consideration (see Alderson & Morrow, 2011; Dockett, Einarsdottir, & Perry, 2009a; Dockett & Perry, 2011; Gallagher, 2009; Harcourt & Einarsdóttir, 2011; Harcourt, Perry, & Waller, 2011; Morrow, 2013; Phelan & Kinsella, 2013; Powell, Fitzgerald, Taylor, & Graham, 2012). So key points in this chapter will focus on 'family members', rather than specifically addressing young children and their involvement in research.

researcher adopting a defined or prescriptive set of techniques and research methods, with the intent of involving participants, but mainly from a perspective of them sharing their perspectives. The methodological strategies adopted by the researcher are usually based on the science of inquiry, underpinned by an interpretivist goal of gaining insight into a phenomenon, and the individuals located within a particular context (Gallacher & Gallagher, 2008).

Surface-level involvement reflects efforts to involve participants, by primarily addressing expectations of ethical processes, including the briefing of participants on the intent of the research, and the seeking of consent. However, methods adopted to involve participants are evidenced purely at a surface level. Researchers who choose to work within this frame are keen to adopt methods that enable participants to be observed and their storied lives and lived experiences to be listened to. These research practices might include narrative methods, case studies, or perhaps capturing experiences with video cameras, interviews, surveys, or focus groups.

Consideration for Participant Rights and Agency

In surface-level involvement participants do have rights; however, these rights and participant input are limited. Participants have the right to accept, or not accept to be involved in, a research project. They have the right to withdraw at any time. However, there are significant limitations in surface-level involvement regarding participant input into the decision-making process (Bergold & Thomas, 2012).

An example of *surface-level* participant involvement is shared by Palaiologou (2014), when he refers to a quote by an early childhood educator in reference to observations they are making in the classroom, "Observations are helping me to explore what children's skills are, but an observation is a skill that comes over time ... the more you do ... the better. Observations are a way to listening to children so I can now, after ten years, guide them [the children] to show ... the possibilities, and help them see how nicely they can play" (p. 694). This example reinforces that surface-level involvement primarily rests on a purpose identified by the researcher, the main goal usually being to collect data in order to better understand a phenomenon, or individual. This type of approach involves researching on and of participants, rather than researching with participants.

Consideration for Power Differentials

Traditionally, the research process in *surface-level involvement* is determined and controlled by the researcher (Mannion, 2007). There also exists in this type of research a power relation between participants and the researcher. In reflecting on ethical praxis with regard to power differentials between the research and participants in surface-level involvement, the holder of power would primarily sit with the researcher (Bergold & Thomas, 2012). They tend to have control over the entire inquiry process, from determining the topic and setting the problem and research questions, right through to the analysis and the way that data is interpreted and conveyed (England, 1994).

While participants may be consulted on matters such as the time and the location of an interview, generally participants tend to be 'objects of research', with limited to no active involvement or input by family members in this approach to inquiry. The major role of members of families is to share their stories, and as 'objects' from which data is collected. There is usually minimal opportunity for participants to voice their interests, or to express how the research is affecting them.

Systematic-Level Involvement

The decision of members of young families to commit to a research project, and their willingness to disclose their lived experiences and personal views, experiences, and opinions, requires a great deal of trust from all those involved in an inquiry. Researchers that have a genuine intent in adopting *systematic-level participant involvement* are committed to an approach to researching 'with' and 'about' others, rather than researching 'on' others. This approach involves engaging in qualitative research and spending significant time in the personal lives of family members, and the contexts in which they are located (Gabb, 2010). However, those committed to adopting a more systematic approach to participant involvement and ethics are cognisant of the fact that when conducting fieldwork one cannot always anticipate at the outset the unexpected challenges that may be encountered, or issues which may emerge during the life of a project, or what Gabb (2009, p. 49) refers to as, the "emotional messiness, uncertainties and fluidity", which come with relational experiences (Cohen, Manion, & Morrison, 2013; Yee & Andrews, 2006).

For example, an unanticipated ethical challenge that I experienced when engaged in fieldwork in the homes of young families as part of my doctoral thesis was being offered a cup of tea, some nibbles, or even being invited for a BBQ and a glass of wine. Although, as an emerging researcher, I had done my due diligence, and had gone to great lengths up front to anticipate ethical issues as part of the ethical clearance process, this did not necessarily prepare me for ethical issues that unfolded, or that I encountered along the way. However I had determined that joining with research participants (in this case members of young families) for a drink or a meal was a valuable part of the process of building authentic relationships, trust, and rapport (Brown & Danaher, 2017) (see Chap. 7 for further details on building trust and rapport with participants).

As a novice researcher, these types of practices and invitations proved challenging, as there were no clear protocols or ethical boundaries that I could refer to guide me, other than reference in the literature to 'keeping professional distance'. And, like Yee and Andrews (2006), I too was "torn between the professional demands" or my researcher role, and the "social obligations of being a 'good guest'" (p. 398). In the end I was left to my own devices, and decision-making, that saw me embracing these invitations as valuable opportunities for building rapport, and authentic relationships with participants, but also in recognising the potential these practices offered for gathering rich data within the home setting.

Gerson and Horowitz (2002) write that "To enter a world in which one is not naturally a part of a researcher needs to present an identity that permits relationships to develop" (p. 212). This raises an interesting challenge in terms of questioning relationships that may occur and develop between researchers and research participants throughout the course of an inquiry. More particularly, these types of considerations have important implications as crucial components to relational dimensions of rapport building, and efforts to maximise the interview's dialogical potential (Brown & Danaher, 2017; Hammersley, 2015).

An interesting dilemma arises for those researchers who choose to embrace relational aspects such as of 'humanness', reciprocity, and the duality of information sharing, as part of the research process, in this case in reference to researching with young families (see Chaps. 6 and 7 for further details). Relational considerations are particularly challenging if our intent is to try to remove the traditional distance between ourselves, and participants, in an effort to establish an environment of informality. In such cases, researchers may choose to adopt an alternative role, other than more traditional roles such as 'the researcher', or 'the interviewer'. In adopting such an approach, we may be faced with a range of unanticipated research dilemmas, particularly in terms of negotiating ethical boundaries, such as how much to divulge and share information about ourselves with others in our efforts to demonstrate our 'humanness'. Or, decisions regarding how much we choose to 'connect' with participants, in efforts to shorten the distance between ourselves and the research participant (Brown & Danaher, 2017; Irvine, Drew, & Sainsbury, 2013).

What becomes clear in exploring examples, and issues such as these, is that in efforts to reposition the participant as part of an inquiry, there is a conscious decision by researchers to move beyond simply employing a set of prescriptive techniques that seek to gain participant perspectives, to an approach that can be referred to as 'responsible knowing' (Gabb, 2010). This genuine commitment to facilitate participation, and build rapport between the participant and the researcher, involves a notion of ethical praxis which is multi-layered, where consideration is given to embedding ethics, ethical conditions, and participation into all aspects of the research design (Palaiologou, 2014). Such an approach entails researchers adopting not only a particular discourse that captures and embraces 'participant' and 'involvement' terminology, but entails efforts to critically examine notions of participation, and how traditional methodological approaches may unintentionally silence participant voices.

More specifically, those who chose to work within such a paradigm may need to critically question traditional data collection strategies and relationships with participants, and consider alternative methods, practices, and processes that are more effective in privileging the perspectives, and positions of others (including children). Furthermore, adopting this perspective requires research and participation to be underpinned by a strong ethical commitment, which would include the layering of ethical considerations into all aspects of the inquiry process, and beyond just the front-ending or compartmentalising of ethics.

Palaiologou (2014) refers to this as a "union of methodology and ethics" and "as a synchronistic relation" (p. 695). On this basis, *systematic-level participant involvement* would move beyond simply referring to up front notions and ethical aspects associated with data collection, driven solely by researchers. Instead, practices would reflect a more equitable distribution of power, which affords opportunities for collaborative decision-making. This approach to ethical praxis would shift boundaries and understandings of involvement and, participation to one which is more sensitive to the context in which participants are located and move within, including: participant values, culture, age, religion, lived history, and any associated political issues which may impact on participant involvement throughout the course of a project.

Adopting such a perspective, or approach, would view participants and their role as more than just an opportunity from which to collect data, to one where individuals are understood to have rights, agency, and respect. Such an approach would impact on many aspects on an inquiry process, including the level of participation shaping the research questions asked, the questions posed to participants, and the involvement of participants in sharing their perspectives and voice (Gabb & Singh, 2015). Other ramifications could include participants being consulted regarding their perspectives on the intent and direction of the project (Hart, 1992). Strategies for involving participant input into inquiry might also include involving participants in the direction of an interview, or even ways in which their perspectives, insights, and stories are conveyed and shared with others (Palaiologou, 2014).

Consideration of Participant Rights and Agency

Excerpt from Palaiologou (2014, p. 697):

Child:	What are you doing?
Researcher:	I am writing down what you just did. It was very interesting.
Child:	I do not like it. (Child stops his activity and walks away.)

When we observe members of young families in the environments and spaces in which they spend significant time, it is worth considering that by engaging in observation or other forms of data gathering we are intervening and interrupting their lives. Systematic involvement would consider this position in terms of reflecting deeply on the degree to which research inquiry violates the rights, dignity, and privacy of family members, including young children (Dockett & Perry, 2011). Practices which reflect these considerations would seek to go beyond simply addressing the process of seeking consent as part of the ethical guidelines and processes. Instead, those working within a systematic approach would seek to minimise the degree of impact that data collection has on the lives and behaviours of individuals. These practices might include consideration given to the degree of agency and the input participants have during the inquiry process. Researchers might also more carefully consider the ways in which they enter spaces where young families reside, and engage in, and in doing so be more cognisant of issues of privacy, and the dignity of the other.

This process would also include practices such as renegotiating and revisiting parameters around data collection, pervasiveness of data collection, and ensuring ethical spaces for research throughout the inquiry process. Dockett, Perry, et al. (2009b) share an example of their teams' efforts to consider the rights of participants by ensuring that discussion was "guided by the participants, as they responded to some open-ended questions about what was happening for their family in relation to the transition to school" (p. 355). This involved researchers actively listening and asking open-ended questions, which usually occurred in the home context with participants.

Systematic-level involvement extends far beyond purely ethical and legal obligations, instead adopting a strong relational approach between the researcher, and those engaged as participants in the research (Gabb, 2010). For example, approaching informed consent at a systematic level, or what Cutcliffe and Ramcharan (2002) refers to as 'process-consent', would extend to a deeper level of reflection on contextual issues, which might impact on 'participation interpretation', such as the right of participants to withdraw at any time. Dockett, Perry, et al. (2009b) share an example of efforts to adopt such an approach, by implementing 'consent strategies' that were negotiated and discussed at multiple touchpoints throughout the research process. They suggest that an underpinning reason for adopting such an approach was due to the diverse contextual backgrounds of their participant groups, some of which had experienced feelings of marginalisation, or voiced concerns with being identified by intervention services.

Finally, Morrow (2009) refers to the process of the seeking of consent, in terms of having multiple touchpoints, and being an ongoing process. This is particularly relevant when research with participants is in multiple parts, or conducted over an extended period of time, where 'checking in', and reminding participants about the intent of the project and the rights they have as participants is important. Adopting such an approach, and perspective to ethical processes, such as the seeking of consent, draws on particular understandings and framing of participants, and contributes to ongoing efforts to maintain respectful and trusting relationships.

Palaiologou (2014) provides another excellent example of a project where children were consulted regarding their involvement in inquiry. In this study, children had the opportunity to help develop the survey in which their perspectives were sought. Palaiologou (2014) points out that this example reinforces the importance of theory informing actions, and researchers going beyond a predetermined set of identified procedures and protocols, or 'how things have always been done'. Instead, researchers were prepared to challenge the status quo, and, if necessary, to modify practices or methodologies to reflect the changing needs and input of all involved.

Adopting *systematic-level participant involvement* practices shifts the emphasis and greater attention to be given to the perspective, rights, dignity, and agency of participants, including those identified as vulnerable. Palaiologou (2014) refers to one such an approach, and the work of Dussel (see 1997, 1998) on ethics intersubjectivity. This approach

emphasises the importance of putting in place procedures for all participants in reaching agreement on the process, implementation, and locatedness of research. In another example, Dockett and Perry (2011) refer to
a paradigmatic shift by researchers, and them adopting a 'participatory
rights perspective', based on an image of the child as "competent social
agents" (p. 231). They raise some important considerations in relation to
research that recognises children's rights and agency, and how this then
influences and flows through to ethical processes such as "children making informed decisions about their participation" (p. 231).

Consideration for Power Differentials

Adopting *a systematic-level participant involvement* approach to inquiry
requires serious consideration, and dedicated effort to break down more
traditional methodological approaches and power differentials between
the 'scientist' and 'subject' (Cook, 2012). This includes efforts to engage
in interactions with participants, such as efforts to consult with participants regularly throughout a research project. Harden, Backett-Milburn,
Hill, and MacLean (2010) share another important aspect of power differential to consider when researching with young families, that of 'generational power relations'. They argue that in our efforts to collect data
with families, researchers need to be cognisant of ensuring that the methods employed do not silence the voice of the child. This means that when
considering generational power differentials efforts are made to ensure
that all family members have the opportunity to share their perspectives.
For example, this may mean the presence of a parent during an inquiry if
the child feels more comfortable with this arrangement in terms of
expressing their views (Harden et al., 2010). It would also be important
that researchers reinforce the value of a child's perspective, and encourage
parents to 'not speak' for the child.

Holistic Paradigmatic Involvement

Located in the outermost layer of LEPPI involvement model is the notion
of *holistic paradigmatic involvement*. As the name suggests, holistic para-

digmatic participation is a particular lens, or underlying philosophical perspective adopted by the researcher. This level of involvement is underpinned by a deep and authentic respect for participation and relationships with the other (Cook, 2012). This level of involvement reflects a deep respect for social justice, democracy, and the acknowledgement of participants' rights and agency, with great consideration given to issues such as power differentials (Foster & Young, 2015; Palaiologou, 2014; Tuck, 2016). Those who choose to work within this paradigm of participant methodology, are often positioned within a critical, feminist, indigenous, or ethical theoretical frame, underpinned by reciprocity and empowerment (Bermúdez, Muruthi, & Jordan, 2016; Brown & Danaher, 2012; Edwards & Mauthner, 2012; Geia, Hayes, & Usher, 2013; Paris, 2011; Rizvi, 2017).

Holistic paradigmatic participant involvement is a particular research approach that embodies and grounds "thinking ethically", and ethical praxis and commitment, fluidly, and authentically, into anticipated, as well as unanticipated situations (Bergold & Thomas, 2012; Miller et al., 2012, p. 1). While still underpinned by ensuring that research addresses the necessary ethical processes, researchers also consider ethical principles more broadly, appreciating that in conducting qualitative research with individuals in multiple contexts, it may be necessary at times to adopt a more idiosyncratic approach to ethical practices (Dockett, Perry, et al., 2009b). As such, researchers working within this frame appreciate that the field in which we enter is constantly changing, and requires us to manoeuvre around unanticipated situations (Rizvi, 2017).

When we engage in fieldwork with participants, there is a system of relationships. This increases the likelihood of encountering diverse and unanticipated ethical issues from different settings, cultures, and context that young families are located in. Those who work within a *holistic paradigmatic perspective* are cognisant of this, including the need to be less rigid in order to be responsive to the challenges that come from working with the idiosyncratic nature of young families as participants. In these instances, researchers would be guided by their paradigmatic positioning, and would respond to individuals with integrity, and in ways that are respectful as well as ethical.

Foregrounded in humanising research principles of integrity, genuine respect for the other, and the valuing of the dialogic process, the ethics praxis of this approach will permeate all aspects of an inquiry. This includes processes that front-end an inquiry, such as: decisions regarding how a project is framed; the way the participants are viewed; the positioning and contexts in which participants are located; the value and respect given to the voices and perspectives of others (including those of children); through to the methods employed, and the considerations given to how findings are communicated to others (Gabb & Singh, 2015; Miller et al., 2012). It is an "orientation to inquiry" underpinned by a union between creating supportive and relational inquiry spaces (Reason & Bradbury, 2008, p. 1). Gabb (2010), adding a valued point that aligns with this level of participant involvement and commitment to ethics, comments that "the researcher is implicated 'in a feminist, caring, committed ethic', shaped through the long-term trusting researcher–participant relationship" (p. 9).

Consequently, such a paradigmatic stance to inquiry in working with young families' challenges researchers to consider reframing methodological processes, which may include the need to push beyond traditional practice. This might mean that as part of engaging in a dialogical process with others, that researchers choose to explore, and employ not only innovative ways for engaging, involving, and communicating with participants, but seek out practices that are humane. These practices privilege the insights and perspectives of the other, as part of the inquiry process (Ellis, 2007).

This type of approach might include care and consideration given to the language and terminology adopted, and communicated throughout a project (Gorin, Hooper, Dyson, & Cabral, 2008). It might also mean the researcher engaging in ongoing negotiation with all members of young families as co-researchers. Such an approach reflects an authentic respect for the other, and where there is a regular 'checking in' on the perspectives and input of individuals, to ensure that there is no mismatch between planning and reality (Given et al., 2016; Palaiologou, 2014). A continual cycle of reflection, between the researcher and participants, also helps to be mindful of whether the inquiry process and the inquiry spaces reflect ethical and respectful practice. In doing so, the intent is that together through these interactions we seek "mutual humanization" and engage in meaning-making related to a phenomenon (Paris, 2011, p. 137).

Those who choose to work within a *paradigm of participant involvement* tend also to adopt a strengths-based perspective. This perspective aligns with an underlying belief in the capacity of others, and the contribution they make to meaning-making throughout the inquiry process (Fenton, Walsh, Wong, & Cumming, 2015; Saleebey, 2012) (see section 'Working Within a Strengths-Based Perspective' in Chap. 2 of this text for details regarding the unpacking a strengths-based perspective). Adopting such a perspective recognises the knowledge and skills that participants bring to the table, and as such embrace and seek out practices and methods that harness this potential (Dockett, Perry, et al., 2009b; McNeil, 2010; Rinaldi, 2006). As a consequence, those researching with young families enter research spaces sensitively, with the intent of ensuring the other is treated with dignity. Researchers are also conscious that participants may bring with them to the inquiry past experiences of being judged, or positioned through a deficit, or pathologised, lens (Bermúdez et al., 2016; Uttal, 2009).

An example of efforts to embrace a *holistic paradigmatic participant involvement* with young families might mean engaging in deeper reflection regarding the place and involvement of young children in an inquiry (particularly those children under the age of five). This may mean researchers seeking out methodological strategies that authentically afford opportunities for children to share their perspectives, or to consider effective ways of listening to children. The challenge comes with accounting for, and considering a child's developmental ability to communicate with words, referred to as 'level of linguistic articulation' (Harcourt et al., 2011; Palaiologou, 2014).

These types of factors can definitely challenge researchers to think outside the box, particularly in terms of exploring innovative strategies for affording young children the opportunity to express themselves and share their perspectives, as an integral aspect of an inquiry (Harcourt & Einarsdóttir, 2011) (see Chap. 3). As Rinaldi (2006) points out, it might mean that researchers need to adopt alternative practices, and ways of listening to children's meaning-making, which could include 'listening with our whole body'. In terms of researching with young children in families, this might entail thinking of other ways in which children can express their ideas, such as through images or body language. From a Reggio Emilia perspective, this is understood as children communicating in multiple ways, referred to as 'the hundred languages' (Edwards, Gandini, & Forman, 1998) (see Chap. 3 for further details on this topic).

You may wish to jump to Sect. 6.3 of Chap. 6, where details are provided of another example of holistic-level involvement discussed in terms of the Mosaic approach. Clark and Moss (2011) reinforce the value placed on participant-centred methods in which children and adults generate knowledge, using methods developed to "play to the strengths of young children, methods which are active and accessible and not reliant on the written or spoken word" (p. 324). The Mosaic approach is underpinned by the genuine belief of children being capable and competent, experts of their own lives, and with the right to be heard, and their views respected (Clark & Moss, 2005).

Authentic participant involvement requires a particular type of commitment, level of reflection, and responsiveness by researchers, in terms of a raised consciousness and sensitivity to the time necessary to build relationships of trust, dignity, and care, or what Paris (2011) refers to as 'humanization' (Paris & Winn, 2014). This involves engaging with participants in ongoing dialogic opportunities throughout the life of a project, and providing the space necessary for all stakeholders to feel safe and supported in communicating perspectives, opinions, and experiences. Adopting such an approach will require considerable time and effort that goes far beyond just talking with participants, to a fundamental and foundational level of interaction that affords deep, rich, and respectful collaborative discussions, and understandings with all involved in an inquiry (Cook, 2012; Wright, Roche, von Unger, Block, & Gardner, 2010).

Bushin (2009) shares a holistic approach to researching with families, referred to as the 'children-in-families' approach. Her work explores family perspectives on migration decision-making, and is underpinned by the 'agentic nature of children', their right to be heard, and for parents and children to be active research participants. Bushin (2009) points out that "adopting a children-in-families approach requires a change of mindset rather than a whole new set of research methods" (p. 430).

Another underlying tenet, considered by those who work within a holistic paradigmatic frame, is seeking input and perspectives from the research team, as well as other professionals who have insight, or a vested interest in the subject of an inquiry. This can be referred to seeking a "shared ethical ground" (Dockett, Perry, et al., 2009b, p. 356). For example, in discussing a research project that investigated family experiences of the 'transition to school', Docket and her team (2009) sought input and advice from the interdisciplinary research group involved in the inquiry, on topics such as the terminology and discourse used throughout the project. This included discussion as to whether to use words such as 'disadvantage' or 'vulnerable' (due to the negative assumptions of these terms). Their efforts also included seeking input from team members regarding the role and responsibilities of the researcher, and other examples such as "engaging with families in positive and respectful ways; compensation for participants ... and the impact of the research on researchers" (pp. 355–356). The team's approach was underpinned by the valuing of diverse backgrounds, ways of knowing, the areas of expertise that each stakeholder brought with them to these conversations, and finally the valuing of ongoing discussion and critically reflective practice.

Those who choose to adopt an approach underpinned by *holistic participant involvement* carefully consider how they choose to represent and communicate interpretations and the storied lives of others (Gabb, 2010; Paris, 2011). Feminist researchers (such as Miller, Birch, Mauthner & Jessop, 2012) refer to this as 'responsible knowing', where, although the intention of research may be to advance knowledge and meaning-making in relation to a phenomenon, the approach adopted in this case is based on respect, ethics, and integrity, conscious of efforts to honour those who afford us the opportunity to engage in research of and with them.

Consideration for Participant Rights and Agency

A *holistic paradigmatic participant involvement approach* is a unifying methodological approach, distinguished by efforts to recognise the rights of participants, including efforts to ensure that participants be included in research that affects their lives (Bergold & Thomas, 2012). Somekh

(2002) comments that, "Knowledge constructed without the active participation of practitioners can only be partial knowledge" (p. 9). Efforts to consider the points of view of participants might entail participants playing an active role in shaping the research questions, debating or contributing to discussion on the purpose of the research or the methodological approach adopted, and even contributing to the interpretations that emerge about their lived experiences.

Consideration for Power Differentials

The deliberate effort by researchers to create a safe place for research, and for communication to be open and respected (Bergold & Thomas, 2012), reflects attempts to equitably involve the other, and distribute power throughout the various phases of an inquiry (Von Unger, 2012). In these cases, while realistically as researchers we may not be able to totally shift the distribution of power, it is possible to be more conscious of power relations that exist in research. This might include critically examining how this power may be adjusted in order for it to be more equitably distributed (Gabb, 2010).

Traditionally, a holistic and genuine attempt to involve participants in inquiry has not been frequently evidenced. Such efforts to distribute power more equitably throughout inquiry requires a process of continual negotiation, and a significant shift in the way that research has always be done. Paris (2011) sets the bar high by suggesting that our aim be "to humanize through research rather than colonize by research" (p. 140). Efforts to adopt such an approach have significant ramifications to the way we choose to collaborate with others, or how others may wish to be involved in an inquiry. There will also be implications for the strategies employed for negotiating and handling disagreement, conflict, and ambivalence, with the aim being to produce a diverse and equitable response.

Gorin et al. (2008) raise another important example of efforts to consider and reflect practices that attempt to shift and increase awareness of the power dynamics during qualitative research with young families, particularly giving consideration to children's involvement. They addressed this aspect of practice in their research, by actively employing methods that constantly negotiated issues of consent. These actions included engaging in a continual process of reminding children that they were able to choose whether they wished to participate in the inquiry, and the option of withdrawing at any time. Efforts involved actively encouraging children to practice stopping the recorder during the interview, using red and green traffic light signs as a fun device for reinforcing that they were able to stop the interview at any time. This was particularly important with issues of a sensitive nature, or where children may have experienced distress or an emotional trigger. They also employed strategies for continually reinforcing to children that their perspectives and stories were valued, reinforcing a sense of agency and that "they were the experts of their own lives" (p. 282).

Efforts to adopt such a dynamic and authentic approach to ethics, and participant involvement, move beyond simply consulting with participants in efforts to encourage involvement, to a more equitable and democratic distribution of power which affords opportunities for productive communication and critical discussion. This type of involvement is dynamic, whereby alternative methods for theorising about strategies, and methods for collecting data can be explored, debated, and, if necessary, lead to the emergence of more innovative approaches being considered and adopted. This perspective seeks to "work towards creating knowledge through bringing together contextualised understanding, practical experience, wisdom, and reasoning" (Cook, 2012, p. 5). Involvement, in this case, "challenges people to work together on 'what could be' rather than 'commenting on what is'" (Foster & Young, 2015, p. 93).

4.4   Conclusion

There is so much potential and insight to be gained in researching with young families, and their lived experiences and contexts. However, in doing so, researchers may step into situations that are not initially anticipated, or for which they may not feel adequately prepared. Each family, each context, each home setting is idiosyncratic, and as such requires us to collaborate differently, and to nuance our relationships and rapport building differently with others.

The LEPPI model, introduced and addressed in this chapter, attempts to capture a range of these perspectives, considerations, and praxis, regarding participant involvement. These include practices that emphasise participant involvement from a visible level of addressing procedural ethics practices, to more a more invisible level that addresses "micro-ethical dimensions", and where notions such as power, and participant agency are more critically scrutinised (Guillemin & Gillam, 2004, p. 278; Palaiologou, 2014). The model offers researchers the opportunity to problematise thinking, and hopefully become increasingly sensitive to the degree to which space is offered within inquiry for authentic and respectful research with young families, as well as the barriers and implications this has on ethical praxis. Further, the layers of the model challenge researchers to confront, and to perhaps reconsider their existing strategies, methodologies, and techniques, in terms of ethical practice, participants' interests, rights and agency, and issues such as power differentials.

The LEPPI model is not offered as a framework or formula. Rather, it is shared as a reflection tool, and as a structure researchers may choose to refer to when reexamining and evaluating their commitment to ethical research, particularly when participation with 'the other' goes beyond simply descriptive, prescriptive, or surface-level participant involvement.

In a way, the LEPPI model offers researchers an opportunity for consciousness-raising, problematising, and deeper level reflection regarding the types of relationships that can potentially be afforded with members of young families as part of the two-way negotiation and inquiry process, as well as the implications this approach may have on the ethical practices we adopt. Research with young families in contemporary times requires us to move beyond rigid methodological approaches to ones which unfold and are more fluid. Such an approach involves interrogation and continual reflection if we are to engage in respectful research spaces and relationships with young families, as well as share in the creation and construction of knowledge in collaboration with others (Bergold & Thomas, 2012; Geia et al., 2013).

Further Reading and Research
Note that it is beyond the scope of this text to address in-depth ethical considerations and associated detail regarding participatory methods of researching with young children. I would argue that there are many excellent books and papers that already address this topic with great expertise and consideration. A number of additional readings and papers on this topic are included here for readers to consider.

Christensen, P., & James, A. (2008). *Research with children: Perspectives and practices*. New York: Routledge.

Clark, A., & Moss, P. (2011). *Listening to young children: The Mosaic approach* (2nd ed.). London: National Children's Bureau and Joseph Rowntree Foundation.

Dockett, S., & Perry, B. (2011). *Researching with young children: Seeking assent. Child Indicators Research*, 4(2), 231–247.

Gallacher, L. A., & Gallagher, M. (2008). Methodological immaturity in childhood research? Thinking through participatory methods. *Childhood, 15*(4), 499–516.

Harcourt, D., & Sargeant, J. (2012). *Doing ethical research with children*. Maidenhead: McGraw-Hill Education.

Kellett, M. (2010). *Rethinking children and research: Attitudes in contemporary society*. London: Bloomsbury Publishing.

Palaiologou, I. (2014). 'Do we hear what children want to say?' Ethical praxis when choosing research tools with children under five. *Early Child Development and Care, 184*(5), 689–705.

Tisdall, K., Davis, J. M., & Gallagher, M. (2008). *Researching with children and young people: Research design, methods and analysis*. Thousand Oaks, CA: Sage.

Warming, H. (2011). Children's participation and citizenship in a global age. Empowerment, tokenism or discriminatory disciplining? *Social Work & Society, 9*(1), 119–134.

References

Alderson, P., & Morrow, V. (2011). *The ethics of research with children and young people: A practical handbook*. London: Sage.

Arnstein, S. R. (1969). A ladder of citizen participation. *Journal of the American Institute of Planners, 35*(4), 216–224.

Baxter, J. (2016). *The modern Australian family*. Retrieved from Melbourne, VIC. https://aifs.gov.au/sites/default/files/families-week2016-final-20160517.pdf

Bergold, J., & Thomas, S. (2012). Participatory research methods: A methodological approach in motion. *Historical Social Research/Historische Sozialforschung, 13*(1), 191–222.

Bermúdez, J. M., Muruthi, B., & Jordan, L. (2016). Decolonizing research methods for family science: Creating space at the centre – Decolonizing research practices. *Journal of Family Theory & Review, 8*(2), 192–206.

Brown, A., & Danaher, P. A. (2012, December 2–6). *Respectful, responsible and reciprocal ruralities research: Approaching and positioning educational research differently within Australian rural communities*. Paper presented at the In: Joint International Conference of the Australian Association for Research in Education and the Asia Pacific Educational Research Association (AARE 2012): Regional and Global Cooperation in Educational Research, 2–6 Dec, Sydney, NSW.

Brown, A., & Danaher, P. A. (2017). CHE Principles: Facilitating authentic and dialogical semi-structured interviews in educational research. *International Journal of Research & Method in Education*, 1–15. https://doi.org/10.1080/1 743727X.2017.13799.

Brown, A., Danaher, P. A., Kenny, M., Hyland, S., Levinson, M., & Quvang, C. (2016). *Leading educational research: Innovative methodologies that maximise rapport and reciprocity in ways that are ethical and empowering (Symposium)*. Paper presented at the European Conference on Educational Research, Dublin, Ireland.

Bushin, N. (2009). Researching family migration decision making: A children-in-families approach. *Population, Space and Place, 15*(5), 429–443.

Chung, K., & Lounsbury, D. W. (2006). The role of power, process, and relationships in participatory research for statewide HIV/AIDS programming. *Social Science & Medicine, 63*(8), 2129–2140.

Clark, A., & Moss, P. (2005). *Spaces to play: More listening to young children using the Mosaic approach*. London: Jessica Kingsley Publishers.

Clark, A., & Moss, P. (2011). *Listening to young children: The Mosaic approach* (2nd ed.). London: National Children's Bureau and Joseph Rowntree Foundation.

Cohen, L., Manion, L., & Morrison, K. (2013). *Research methods in education* (7th ed.). New York: Routledge.

Cook, T. (2012). Where participatory approaches meet pragmatism in funded (health) research: The challenge of finding meaningful spaces. *Forum: Qualitative Social Research, 13*(1), 1–21.

Cornwall, A. (2008). Unpacking 'participation': Models, meanings and practices. *Community Development Journal, 43*(3), 269–283.

Cutcliffe, J. R., & Ramcharan, P. (2002). Leveling the playing field? Exploring the merits of the ethics-as-process approach for judging qualitative research proposals. *Qualitative Health Research, 12*(7), 1000–1010.

Daly, K. J. (2007). *Qualitative methods for family studies and human development.* Thousand Oaks, CA: Sage.

De Fina, A., & Perrino, S. (2011). Introduction: Interviews vs. 'natural' contexts: A false dilemma. *Language in Society, 40*(1), 1–11.

Dockett, S., Perry, B., Kearney, E., Hamshire, A., Mason, J., & Schmied, V. (2009). Researching with families: Ethical issues and situations. *Contemporary Issues in Early Childhood, 10*(4), 353–365.

Dockett, S., & Perry, B. (2011). Researching with young children: Seeking assent. *Child Indicators Research, 4*(2), 231–247.

Dussel, E. (1997). The architectonic of the ethics of liberation. In D. Bastone, E. Mendiete, L. A. Lorentzen, & D. N. Hopkins (Eds.), *Liberation theologies, postmodernity and the Americas* (pp. 273–304). New York: Routledge.

Dussel, E. (1998). *Ética de la Liberación en la Edad de la Globalización y de la Exclusión.* Madrid, Spain: Trotta.

Edwards, C., Gandini, L., & Forman, G. (1998). *The hundred languages of children: The Reggio Emilia approach advanced reflections* (2nd ed.). Norwood, NJ: Ablex Publishing.

Edwards, R., & Mauthner, M. (2012). Ethics and feminist research: Theory and practice. In T. Miller, M. Birch, M. Mauthner, & J. Jessop (Eds.), *Ethics in qualitative research* (2nd ed., pp. 14–28). London: Sage.

Ellis, C. (2007). Telling secrets, revealing lives: Relational ethics in research with intimate others. *Qualitative Inquiry, 13*(1), 3–29.

England, K. (1994). Getting personal: Reflexivity, positionality, and feminist research. *The Professional Geographer, 46*(1), 80–89.

Fenton, A., Walsh, K., Wong, S., & Cumming, T. (2015). Using strengths-based approaches in early years practice and research. *International Journal of Early Childhood, 47*(1), 27–52.

Foster, V., & Young, A. (2015). Reflecting on participatory methodologies: Research with parents of babies requiring neonatal care. *International Journal of Social Research Methodology, 18*(1), 91–104.

Gabb, J. (2009). Researching family relationships: A qualitative mixed methods approach. *Methodological Innovations Online, 4*(2), 37–52.

Gabb, J. (2010). Home truths: Ethical issues in family research. *Qualitative Research, 10*(4), 461–478.

Gabb, J., & Singh, R. (2015). The uses of emotion maps in research and clinical practice with families and couples: Methodological innovation and critical inquiry. *Family Process, 54*(1), 185–197.

Gallacher, L.-A., & Gallagher, M. (2008). Methodological immaturity in childhood research? Thinking through participatory methods. *Childhood, 15*(4), 499–516.

Gallagher, M. (2009). Ethics. In K. Tisdall, J. M. Davis, & M. Gallagher (Eds.), *Researching with children and young people: Research design, methods and analysis* (pp. 11–64). Thousand Oaks, CA: Sage.

Geia, L. K., Hayes, B., & Usher, K. (2013). Yarning/aboriginal storytelling: Towards an understanding of an Indigenous perspective and its implications for research practice. *Contemporary Nurse, 46*(1), 13–17.

Gerson, K., & Horowitz, R. (2002). Observation and interviewing: Options and choices in qualitative research. In T. May (Ed.), *Qualitative research in action*. London: Sage.

Given, L., Cantrell Winkler, D., Willson, R., Davidson, C., Danby, S., & Thorpe, K. (2016). Parents as coresearchers at home: Using an observational method to document young children's use of technology. *International Journal of Qualitative Methods, 15*(1), 1609406915621403.

Gorin, S., Hooper, C. A., Dyson, C., & Cabral, C. (2008). Ethical challenges in conducting research with hard to reach families. *Child Abuse Review, 17*(4), 275–287.

Guillemin, M., & Gillam, L. (2004). Ethics, reflexivity, and "ethically important moments" in research. *Qualitative Inquiry, 10*(2), 261–280.

Guillemin, M., & Heggen, K. (2009). Rapport and respect: Negotiating ethical relations between researcher and participant. *Medicine, Health Care and Philosophy, 12*(3), 291–299.

Hammersley, M. (2015). On ethical principles for social research. *International Journal of Social Research Methodology, 128*(4), 433–449.

Harcourt, D., & Einarsdóttir, J. (2011). Introducing children's perspectives and participation in research. *European Early Childhood Education Research Journal, 19*(3), 301–307.

Harcourt, D., Perry, B., & Waller, T. (2011). *Researching young children's perspectives: Debating the ethics and dilemmas of educational research with children.* New York: Taylor & Francis.

Harcourt, D., & Sargeant, J. (2012). *Doing ethical research with children.* Maidenhead: McGraw-Hill Education.

Harden, J., Backett-Milburn, K., Hill, M., & MacLean, A. (2010). Oh, what a tangled web we weave: Experiences of doing 'multiple perspectives' research in families. *International Journal of Social Research Methodology, 13*(5), 441–452.

Hart, R. (1992). *Children's participation: From tokenism to citizenship.* Retrieved from Florence, Italy. https://www.unicef-irc.org/publications/pdf/childrens_participation.pdf

Hart, R. (2008). Stepping back from 'the ladder': Reflections on a model of participatory work with children. In *Participation and learning* (pp. 19–31). New York: Springer.

Irvine, A., Drew, P., & Sainsbury, R. (2013). 'Am I not answering your questions properly?': Clarification, adequacy and responsiveness in semi-structured telephone and face-to-face interviews. *Qualitative Research, 13*(1), 87–106.

Kirby, P., Lanyon, C., Cronin, K., & Sinclair, R. (2003). *Building a culture of participation: Involving children and young people in policy, service planning, delivery and evaluation.* Retrieved from London. https://www.unicef.org/adolescence/cypguide/files/Building_a_culture_of_participation.pdf

Mannion, G. (2007). Going spatial, going relational: Why "listening to children" and children's participation needs reframing. *Discourse: Studies in the Cultural Politics of Education, 28*(3), 405–420.

Mapedzahama, V., & Dune, T. (2017). A clash of paradigms? Ethnography and ethics approval. *SAGE Open, 7*(1), 2158244017697167.

McNeil, T. (2010). Family as a social determinant of health: Implications for governments and institutions to promote the health and well-being of families. *Healthcare Quarterly, 14*(Special Issue, Child Health Canada), 60–67.

Miller, T., Birch, M., Mauthner, M., & Jessop, J. (2012). Introduction. In T. Miller, M. Birch, M. Mauthner, & J. Jessop (Eds.), *Ethics in qualitative research* (2nd ed.). London: Sage.

Mohan, G. (2001). Beyond participation: Strategies for deeper empowerment. In B. Cooke & U. Kothari (Eds.), *Participation: The new tyranny?* London: Zed Boos.

Morrow, V. (2009). *The ethics of social research with children and families in Young Lives: Practical experiences* (Working paper no. 53). Retrieved from University of Oxford, Oxford, UK. https://www.younglives.org.uk/sites/www.young-lives.org.uk/files/YL-WP53-Morrow-EthicsOfResearchWithChildren.pdf

Morrow, V. (2013). Practical ethics in social research with children and families in young lives: A longitudinal study of childhood poverty in Ethiopia, Andhra Pradesh (India), Peru and Vietnam. *Methodological Innovations Online, 8*(2), 21–35.

National Health and Medical Research Council Australian Research Council. (2007). *National Statement on Ethical Conduct in Human Research (2007) - Updated December 2015 (the National Statement).* Retrieved from Canberra, ACT. https://nhmrc.gov.au/about-us/publications/national-statement-ethical-conduct-human-research-2007-updated-2018

Palaiologou, I. (2012a). Ethical praxis when choosing research tools for use with children under five. In I. Palaiologou (Ed.), *Ethical practice in early childhood* (pp. 32–46). London: Sage.

Palaiologou, I. (2012b). Introduction: Towards an understanding of ethical practice in early childhood. In I. Palaiologou (Ed.), *Ethical practice in early childhood* (pp. 1–12). London: Sage.

Palaiologou, I. (2014). 'Do we hear what children want to say?' Ethical praxis when choosing research tools with children under five. *Early Child Development and Care, 184*(5), 689–705.

Paris, D. (2011). 'A friend who understand fully': Notes on humanizing research in a multiethnic youth community. *International Journal of Qualitative Studies in Education, 24*(2), 137–149.

Paris, D., & Winn, M. (Eds.). (2014). *Humanizing research: Decolonizing qualitative inquiry with youth and communities.* London: Sage.

Phelan, S., & Kinsella, E. (2013). Picture this ... safety, dignity, and voice—Ethical research with children practical considerations for the reflexive researcher. *Qualitative Inquiry, 19*(2), 81–90.

Powell, M. A., Fitzgerald, R. M., Taylor, N., & Graham, A. (2012). *International literature review: Ethical issues in undertaking research with children and young people (Literature review for the Childwatch International Research Network).* Retrieved from Lismore, NSW: Southern Cross University, Centre for Children and Young People/Dunedin, New Zealand: University of Otago,

Centre for Research on Children and Families. http://epubs.scu.edu.au/cgi/viewcontent.cgi?article=1041&context=ccyp_pubs

Reason, P., & Bradbury, H. (2008). Introduction. In P. Reason & H. Bradbury (Eds.), *The Sage handbook of action research. Participative inquiry and practice* (2nd ed., pp. 1–10). London: Sage.

Rinaldi, C. (2006). *In dialogue with Reggio Emilia: Listening, researching, and learning.* London: Routledge Falmer.

Rizvi, S. (2017). Treading on eggshells: 'Doing' feminism in educational research. *International Journal of Research & Method in Education*, 1–13. http://dx.doi.org/10.1080/1743727X.2017.1399354

Roulston, K. (2014). Interactional problems in research interviews. *Qualitative Research, 14*(3), 277–293.

Saleebey, D. (2012). *The strengths perspective in social work practice* (6th ed.). Boston: Pearson.

Shier, H. (2001). Pathways to participation: Openings, opportunities and obligations. *Children & Society, 15*(2), 107–117.

Somekh, B. (2002). Inhabiting each other's castles: Towards knowledge and mutual growth through collaboration. In C. Day, J. Elliott, B. Somekh, & R. Winter (Eds.), *Theory and practice in action research: Some international perspectives* (pp. 79–104). Oxford, UK: Symposium Books.

Sumsion, J., & Goodfellow, J. (2012). 'Looking and listening-ein': A methodological approach to generating insights into infants' experiences of early childhood education and care settings. *European Early Childhood Education Research Journal, 20*(3), 313–327.

Tuck, E. (2016). In conversation with Michelle Fine. Inner angles: Of ethical responses to/with indigenous and decolonizing theories. In N. D. M. Giardina (Ed.), *Ethical futures in qualitative research: Decolonizing the politics of knowledge* (International congress of qualitative inquiry series) (pp. 145–168). London: Routledge.

Uttal, L. (2009). (Re)visioning family ties to communities and contexts. In S. A. Lloyd, A. L. Few, & K. R. Allen (Eds.), *Handbook of feminist studies* (pp. 134–146). Thousand Oaks, CA: Sage.

Vähäsantanen, K., & Saarinen, J. (2013). The power dance in the research interview: Manifesting power and powerlessness. *Qualitative Researcher, 13*(5), 493–510.

Von Unger, H. (2012). Participatory health research: Who participates in what? *Forum Qualitative Sozialforschung/Forum: Qualitative Social Research, 13*(7), 1–28.

Wright, M. T., Roche, B., von Unger, H., Block, M., & Gardner, B. (2010). A call for an international collaboration on participatory research for health. *Health Promotion International, 25*(1), 115–122.

Yee, W. C., & Andrews, J. (2006). Professional researcher or a 'good guest'? Ethical dilemmas involved in researching children and families in the home setting. *Educational Review, 58*(4), 397–413. https://doi.org/10.1080/00131910600971859.

5

Gathering Layers of Meaning in Context

Scenario 5: Deliberating Over Research Methods and Data Collection Tools

Jane and her team have been making great headway in planning for their research project. Their goal is to explore interpretations of 'risky play', and the impact these understandings have on child agency, and restrictions on active play opportunities. Their plan is to better understand this phenomenon by seeking insight into the multiple perspectives of parents and children in families. The team have already engaged in reflection and professional conversations to discuss their paradigmatic perspectives (epistemology, ontology, and axiology), and how they are positioned within the research. This has helped to ensure their methodological approach aligns and intersects with the direction of the inquiry. Several key themes that have emerged from their discussion are that their study be positioned within an interpretivist paradigm, and the value their group places on collective and individual storying. There was also mutual agreement regarding the importance of considering power differentials which may exist between researcher and participants, and between adults and children, as well as questioning notions of truth.

Based on their experience, and after reflecting on their positioning, and the direction they wished their project to head, the researchers have come to a

© The Author(s) 2019
A. Brown, *Respectful Research With and About Young Families*, Palgrave Studies in Education Research Methods, https://doi.org/10.1007/978-3-030-02716-2_5

consensus that the methodological approach they wish to employ will be that of a single case study with multiple sites (approximately 25 families in total, with at least one child in each family being aged five years or under; and families from a broad range of contexts). They agreed that this approach would help to 'situate participants' views in the context of the social relationships within which they are constructed', and illuminate understandings and complexity of the phenomenon being investigated (Harden, Backett-Milburn, Hill, & MacLean, 2010, p. 441). *However, currently they have been deliberating over the methodological drivers impacting on their decision-making, particularly regarding the type of data collection tools that would best support their position, and afford them in collecting rich data.*

Great consideration has also been invested in how the data collection tools would reflect the value they collectively had regarding the position of voice being 'heard alongside others', a heightened awareness of the power dynamics that would exist between the researchers and the family, the rights of the child, and supporting the agency of all family members within 'existing generational power relations' (Christensen & James, 2008a, 2008b). *This was identified as particularly poignant, given their desire to ensure that all family members, including children (particularly younger children), had an opportunity to share their stories* (see Chap. 2), *and voice their perspectives, thoughts, and feelings* (see Chap. 4). *The type of questions they were deliberating over in relation to considering research methods and data collection tools included: How could these methods best afford the gathering of data from different perspectives? What methods would best afford all members of young families' opportunities to share, and feel comfortable in sharing their stories? What research methods would be effective in informing our questions, yet flexible enough to account for the context, agency, and needs of participants? Where should the researchers position themselves when collecting data?*

Note: This scenario has been inspired by the research and paper of Jeni Harden and her team (2010).

Chapter Synopsis

Why dedicate a chapter to research methods for supporting inquiry about, and with, young families? Wouldn't these methods be similar to that of other types of qualitative research approaches? Well, yes, in principle this may be the case, in that the data collection methods one chooses to explore, and eventually adopt, may have a number of similarities with other interpretivist methods. Perhaps also, our background research into the methods we wish to adopt could certainly draw upon, and be informed by the many excellent books and papers dedicated to "how to employ a particular method and how to use it well" (Tudge, 2008, p. 88). However, the distinction, and where the paucity of information exists for those seeking insight and direction in the choice of research methods for engaging in inquiry with young families, is with regard to the nuanced and contextual differences of phenomena associated with young families and its members.

> What methods best afford opportunities for the social actors in domestic spaces to share their stories and lived experiences?
> Does our choice of participatory tools necessarily engage both parents and children, particularly young children from birth to five years of age?
> How will research of or with young families impact on the choice of data collection tools we employ?
> How will our perspectives, beliefs, and the lens in which we view children and families impact on the methods we choose, and our actions as researchers (including the way we enter domestic spaces and interact with individuals in these environments)?

For those seeking to research with, or about, young families, there is also the desire to 'walk in another's shoes', and to see the world through the lens of another. Each of these goals requires the careful selection and employment of data-gathering tools. This requires a combination of a considered approach, and the integration of a range of methods that are respectful, ethical, enabling "the fabric of family relationships to be unpicked" (Gabb, 2009, p. 37).

However, at this point, insights into strategies to support inquiry with, or about, families are still scarce. Further, there is limited guidance within the literature offering a distinctive rationale necessary for adopting a particular suite of tools to address this type of inquiry. Such a response would benefit from creative research design, and would need to reinforce the importance of a set of tools that open up the possibility of gaining an in-depth understanding of the full complexity of contemporary young families (Daly, 2007; Gabb, 2009; Harden et al., 2010).

Young families are a collection of individuals, but they are also members of a distinctive and idiosyncratic group. Families are situated in a complex social system of relationships, while being located in dynamic contexts that change over time (Flyvbjerg, 2001). Families also have a hierarchy of age, standpoints of generation, nuanced family practices, and multiple memberships and positions, all of which need to be acknowledged, and taken into account, as part of the methodological decision-making process.

Let's pause for a moment before moving forward, to reflect back on the project that Jane and her team were planning. Quite a number of the questions they raised regarding considerations for data collection strategies are distinctive to researching with young families, such as needing to consider the dynamics of existing generational power relations (Christensen & James, 2008), and the impact this might then have on affording all members of young families the opportunity to share their stories, and feel comfortable in doing so. You can appreciate that for their project, engaging in inquiry with young families presents a unique set of circumstances, and considerations that will require a careful selection and application of tools, effective for gathering layers of meaning. The research team also identified that it was important that their decision-making was cognisant of participant agency, and the rights of others to share their perspectives.

Unique to family research is also the matter that family life is private and, as such, being 'invited in', and researching in the field to investigate a phenomenon related to young families and its members, is a privileged position. It requires a particular mindset and approach, which includes being fully present in the spaces and places where young families move, live, and work. And like an artist, builder, or teacher, it requires a specialised set of tools, chosen specifically to efficiently and effectively support the act of 'seeing' and 'being' in the environments, wonderings, and social processes of others (Greenstein & Davis, 2013; Torin & Fisher, 2010).

In our pursuit of inquiry with young families we are afforded with data being potentially everywhere and all around us. As such, it will be essential that in planning for our inquiry, we are mindful and conscious to select the right tools for the right job, the intent being that the combination of these will support the co-construction, and a rich portrayal of the multiple layers of meaning of individuals within contexts (Cohen, Manion, & Morrison, 2007; Stark & Torrance, 2005). Careful consideration also needs to be given to how the methods we employ are both ethical and respectful of the children and families involved.

At the same time, we need to be cognisant that the methods employed recognise the competency, capacity, and agentic nature of family members (Hägglund, 2012). Further, consideration will also need to be given to how the methods chosen will realise, and in turn value, participant perspectives and voice. It will be important that these voices also include those of young children, and their insights as significant members of young families, and what they can teach us about their lived experiences (Harden et al., 2010; Palaiologou, 2014). And, in a process, rather likened to making a television documentary, hopefully the various data collection tools, and innovative methods we choose to employ, will together help build a mosaic (Clark & Moss, 2011)-this being a composite, or picture, that collectively attempts to capture what is happening in a micro-environment in a particular moment in time (Gabb, 2009).

With these points in mind, this chapter offers a range of tools that researchers may wish to consider, adapt, or combine, to support their quest of inquiry focussed on young families and its members, the intent of this being to 'give flesh' to participants' stories (Warr, 2004). Cognisant that each study is unique, and reflects the phenomenon being investigated, and the epistemology of the study, the intent of this chapter is not to recommend one tool or method over another, but to showcase a range of popular and innovative qualitative methods, the careful selection and combination of which might serve to support inquiry that seeks to gain a deeper appreciation and understanding of the idiosyncratic experiences and motivations of young families.

The methods, carefully selected and shared here, are particularly effective in generating context-dependent knowledge, and supporting the type of inquiry that recognises the situatedness of human behaviour. Further, it will be important that these methods are effective in exploring the contextual nuances that operate on, or are embedded in, the lives of individuals, and give meaning to their thoughts and actions (Flyvbjerg,

2001). Finally, appreciating that both adults and children are fundamentally situated in context (Brown, 2012), and embedded in a series of complex socio-cultural negotiations, the methods and tools included in this chapter have been chosen for their effectiveness in better understanding the pervasive influence that multiple factors have on the lives of individuals.

This chapter starts by introducing strategies that support efforts to scan the home environment, a critical space where the learning and development of young children take place, and is supported. Behaviour mapping and contextualised observation are then discussed, as effective methods for documenting evidence of 'household happenings', practices, and environment in situ. A multi-method framework, referred to as the Mosaic approach, is then introduced as an effective and innovative approach to support the piecing together of meaning, through the adoption of multiple forms of documentation. The chapter concludes by exploring the valuable research tool of interviews, and offers a range of considerations for employing this method to engage in active listening, and for capturing the situated stories of young families.

Throughout this chapter conscious reflexivity (the act of being critically self-aware), is promoted as being an important strategy for ensuring rigour and trustworthiness in qualitative research. This process involves an interpretive awareness of being "self-examining, self-questioning, self-critical and self-correcting" (Lincoln & Guba, 1988, p. 11). Ideally, this process is most effective when embedded into all aspects of our methodology and data collection which would also include personal self-reflection, and co-construction and reflection with peers (Guillemin & Gillam, 2004). These collective voices and multiple perspectives of self and others help to clarify subjectivity, to interrogate more deeply our view of the world, our interpretations of the data, and the meaning-making and the storying of others (Finlay, 2003). Other researchers have also seen value in the process of "inward gazing" as a means of articulating the assumptions that underline their work, and in more fully interpreting the data particularly in relation to those we are researching (Leung & Lapum, 2005, p. 9).

A Stocktake of the Tools Required to Do the Job

An essential step, and part of the methodological process of inquiry, is dedicating time and reflection to selecting the right tools for the right job. This is particularly important for inquiry with and about young families, where great thought will need to be given to the methods that will afford all members of families (including young children) opportunities to share their stories, insights, and ideas. With this in mind, and before reading further, you may wish to pause and take this opportunity to conduct a stocktake of factors that will impact on the decision-making process.

- Who is your audience? Where are they located (physically, temporary, socially)?
- Where are you located and positioned as you enter into the private lives of young families?
- What type of tools will you need to employ to account for the position of yourself and 'the other'?
- What role and how much agency will participants have in your study, including their input into the tools that will be used?
- What is the phenomenon you are interested in investigating? What types of tools will support this quest?
- To what extent might the tools you have chosen impact on your researching 'on', rather than perhaps researching 'about' or 'with' young families?

5.1 Scanning the Environments of Young Families: Seeing into Their World

Daly (2007) so aptly sets the scene for this section of chapter. He writes, "The most important skill that we can cultivate when doing qualitative work is learning how to see" (Daly, 2007, p. 16). Interpretivist researchers of young families will usually have a strong valuing for context-dependent understandings of a phenomenon (including 'household happenings'), where importance is placed on observing social interactions, uncovering behaviours and practices, and gaining insights into the environments in which member of young families are embedded (Stake, 2010). Scanning of the environment provides insight into the reality of families, and the natural unfolding of these types of domestic events, behaviours, and environmental contexts (Brown, 2012).

Scanning the environment offers a naturalistic approach for inquiry. This strategy is particularly adept at data gathering to inform an in-depth understanding of the social/emotional environment, the temporal environment (time, schedules, routines, and time pressures), and the physical environment of young families (e.g. the home, education are care settings, and social and sporting settings) (Gabb, 2009). Employing a range of data collection tools for this purpose can help uncover the idiosyncratic nature of these sites, and the bi-directional relationship that exists between the interaction of people and place (Tudge, 2008). These tools require the skill and practice of being 'self in context', and could include time sampling, direct and indirect observation, photo-documentation, and environmental scanning and auditing tools (Given et al., 2016).

Observing in, and Reflecting on, Context

Observation is a significant tool for generating data, and effective for scanning the environment (Merriam & Tisdall, 2016). Observation can be tracked to a long tradition adopted in the social sciences for 'surveying the terrain', but also an important starting point for listening to participants (Bratich, 2017; Clark & Moss, 2011; Rinaldi, 2006). The term 'observation' is used when referring to the process of documenting and 'the gazing' at, of, or about individual behaviours, actions, interactions, and environments (physical, temporal, or human) (Patton, 2015). In particular, observation refers to the act of observing and being situated in context, as well as reflecting on context.

Traditionally this process conjures up images of a scientist with notebooks, exercising objectivity, and using tools such as checklists to track, categorise, and assess behaviours, similar to that of observing a specimen (researching on individuals). However, for interpretivists, observation becomes a legitimate scientific pursuit when there is a specific goal, has a particular focus or plan (including key areas to focus on), where notes are taken and recorded (sometimes referred to a "field jottings"), and more detailed notes and reflection on context follow observational pursuits (Greenstein & Davis, 2013, pp. 108–109). Further, rather than being disassociated from context, naturalistic observations are understood to be located and embedded in context. As such, observations are understood to be embedded in social process, including the agency of the other, and their part in the active meaning-making process.

Why Observations Are of Value?

The tool of observation is of particular value to researchers that recognises that adult and child learning is a series of continual, 'complex social negotiations', "fundamentally situated" in context (Brown, Collins, & Duguid, 1989, p. 33). Qualitative observational tools are effective in better understanding, and seeing family practices and behaviours unfolding. Contextual observation and "learning from observing others" offer a meaningful data collection technique that provides a heightened sense of awareness of social life processes such as body language and behaviours (Fraser, 2004; Stake, 2005, p. 4).

Observational data collection tools provide great insight into a phenomenon, and the characteristics of a setting. These include gaining insight into the unfamiliar territory, meaning-making, and the lived experiences that unfold within the micro-environment of the family home (Gabb, 2009; Given et al., 2016). The practice and employment of these tools allow one to sit, observe, and reflect upon very specific moments, behaviours, and aspects of family life and family members, located in situ in a specific micro-context, as well as holistically (Harden et al., 2010). In conjunction with other methods, and scanning techniques, observational tools afford opportunities to interpret what is being observed, while gaining a richer and more complete picture of domestic places and social spaces of young families, and the heightened awareness of the impact environments (physical, social, temporal) have on the meaning-making and behaviour.

Skills and Considerations

Learning to use a tool as an artist, for a trade, or for research, requires mental effort, commitment, and great skill. The tool of observation, and "learning to see", is no different. Daly (2007) likens the process and conditions similar to that required for meditation (p. 16). And, just like learning to meditate, or any other skill, learning the skill of observing requires regular practice, both practically, in terms of what to look for, how to record, what to record (what details are important), the choice of tools, but also with regards to where we position ourselves to have minimum impact on others. Effectively mastering the skill of observation also requires preparation in order to be truly open to being 'in the field' (Greenstein & Davis, 2013). This requires us to 'listen with our whole bodies', to the social processes, lived experiences of others, and 'the unfolding of the everyday' (Gabb & Fink, 2015).

Observers also require a particular mindset, which includes humbleness, and a sensitivity to others. This includes appreciating that we are being invited in to the private spaces of young families, and mindful that by the very nature of the world in which we live, families will feel vulnerable and a sense of being judged and under surveillance (Bratich, 2017; Gabb, 2009). As such, it is important that researchers enter these spaces, and engage with others respectfully, and sensitively. At times, the role of the observer in these contexts may require obtrusive measures, such as that of shadowing of family members, sitting in context making notes while observing. However, another option is to consider more subtle forms of observation, with the intent of becoming less visible or employing strategies where "the researcher's presence melts into the background" (Given et al., 2016, p. 2).

There is the potential of data being present everywhere. As such, researchers will face a number of decisions regarding how best to engage in the process of 'observing in', and 'reflecting on' context. For young families, these observable moments include mealtime, times when parents are busy parenting, or when families are engaged in domestic routines, such as organising children for bed or a bath, making dinner, or hanging out the clothes. Depending upon the phenomenon being investigated, observational pursuits might include behaviours such as television viewing habits, children's use of technology in their daily lives, or perhaps a focus on quality family time.

Inventory Approaches, Environmental Mapping, and Contextual Audit Tools (or CATs)

A contextual audit, or an environment scan, refers to the systematic practice of drawing upon and making sense of a range of data (i.e. observations, photo-documentation, artefacts, and interviews). Researchers employ this strategy to help build a picture of a particular context, setting, or environment. Contextual audits and environment scans are frequently used in business practices and organisations to gain a detailed understanding of where a company has come from, is currently at, or is heading towards. However, for inquiry focussed on young families, contextual audits and scans refer to the process of collecting focussed data on a particular micro-environment.

Researchers who believe in the situatedness of meaning-making, and the impact that the environment has on individual behaviour, perspectives, and practice, will see value in tools such as contextual audits and environmental scans. These types of tools support researchers in drawing attention, and engaging in a heightened sensitivity to key features and practices within micro-environment, that are relevant to the phenomenon being investigated. The tools can be used in isolation, or in combination with other scanning tools, such as that of observations, and interviews, and aid in prompting researchers to look beyond the observation, to the contextual details and the physical, social, and temporal environments in which individuals are located.

Scans and audits often draw upon a contextual audit template to guide the focus of the scan. In researching with young families, scans are effective in extending our observations beyond the home environment, including making notes on the neighbourhood, early learning service that young children attend, or other environments where families socialise and spend time (such as at church, or within a playgroup setting, or sporting/leisure activity). Scan and audit tools are important in helping to focus a researcher's attention on a particular aspect of the micro-environment, or context, in which families move, work, and live.

With regard to inquiry with young families, the employment of such tools helps to create a picture, or contextual overview, in efforts to make sense of, or provide insight into a phenomenon. This includes helping to build a holistic and ecological picture of the case or place in which individuals are located. Contextual scanning and contextual audit templates help alleviate some of the complexity of gathering contextual details of people's lives, and supports in the illumination of environmental factors that impact on practice, behaviours, or the perspectives of others. Finally, an audit template can serve as a useful prompt for reviewing and making notes on a focussed environment, or aspects that need to be investigated and to gather contextual details on the family, and setting.

For researchers of young families, environmental scanning tools, such as behaviour mapping or emotion mapping (a popular tool in family therapy research) (Gabb & Singh, 2015), offer an innovative research method for observing and investigating the behavioural dynamics of the environments in which family members live, work, or play. The value of this type of research method is that it helps inform understandings of the types of environments that support and impact on particular social and individual behaviour. This type of evidence also helps inform and aids in designing policy and practices related to the associated phenomenon.

Further, behaviour and emotion mapping is a valuable addition to a methodological toolkit, as the tool does not rely on high literacy or language skills. As such, the research method is capable of privileging the voices and perspectives of all family members, and cab "help overcome the generational competencies which ordinarily divide parents and children", or where English may not be the first language (Gabb & Singh, 2015, p. 186). For interpretivist researchers, emotion mapping makes a valuable contribution to a suite of data collection tools one might choose to employ, as it provides an opportunity to engage in a strengths-based research method. In this way, employing emotional mapping strategies affirms dialogue with family members, and primary carers, rather than focussing only on deficits (Gabb & Singh, 2015).

Skills and Considerations
Similar to the skills a detective might employ to collect evidence on a case, researchers seeking to scan the environment may benefit from referring to a CAT—contextual audit template. This strategy is employed as a guide to aid researchers in focussing their attention on a range of contextual details related to the environment, and the individuals situ-

ated within the micro-environment. (Refer to details and definition of the micro-environment outlined in Chap. 1 of this text.) This process ideally occurs over several visits to a context, in order to build a detailed picture and understanding of the phenomenon being investigated.

For example, in my own doctoral research (Brown, 2012), each site (the micro-environment of the family home) was visited a minimum of three times. Each time, while engaged in other data collection pursuits, a scan of the environment was also ongoing and integrated into the site visit. During these visits, attention was focussed on gathering evidence of the environments, and resources that supported or inhibited active play practices, and opportunities for young children in families (Brown, 2012).

For example, during the first visit, a particular focus was on collecting contextual background details on family members (including socio-demographics, employment status, education level of each parent, family structure, work commitments and hours of work, etc.). However, it was often the case that children in families wished to show me their rooms and play spaces during these times, so photo-documentation helped capture these environments, resources, and the play toys children had available to them. Again, prompted by key areas of focus identified in the CAT scan of the environment, the second and third visits focussed more specifically on collecting further evidence of the physical environment (such as outdoor play spaces, indoor play spaces, and resources such as toys).

The contextual audit tool, referred to as of 'behaviour mapping', works by the researcher, or participants as co-researcher, creating a visual map, and then documenting and coding of particular behaviour associated with a specified environment. For example, Cosco, Moore, and Islam (2010) explored the types of physical and sedentary behaviours evidenced in a range of early childhood settings. Other examples might include gathering data observed within the environmental places and spaces that families socialise and communicate. These spaces may include observing the feeding habits of parents with infants, or perhaps the formal and informal eating habits of family members. The employment of 'geographical information systems' and handheld digital coding devices are another type of 'scanning tool' that helps track the behaviours of participants, which could include tracking the places and spaces that young children are allowed to play and engage in active play around the home, or in the surrounding neighbourhood.

Researchers usually start this process, by creating a map or sketch of the environment, which will be the focus of the observation. This would include a symbolic identification of key physical features with this space. For example, when exploring the active play spaces within the indoor environment of a family home, this may include sketching out the family home with efforts to draw to scale all areas (including hallways), and then noting key physical features and key resources in these spaces (sofas, play boxes, entertainment units, dining table, beds, doll houses, etc.).

The process of emotion mapping starts again with creating a floor plan of the physical environment aligned with the focus of the study, and phenomenon being investigated. Gabb and Singh (2015) then suggests that a designated length of time for emotion mapping is identified, such as several days. Family members are then given a selection of emoticon stickers "denoting laughter, happy, indifference, sadness, upset, grumpiness or anger, and love/affection" (with each member of the family represented by a specific colour of sticker, such as red for dad, and yellow emoticon stickers for mum (Gabb & Singh, 2015, p. 188). Family members would then be encouraged to place an emoticon sticker on the relevant place on the floor plan when an interaction occurs for which they wish to express their feelings. In Gabb's study, family members would then be encouraged to draw their own representations and floor plans, with each family member invited to participate in adding their emoticon stickers to their floorplan throughout a designated period of time.

After a designated time of families engaging in the process of emotion mapping, the researcher would visit the family again, and engage in dialogue to explore the various maps of family members. Of course, as most researchers are not qualified psychologists or psychotherapist in family studies, the process of engaging in dialogical relations with family members regarding their experience and interpretations of events will need to be considered and approached very carefully, in order to best support ethical and respectful research. However, it doesn't discount the usefulness of employing such an innovative tool for engaging in authentic meaning-making with families, and is worth exploring further opportunities and possibilities.

Note that researchers interested in employing a scan, audit or mapping tool, may wish to consider modifying or customising an existing tool, template, or technique, rather than creating a completely new tool. For example, in my doctoral study (Brown, 2012), which focussed on the phenomenon of active play and young children in domestic contexts, the contextual audit template I employed drew upon my previous knowledge and application of environmental scans. However, the scan I eventually developed was drawn from inspirations, and ideas from other valued scanning techniques, such as those employed by Egger, Pearson, Pal, and Swinburn (2007), and Swinburn, Egger, and Raza (1999), for diagnosing and dissecting obesogenic environments.

Photo-Documentation

Photo-documentation refers to a visual research method. Efforts of data collection that employ this method focus on the process of capturing behaviour, practices and context via photograph/or video, to gain insight into a phenomenon. If approached in a scholarly and rigorous way, rather than just a matter of simply 'snapping shots', the process of photo-documentation can be viewed as a critical visual methodology for data generation (Merewether & Fleet, 2014; Rose, 2016).

Photo-documentation is a powerful interpretivist research tool employed by itself or in combination with other data collection tools, for capturing images of the individuals, spaces, and places. It is a meaningful data-gathering tool for gaining insight into the physicality of context, such as the micro-environment of the family home, and world of young families (Markwell, 2000). Photo-documentation contributes to a holistic, rather than reductionist, interpretation, and investigation of a phenomenon.

A powerful bonus of employing photo-documentation as a data collection tool is that these snapshots, or visual imagery of domesticity, or other contexts relevant to research about families, can in fact be an excellent prompt for extending conversations on a range of interview topics, beyond those questions originally anticipated. The presentation of photo-documentation to family members, or what Fleer and Ridgway (2013) refer to as 'photo-based interviews', can be a powerful tool to invite, or trigger, conversations beyond the original intent of the interviews, and adding an additional layer or window into viewing the lives of families, often referred to as photo-elicitation (Bridger, 2013; Gabb, 2009).

Notwithstanding, photo-documentation has been successfully used by myself on a number of occasions, including being used in conjunction with other data collection tools (a contextual audit template and semi-structured interviews) as part of my doctoral research (Brown, 2012). For this inquiry, photo-documentation proved to be an excellent data collection tool to heighten and help to focus on the meaning behind the choices, and uses of the various resources and environments dedicated, to active play experiences in the domestic spaces of young families. During site visits, and interviews with each family, photo-documentation of captured images would be shown. These images would often stimulate conversation, and encourage parents to share their ideas, excitement, and extend on their stories about the role of active play opportunities in their context.

Included here is an example of how a prompt from a photo of a child's plastic cubby house (see Fig. 5.1), taken during a previous visit with the

Fig. 5.1 The plastic cubby: an example of photo-documentation

Mason family, led to a detailed conversation between Sarah (mother) and myself, at the kitchen table. This conversation then led to us revisiting the outdoor environment, where we watched Helen (daughter) play and talk about the outdoor play spaces and the recreational activities Helen liked to engage in, in the backyard.

Alice   *Does she play in that very much? (A photo of a plastic cubby house taken on a previous visit is shown.)*

Sarah   *Ah, the thing is that she's never been very interested in playing in that house, which is kind of curious, but she always loved the sandpit. Helen, do you want to go outside and take the lid off the sandpit and show Alice what's in there so she can see it?*

Alice   *It's interesting though, because she'd rather make something else into a house instead of playing in the playhouse. Perhaps it's too claustrophobic?*

Sarah   *Yeah, that's exactly right and this is one of those things that people think kids will like, but she's never really been interested. And when she was very small I used to put the little kiddies tables and chairs in it and say, 'let's play tea parties' and say, 'come on' and set up the play. And it's ended up as a storage shed because she's never been interested. She'd prefer to get the tea party out, pull out a picnic rug and sit out here and have the tea party.*

The genuine interest that is demonstrated by the researcher to 'better understand', and seek explanation of an image that has been documented with family members, also proves to be an authentic rapport-building technique. It is a way to embed strengths-based practices, and perspectives, as part of the data collection process, as conversation to explore meaning behind the images unfolds. The collaborative moments of the co-construction of meaning are an authentic way of affirming the efforts, practices, and contexts of young families. Adopting a lens of affordances to documentation, celebrates the voice, storying, places, and spaces of young families. This will be addressed in the next section of this chapter.

Skills and Considerations

It is easy to get carried away in the moment, and perhaps even be over-whelmed by the potential of great photographic moments being evidenced everywhere, and all around us, while 'in context'. Therefore, a tip for engaging in effective photo-documentation, with, or about, young families, is having an anticipated focus for the type of images you wish to document (Rose, 2016). Of course, these decisions will be primarily informed by the goals, focus of an inquiry, and the associated research questions. Daly (2007) refers to the practice of 'bracketing' as a process to help "bring attention to a particular aspect of our conscious awareness" (p. 24).

Adopting the practice of narrowing our gaze enables researchers to make decisions on the subject matter which is important to hone in on, or "commit to a composition that holds promise for our inquiry" (Daly, 2007, p. 24). However, photo-documentation can also be guided through the aid of a contextual audit template/tool. And, while it is important to plan for the focus of documentation, it is also important to leave room for spontaneity, and be ready and open to capture the unanticipated moments, behaviours, practices, and environments that are presented to us.

It is important that photo-documentation is approached with great care, respect, and sensitivity to the people and spaces at the heart of an inquiry. For example, if there is a desire to take photos of the play toys and spaces of young children, even if permission has already been 'officially' granted, it is important, as part of respectful and ethical practice, to verbally seek permission with the children involved. Of course, this request needs to be posed in a sincere and authentic way, as part of expressing a genuine interest in their world, resources, and spaces.

5.2   Identifying Affordances in the Environments Families Live, Move, and Work In

In the previous section of this chapter we addressed a range of tools that can support researchers in scanning the environments in which young families live, work, or play. One of the tools introduced was that of contextual audit templates, or contextual scans. We continue to build on scanning techniques and tools now, by introducing a methodology, and set of tools, that help to identify specifically the affordances evidenced within these environments.

Notions of 'affordance' have their roots within the ecological branch of psychological theory (Gibson, 1977, 1979), in which significant writing and research have been conducted (Bjørgen, 2016; Heft, 2010). Over the last few decades the adoption and interpretation of affordance theory has continued to be embraced by environmental psychologists, the field of environmental design, and with increased popularity in other fields such as education and physical activity, to better understand the physical components of the built environment (Cosco et al. 2010; Falcini, 2014). Researchers have also drawn on affordance theory to develop scanning, observation, and coding tools, in efforts to help make sense of the environments and behaviour settings of individuals, including the daily lives of children (Cosco et al., 2010; Little & Sweller, 2015).

However, in relation to the topics and themes addressed in this chapter, and indeed throughout this text, the term 'affordance' will be referred to and used slightly differently. The distinction is significant, in that adopting the term affordances does not directly link to the functional significance that the environment affords an individual (Heft, 2010). Rather, affordance, and reference to this term, is positioned within a strengths-based, multi-dimensional, and ecological lens for seeing the world and aspects of the environment (human, temporal, or physical). This includes what we see, feel, hear, and the relationship these aspects have on behaviours, practices, values, and perspectives (Mori, Nakamoto, Mizuochi, Ikudome, & Gabbard, 2013). Reference to affordance in this way also includes viewing the environment through a positive lens, in terms of what resources, behaviours, practices, and environments are evidenced, and how these features might support or enable a phenomenon, rather than viewing these factors and environments from a deficit of perspective of 'what isn't there', or 'what's not happening'. (See Chap. 2 of this text for further details and unpacking of a strengths-based perspective.)

With reference to notions of affordance related to environments in which young families live, move, or work, the term could be understood as the appreciation and evidencing of multi-dimensional environments which include:

- social/human environments, such aspects as socio-economic/demographic factors, personal and interpersonal factors of family members, personal health and wellbeing, social networks and playmates, social culture, access to social capital, parental/child values, beliefs/practices;
- the physical environment, such as features of the home—indoor/outdoor; neighbourhood, and resources; and
- temporal, such as lived experiences across time, routines, schedules, within a specified environment.

In this case, affordances would be noted, in terms of their enabling, or 'actualisation', being in relation to positively influencing a phenomenon, or behaviour occurring, rather than constraining a behaviour or phenomenon (Kyttä, 2004).

Interpretivist Approach to Affordance Scanning

Affordance audits and scanning tools are effective in supporting researchers focussing attention on resources and behaviours within an environment. These efforts provide insight into the factors impacting on the phenomenon being investigated. From an interpretivist perspective, there is much that we can gleam, adapt, and adopt in terms of the usefulness of the concept of affordance, particularly in terms of its application to research methods and data collection tools, related to phenomenon associated with, or about, young families.

For example, adopting an affordance approach for interpretivist research would be valuable in providing insight into the transactional-ecological, or interrelational ways in which environments and behaviour interact, with each influencing and impacting on the other (Falcini, 2014). Affordance tools are also effective for investigating the agency of families and children in context, rather than adopting a deficit lens. Affordance tools enable researchers to view 'what is evidenced' within the home environment or other environments where families live, work, or play. Adopting this reframed lens to affordance would alter the way in which audit, mapping, and scanning methods are used, and the way in which we enter and view these domestic spaces. Our lens, or approach, would change from one of being a researcher that stands back at a distance and views the environment unemotionally, to an approach which views the people in the environment connected to, and embedded in, a phenomenon.

Further, from a post-structuralist perspective, the notion of agency is framed through this interpretation of affordance, in terms of the influence that individuals (in this case, family members) directly and indirectly have on the environment. Lynch (2011), captures this perspective, referring to affordances as operationalising a 'transactional approach' that considers the social and cultural environment, as much as the physical environment. Therefore, it is important to reflect upon affordance scans, and how the factors identified, and objects/data collected as part of these scans, are socio-culturally mediated (Waters, 2017).

Interpretivist affordance tools and scans, combined with other qualitative methods, would also ideally be conducted 'with', rather than 'on', families. This might mean adopting tools where families join us in inquiry as co-researchers, in both sharing their perspectives and engaging in the task of 'looking out for' affordances related to the topic of the research, and phenomenon being investigated. Affordance tools that are able to support the task of families and researchers 'looking for', and 'seeking out', would embrace tools where participant voices are privileged and their storying and meaning-making evidenced in the data collection process. Adopting this lens to affordances extends the scope, potential, and possibilities of this tool, far beyond traditional affordance approaches.

Affordances Within the Home Environment

Studies focussed on determining the relationship and affordances within the home environment have become an increasingly popular field of inquiry. This has particularly been the case with studies focussed on investigating the relationship between the multi-dimensional home environment and behaviours such as motor development, play, physical activity, and relationships (Caçola, Gabbard, Montebelo, & Santos, 2015;

Gabbard, Caçola, & Rodrigues, 2008; Mori et al., 2013). As pointed out earlier, exploring affordances within the home environment ideally means adopting a multi-dimensional, ecological, strengths-based approach. This could include investigating not only the physical environment and resources, but also the human/social (such as the presence of siblings, social networks, and social spaces), and temporal environments, resources, and considerations. It could also mean exploring affordances in terms of 'what is' evidenced, rather than what is not present. Studies which focus on observing affordances open up a range of possibilities to dig deeper into a phenomenon, situated within the home environment, in order to more fully explore and understand the contextual and idiosyncratic nuances that exist with and between these spaces.

5.3   Listening to, and Hearing the Storying of, Families: 'The Mosaic Approach'

Piecing Together for Meaning

Adopting the multimodal possibilities of the Mosaic approach as a research strategy helps us to shift our gaze or approach to strategies for data collection (Daly, 2007). In doing so, we not only privilege the stories of children and families, but seek out methods that afford for all voices, even the voices of our youngest people, to be heard more clearly. This rethinking, or reframing, of ethical and respectful research methods calls on a commitment to not only seek out, but to employ, innovative tools and strategies that enable us to listen to the stories, and share in the co-creation of meaning-making with, and about, others. In doing so, the agenda is more intently focussed on exploring, seeing, hearing, listening, and responding to the multiple perspectives of others (Clark & Moss, 2011).

The Mosaic approach, in this chapter and text, is introduced and explored from the perspective of learning from, and being inspired by, the work of early adopters such as Clark (2001), Clark and Moss (2001), Clark and Moss (2005), Clark and Moss (2011), Clark and Statham (2005), Clark, Kjorholt, and Moss (2005); and others such as Fraser (2012), and

Harcourt (2008) and Stephenson (2009), Each of these authors, their own way making a contribution to opening up the possibilities of communication, and challenging us to rethink ways for integrating approaches for co-constructing meaning. The Mosaic approach has emerged from the desire to privilege the voices of young children, yet the approach and methods are just as relevant, in terms of engaging in themes related to ethical, respectful, and reciprocal relationships and research with, and about, families. The approach employs methods that seek out and are effective in documenting the insights, interests, and experiences of children on matters which concern them, or in which they have a vested interest. This 'listening' and 'piecing together for meaning' requires both skill and a particular disposition. It also requires us setting a particular tone, or climate for engagement, and inquiry, one that holds as integral the value of voice, the right for others to be heard, and the steadfast belief in the capacity of others, referred to by some as individuals having 'funds of knowledge' (González, Moll, & Amanti, 2005).

Back in 2001 Clark and Moss (2001; Clark, 2001) introduced the Mosaic approach as a multi-method approach and framework. The approach included a range of different techniques, employed for listening to and privileging the voices of young children five years of age and under. The 'framework for listening' was understood as one that went beyond just that of just the spoken word, to include verbal and nonverbal processes. This approach afforded and considered strategies for even preverbal children, or children that speak languages other than English to communicate, to ensure they were not overlooked (e.g. through actions, drawing, photographs, play, and facial expressions).

The Mosaic approach is underpinned by the deep respect for the rights of the child, including their 'right to express themselves on matters which affect them' (Article 12 from the UN Convention on the Rights of the Child). Clark (2001) defines the Mosaic approach as a "multi-method framework, which combines the traditional methodology of observation and interviewing, with the introduction of participatory tools including the use of cameras, tours and mapping", that could be combined with other tools "such as drawing and role-play" that, brought together, help to form and create a larger picture (p. 334). The Mosaic approach includes a second stage, or another layer, which draws together the different pieces of data, as a basis for co-construction, dialogue, reflection, and meaning-making with children and adults, as a way of gaining greater insight into the perspectives of young children (Clark & Moss, 2011).

Since its introduction in 2001, the Mosaic approach has continued to evolve, drawing upon and being informed by a range of perspectives, positions, and pedagogical approaches, such as from Rinaldi (2006), Fraser (2012), and other innovative scholars that have chosen to embed the Reggio Emilia approach into their practice (Edwards, Gandini, & Forman, 1998). The underpinning positioning of the approach has motivated practitioners, educators, and researchers to rethink and explore how research strategies might be employed more effectively, to gain insight into the perspectives of young children and adults. Examples of these perspectives have included:

- Belief in the capacity of the other (funds of knowledge) (González et al., 2005);
- The importance placed on listening, rather than assuming answers;
- Listening being an active process of hearing, but also interpreting and responding;
- Recognising children as capable and competent experts in their own lives;
- The importance placed on the responsiveness to the voice of the child;
- The rights to child to express their point of view; and
- The agency of the child in the research process, and the world in which they invested and embedded in.

This Mosaic approach goes beyond just the reliance or focus on the written word, to research strategies that afford for making the perspectives of others more visible (Clark & Moss, 2011; Rinaldi, 2006). Further, adaption and consideration of this approach, from a range of disciplines and special interest groups, have led to challenging the boundaries and possibilities of the Mosaic approach. This has included the continued development and rethinking of methods and strategies that might reposition the role and level of involvement of young children, but also families and practitioners in the research process (Baird, 2013).

Moving from 'Knowledge Extraction' to Meaning-Making and Knowledge Creation

An important underlying principle of the Mosaic approach is a shift in thinking about the process of data collection in research to one which focusses on meaning-making and 'knowledge creation, construction, or generation' (Clark, 2011). Facilitating the process of knowledge production, as an integral part of the inquiry process, is a shift towards more participatory research methods. This process embraces social cultural notions of participation, where participants are viewed as being an integral part of the research process, including involvement in data gathering, and as collaborators and reflectors on data for meaning-making (Clark & Moss, 2005).

By gathering layers of meaning, referred to as 'documentation' (which is part of the first stage of the Mosaic approach), co-researchers are better able to engage in what Rinaldi (2005) refers to as 'internal listening'. These strategies help create a context which supports those engaged in the research process, which includes children and adults, to reflect on and explore understandings of their lived experiences, as a way of co-constructing meaning, and for gaining more explicit knowledge and perspectives of others. Clark (2011) continues, by pointing out that "these forms of expression were chosen to be closely aligned to how young children might choose to communicate with friends and family" (p. 19).

The Creation of 'Mosaics'

The Mosaic approach comprises of multiple methods and inquiry strategies that work with the strengths and communication preferences of participants as co-researchers. The focus is on exploring strategies which may help reveal, or crystallise, the multi-dimensional and complex nature of the lived experiences of others (Clark, 2011; Richardson & Adams St. Pierre, 2008). The process of the Mosaic approach is now briefly unpacked, by sharing a case study by Clark (2001), from one of her earlier projects.

Clark (2001) outlines how the Mosaic approach was employed to gain the insights and perspectives of Gaby's nursery experiences, a three-year-old girl that she was working with in an early childhood service, near Kings Cross, London. Note, if any of this information sparks an interest to readers, or if readers are interested in exploring this approach more, they are invited to seek out a range of papers and writings on this topic (Baird, 2013; Clark, 2001; Clark & Moss, 2011; Stephenson, 2009).

The first stage of the Mosaic approach is the use of a range of data collection methods to gain insight into a young child's perspectives of the world in which they are connected to. In the Mosaic approach, observing is understood as a data-gathering strategy that calls on researchers to 'listen with all of our senses' (Rinaldi, 2006). For Clark (2001), the act of observation also utilised documentation, in a style referred to a 'nursery stories', or 'learning stories', as a strategy employed for focussing on the details.

Child conferencing was then employed as a research strategy, which took place between Clark, Gaby, and other children in the group. This process required talking to young children about their understandings of their environment and experiences, and entailed a process of formal and informal conversations and dialogue. Children were asked to share their insights on their friendship groups, the role they understood of the adult in the nursery, and concluded with an open-ended question which enabled young children to share their thoughts and perspectives on what 'they thought was important', in perhaps another form of communication such as drawing a picture. The process of 'checking in' and child conferencing was conducted twice over a four-month period.

Another strategy that Clark (2001) employed was photography. She provided instruction, and the provision of single use cameras, to help build up individual and collective mosaics. The intent behind this strategy was to afford children the opportunity to express themselves, and share their perspectives through another 'language of communication'.

Children were encouraged to photograph 'things that they saw as important to them'. This approach also helped children capture their worlds in images, as well helping to reveal and record these environments, 'what an individual sees of their world', for adults. In Clark's study (2001), children were also provided with a hard copy set of the photos they had taken, and encouraged to choose a selection of their photos to create into a book. (For more on this approach or the multiple or 'hundred languages of children' refer to writings from Edwards et al. [1998], and another reference by Fraser [2012], as well as Chap. 3 of this text.)

Gaby and other children in the study—in this instance Gaby's friends Merly and Kirsty—were also encouraged to take Clark on a guided walk of the different environments within their setting, and encouraged to record this walk, or 'tour', through photographs and a small tape-recording device, and notepad. The tour started where the children began their day at the service, with the girls guiding Clark through a number of rooms where they played and had friends or siblings. Dialogue occurred throughout the journey, where the girls explained what happened in each room, and introduced Clark to other children and their places, spaces, and interpretations of these events. Gaby was then encouraged to choose the images she felt were important in capturing this tour.

The 'mapping strategy' made up another piece of the mosaic, and afforded Clark (2001) a tangible opportunity to engage with children in the co-construction of meaning. The process, which included combining photographs taken by children along the journey, and the drawings of their route, has similarities to a 'child-friendly' version of environmental scanning, referred to earlier in this chapter. This process afforded an opportunity to listen, and to gather detailed information on the world of a child, from the perspectives and 'local knowledge', from those embedded in context (Clark, 2001). For the researcher, the privileged position of being in context, and participating in this guided tour, is another authentic opportunity for asking questions, observing, listening, and learning.

At this point, and at other steps along the way, Clark also sought out the perspectives of others, including Gaby's parents, using similar interview questions to those posed to Gaby. This was seen as a way of gaining further contextual insight of her life at the centre, and as a way of continuing to add to the mosaic. As such, throughout the process of research at the centre, Clark coordinated collaboration and discussion, referred to as 'meaning-making', between and with children, practitioners and researchers, children and researchers, and parents and researchers, as well as between parents and children. These collaborative discussions were also understood to provide opportunities to explore ideas, engage in lively exchanges, and share multiple interpretations and perspectives, with children's ideas being central in these exchanges (James & Prout, 2015).

Adapting the Mosaic Approach for Research with and of Young Families

It is worth pausing at this point to consider the innovative research strategies and perspectives associated with the Mosaic approach, and the relevance and application, and techniques have to researching with, and of, young families.

Time for Reflection

The questions below may help to facilitate this process of reflection:

- What aspects and perspectives of the Mosaic approach align with your positionality and perspectives on conducting research with young families?
- How might the belief in the capacity of 'the other' impact on the methods we choose to research with, or about, young families?
- Which tools or approaches outlined in the Mosaic approach might afford opportunities for family members to communicate in multiple forms to share their perspectives?

What becomes apparent in reviewing the ideas, strategies, and perspectives associated with the Mosaic approach are the mechanics employed in supporting listening. These strategies reflect the authentic valuing of the insights, capacity, and the perspectives of others (Clark, 2001; Clark & Moss, 2011). The high visibility of listening and communication embraced in the Mosaic approach to data collection and documentation is so valuable to apply and consider in researching with young families as well. These types of strategies help reinforce the genuine respect for the other, and the valuing of the insights that family members can provide of their experiences of the everyday.

The Mosaic approach reinforces the value and possibilities of adopting a multi-method approach to knowledge creation and meaning-making. This is particularly valuable in terms of employing a set of tools that would aid in family members expressing themselves, and capturing their thoughts, values, practices, and experiences. These 'pieces' of the mosaic, referred to as forms of documentation, also open up different types and opportunities for dialogue from all the social actors involved in an inquiry (Clark & Moss, 2011), enabling the rich and unique "mosaic patterns" to emerge (Stephenson, 2009, p. 136).

5.4   Capturing the Situated Stories of Young Families Through Interviews

Interviewing: Probing or Conversational Encounters?

Capturing the situated stories of young families, "recounting narratives of experience", and engaging collaboratively in the process of meaning-making require seeking out methods that enable researchers to gain a context-dependent understanding (Irvine, Drew, & Sainsbury, 2013, p. 8; Warr, 2004). Traditionally, interviews tended to be the default technique, or tool of choice, for achieving such a goal (Denzin & Lincoln, 2017). In the broadest and most simplistic terms interviews are encounters that usually involve actually sitting down, engaging in conversation, or "probes", on an identified topic (or "conversations with an agenda"), and listening to someone talk about their storied lives, on their "own turf" (Daly, 2007, p. 141; Patton, 2015).

Interviews, as a qualitative technique, have occupied a central position in historical and contemporary research methods (Kvale, 1996, 2006; Seidman, 2013). Interviews are also deployed as a valued method of choice, for collecting data with children and families. Interviews provide families with an opportunity to engage in storytelling, yarning, and to share what the world looks like through their eyes (Brown & Danaher, 2017; Daly, 2007; Gabb & Fink, 2015; Rizvi, 2017).

Approaches to interviewing are positioned between those that provide more, or less, structure. On one end of the interview continuum are more open-ended and unstructured interview styles (which include focus groups), where the research questions emerge, and flow more freely, and adopt a more conversational or friendly tone. This style of interview provides significant dialogical opportunity for participants to share insights about their lives, and their idiosyncratic biographical details, backgrounds, and stories (Harden et al., 2010; Harding, 2006).

Highly structured interview techniques are situated on the other side of the continuum where the interviewer has a rigid plan, which they are not prepared to deviate from. The more flexible the approach, the more participants are afforded the opportunity to help set the pace for the conversation, and for the direction of the interview to unfold and be guided by the stories and experiences being shared (Patton, 2015). In the broadest sense, semi-structured interviews are positioned somewhere in the middle range of the interview continuum, in terms of being not entirely naturalistic, or rigid. In these cases, the researcher usually brings to the interview context a set of questions, loosely based on general topics, yet prepared to deviate, discard, or modify these to seek out authentic details on individuals' interpretations and perspectives of their storied lives (Madill, 2011).

While in-depth, semi-structured, and unstructured interview techniques have been a popular style of inquiry between the researcher and research participant, interview techniques continue to evolve and be shaped by the changing paradigms and perspectives that exist. For example, critical feminist research and post-structuralist perspectives are pivotal in impacting both on the positionality of the researcher, methodological approaches, and the way in which participants are viewed, and their voices privileged, as part of an inquiry (Rizvi, 2017). Rizvi, in her study (2017), was critical of how the in-depth interview process may have led to unanticipated triggering, participants "re-living" an emotional trauma (p. 11). She questioned, ethically, the role that she may have played in causing participants to 'recall painful memories'. These types of considerations, and positions, are pushing the boundaries on traditional interview techniques in term both challenging, and motivating researchers to explore, reflect on, and adapt the techniques and approaches employed for interviewing (Gabb, 2010; Harden et al., 2010).

Interviewing: Techniques for Eliciting 'Lived Experiences' and 'Sense-Making'

Interviews and active listening techniques are recognised as important data collection strategies to employ for gaining a deeper level of under-standing, and insight into the embodied lived experiences, and storied lives of others (Rinaldi, 2005). For researching with, or about, young families, these techniques are effective in eliciting personal opinions, experiences, and beliefs, and gathering rich details of their 'sense-making' practices, taken-for-granted accounts, and the complexity of individual and group contexts (Berg, 2016; Denzin & Lincoln, 2017). By inter-viewing families, it is possible to explore the dynamic ways that family members make sense of their everyday lives, and to share their opinions on matters in which they have a vested interest (Harden et al., 2010). For example, researchers of, and about, families, such as Harden et al. (2010), explored and challenged existing interview strategies and techniques. They were motivated by the desire to ensure that notions of power and truth were considered, and reflected in their methodological approach. The researchers were cognisant to ensure that the interview techniques employed privileged the voices of all family members, including those of children, in order to gain the multiple perspectives of families.

Interviewing: Deceptively Simple, or Fraught with Complexity

To those unfamiliar, or the neophyte researcher, the act of engaging in interviewing for qualitative inquiry may, on the surface, appear to be deceptively simple. However, to those more experienced, it is appreciated that interview techniques, considerations, and approaches are complex and fraught with a range of ethical and practical dilemmas, and con-straints (Brown & Danaher, 2017). To be done successfully, and effec-tively, researchers require training and ongoing practice in this technique, as well as commitment to ongoing reflection.

As a research tool, approaches to, and styles of interviewing also vary greatly, and are dependent on a number of factors, which include a researcher's epistemology and the way in which they are positioned, such as being positioned as a 'neopositivist' or a 'romanticist', in terms of a researcher's perspectives on interviews (Brown & Danaher, 2017). There is also increasing flexibility of interviewing approaches that goes beyond face-to-face and telephone interviews, to now include e-interviewing and online techniques (Bryman, 2015; Iacono, Symonds, & Brown, 2016), However, regardless of the medium, like other data-gathering techniques, interviews require fundamental critiquing, with regard to the purpose and alignment to the intent, and outcomes of an inquiry.

There are also specific, and crucial, elements a researcher will be required to consider (Patton, 2015). These elements range from deciding how many participants to interview and how to recruit them, to structuring the interview questions to best address the focus of an inquiry, to knowing how to listen, how to prompt participants to talk, when to interrupt or steer a conversation or story. Considerations also include knowing when to probe further, and which strategies to employ to maximise "the authentic interactional encounters afforded by the interviews" (Berg, 2016; Brown & Danaher, 2017, p. 3) (see Chap. 6 for extensive details on this point). At this point, it is timely to note that there are a plethora of books, chapters, and papers to guide researchers regarding consideration, and the use of interview techniques. Readers are invited to pursue these if they wish to explore this topic further. However, several of these considerations, 'the importance of active listening', and the 'consideration of place', are worthy of particular mention as part of this chapter, in terms of affording the stories, perspectives, and lived experiences of young families.

Interpretivists do what they do well by their adeptness in asking a particular set of questions, and by creating dialogical opportunities for others to share their stories (Harden et al., 2010). This requires being skilled in the mechanics of listening, and the practice of active listening. For those focussed on the co-construction of meaning and research with young families, and affording them opportunities to engage in storytelling and to shared their lived experiences, these skills are particularly important (Dockett et al., 2009). Great consideration also needs to be given to 'child voice within family', and strategies that not only afford for voices, but that those voice be heard (Bessarab & Ng'andu, 2010).

The art of listening is an important technique, a skill that many would consider comes naturally and is inherent. However, in reality these skills require practice when employing this technique as a part of the data collection tool of interviewing (Alasuutari, 2013). The skill of active listening and interviewing requires an attunement and attentiveness to the other, and a strong desire to seek insight in what they have to say.

The art of listening requires the knowledge of when to extend, and how to extend on a narrative, as well as how to prompt a conversation to elicit more details (Daly, 2007; McCashen, 2005). An important aspect of successful interviewing is employing a range of interpersonal skills (Brown & Danaher, 2017; Macnamara, 2015). The act of listening also involves a heightened sense of awareness of the other, and goes beyond just the mechanics of listening, but requires a degree of 'authentic connectivity' and openness with the participant (Geia, Hayes, & Usher, 2013). (Note this topic is addressed in section 'Engaging in the Act of Attentiveness, Listening, and Hearing' of Chap. 3, and expanded upon further in Chap. 6 of this text.)

As the intent of an interpretivist is to illuminate the multiple realities and social worlds of others, the consideration of place and the situatedness of the interview process are critical. Positioning the interview process in a naturalistic setting, or sitting within the lived environment, offers a 'researcher in context' with an invaluable opportunity to observe families within their micro-environment, or another context of relevance, in order to uncover behaviours, and to develop a context-dependent understanding of a phenomenon (Berg, 2016; Denzin & Lincoln, 2017). This is based on the understanding that meaning-making and the co-construction of meaning are inextricably connected to the contexts, and social systems in which individuals are located and embedded (Daly, 2007; Merriam & Tisdall, 2016).

Although often busy, and even chaotic, situating interviews within natural settings offers the researcher an opportunity to be in a context that will better afford insight into another's reality, and how individuals make sense of, and experience, their surroundings, and enable meaning-making to be exposed (Berg, 2016). These settings may include domestic spaces such as the family kitchen, backyard, over a family dinner or meal, or in a local park where young families play together, or other sites such as those linked to education, care, culture, or health. Each of these contexts, and ecological niches, are understood as environments where individuals are influenced by the interplay of multiple systems and environments.

Situating interviews on 'the turf' of young families offers a relaxed setting for parents' meaning-making to take place (Warr, 2004). If intending to conduct interviews within the domestic space of the family home, researchers may wish to consider whether it is worth setting up permeable boundaries "between the interview and the rest of household happenings" (Chavez, 2008, p. 484). Although often busy and even chaotic at times, considering a more naturalised approach offers 'researchers in context' the opportunity to observe environments, uncover behaviours, and develop a context-dependent understanding of the domestic settings. An example from my doctoral research of these interview events is now shared (Brown, 2012):

> *Observing the unfolding 'household happenings' often occurred while I was present with families during meal times, where almost invariably, as I sat and conversed with the parents around a table or in the kitchen, family members would talk to one another, and move off task or into 'routines of parenting'. In these cases, it was important to just 'go with the flow' and observe the natural unfolding of domestic events. This approach provided insight into the reality of family routines, the spaces where children played, the busyness of a young family, and the benefit of collecting authentic data.*

5.5   Anticipating the Challenges

The research methods and tools unpacked in this chapter have been chosen for the value and effectiveness they offer for researching with, or about, young families, and gathering layers of meaning in context. However, it is important to note that like any other tools that one chooses to use or adopt, each tool is not without its anticipated challenges. One of the major challenges when conducting research with family members, either in the domestic space of the family home, or in another context relevant to families and the phenomenon being investigated, is establishing and building trust, rapport, and being 'invited in' (see Chap. 6 for further details on this topic). The other anticipated challenge is the significant time required for employing a number of these research methods.

If the aim of our research is to gather layers of meaning of a particular context, and insight from the individuals that reside within this space, then it is important that no matter which research methods and data collection tools we employ, we establish an environment in which young families feel comfortable in sharing their stories, and opening up their private spaces to support our investigation. Integral to achieving optimum dialogic opportunities with young families, which are both ethical and respectful, is the building of rapport and trust. This approach requires researchers to rethink their methodological techniques and theoretical orientations to ensure authenticity, relevance, and rigour (Brown & Danaher, 2017; Palaiologou, 2014).

At this point, there is limited literature available that explores or addresses such practices and considerations, particularly regarding considerations for establishing rapport and trust, maintaining heightened interpersonal relationships, and maximising ethical, dialogical, and meaningful research encounters with young families. As such, the next chapter of this text is dedicated specifically to this topic. This will include unpacking the CHE principles (connectivity, humanness, and empathy) as a rigorous framework for guiding researchers in their decision-making for facilitating and sustaining positive and authentic relationships with young families.

5.6 Conclusion

The dynamic and complex lives of contemporary young families require a particular set of tools and associated skills for engaging in inquiry. This calls on researchers to reimagine and rethink the strategies employed, in order to best afford family members opportunities to communicate in ways their perspectives and voices are not only privileged, but also heard. Whether on their own, or in combination, it is important that the tools researchers choose to employ for inquiry effectively enable the co-

construction of meaning-making with family members. The idiosyncratic nature of the families we research with and about will mean that the methods and tools we choose will also not be just a matter of 'one size fits all', or adopting a cookie cutter approach (Baird, 2013).

Of course, one might question the necessity for using specific research tools, or developing a specific set of research methods, for engaging in inquiry with, and about, young families. However, perhaps it is not the need to develop 'new methods', but more importantly to look at the methods that currently exist, and consider how these tools and strategies may potentially be used differently. This calls on researchers to think critically about the children and adults that may engage in co-researching with us, and the methods and tools that can best support these goals. This chapter has attempted to present just some of the methods and tools available that may serve this purpose, with the intent being not to privilege one approach over another, but to showcase the types of tools that are out there. In doing so, the intent is that the reader may be prompted to further explore the possibilities of employing such tools, in terms of their effectiveness for helping to reveal the world of others, and the possibilities of learning from and with families, in ways which are ethical and respectful.

References

Alasuutari, M. (2013). Voicing the child? A case study in Finnish early childhood education. *Childhood, 21*(2), 1–8.

Baird, K. (2013). Exploring a methodology with young children: Reflections on using the Mosaic and Ecocultural approaches. *Australasian Journal of Early Childhood, 38*(1), 35–40.

Berg, B. (2016). *Qualitative research methods for the social sciences* (9th ed.). Boston: Pearson.

Bessarab, D., & Ng'andu, B. (2010). Yarning about yarning as a legitimate method in indigenous research. *Journal of Critical Indigenous Studies, 3*(1), 37–50.

Bjørgen, K. (2016). Physical activity in light of affordances in outdoor environments: Qualitative observation studies of 3–5 years olds in kindergarten. *SpringerPlus, 5*(1), 950.

Bratich, J. (2017). Observation in a surveilled world. In N. Denzin & N. Lincoln (Eds.), *The Sage handbook of qualitative research*. Thousand Oaks, CA: Sage.

Bridger, L. (2013). Seeing and telling households: A case for photo elicitation and graphic elicitation in qualitative research. *Graduate Journal of Social Science, 10*(2), 106–131.

Brown, A. (2012). *The new frontier: A social ecological exploration of factors impacting on parental support for the active play of young children within the micro-environment of the family home.* PhD, University of Southern Queensland, Toowoomba, QLD.

Brown, A., & Danaher, P. A. (2017). CHE principles: Facilitating authentic and dialogical semi-structured interviews in educational research. *International Journal of Research & Method in Education*, 1–15. https://doi.org/10.1080/1 743727X.2017.13799.

Brown, J., Collins, A., & Duguid, P. (1989). Situated cognition and the culture of learning. *Educational Researcher, 18*(1), 32–42.

Bryman, A. (2015). *Social research methods.* Oxford: Oxford University Press.

Caçola, P. M., Gabbard, C., Montebelo, M., & Santos, D. C. (2015). Further development and validation of the affordances in the home environment for motor development–Infant Scale (AHEMD-IS). *Physical Therapy, 9*(5), 1–23.

Chavez, C. (2008). Conceptualizing from the inside: Advantages, complications, and demands on insider positionality. *The Qualitative Report, 13*(3), 474–494.

Christensen, P., & James, A. (2008a). Introduction: Researching children and childhood cultures of communication. In P. Christensen & A. James (Eds.), *Research with children: Perspectives and practices* (pp. 1–9). London: Routledge Flamer.

Christensen, P., & James, A. (2008b). *Research with children: Perspectives and practices.* New York: Routledge.

Clark, A. (2001). How to listen to very young children: The Mosaic approach. *Child Care in Practice, 7*(4), 333–341.

Clark, A. (2011). Breaking methodological boundaries? Exploring visual, participatory methods with adults and young children. *European Early Childhood Education Research Journal, 19*(3), 321–330.

Clark, A., Kjorholt, A. T., & Moss, P. (2005). *Beyond listening: Children's perspectives on early childhood services.* Briston: Policy Press.

Clark, A., & Moss, P. (2001). *Listening to young children: The Mosaic approach.* London: National Children's Bureau for the Joseph Rowntree Foundation.

Clark, A., & Moss, P. (2005). *Spaces to play: More listening to young children using the Mosaic approach*. London: Jessica Kingsley Publishers.

Clark, A., & Moss, P. (2011). *Listening to young children: The Mosaic approach* (2nd ed.). London: National Children's Bureau and Joseph Rowntree Foundation.

Clark, A., & Statham, J. (2005). Listening to young children: Experts in their own lives. *Adoption & Fostering, 29*(1), 45–56.

Cohen, L., Manion, L., & Morrison, K. (2007). *Research methods in education*. New York: Routledge.

Cosco, N., Moore, R., & Islam, M. (2010). Behavior mapping: A method for linking preschool physical activity and outdoor design. *Medicine & Science in Sports & Exercise, 42*(3), 513–519.

Daly, K. J. (2007). *Qualitative methods for family studies and human development*. Thousand Oaks, CA: Sage.

Denzin, N., & Lincoln, N. (2017). *The Sage handbook of qualitative research* (5th ed.). Thousand Oaks, CA: Sage.

Dockett, S., Perry, B., Kearney, E., Hamshire, A., Mason, J., & Schmied, V. (2009). Researching with families: Ethical issues and situations. *Contemporary Issues in Early Childhood, 10*(4), 353–365.

Edwards, C., Gandini, L., & Forman, G. (1998). *The hundred languages of children: The Reggio Emilia approach advanced reflections* (2nd ed.). Norwood, NJ: Ablex Publishing.

Egger, G., Pearson, S., Pal, S., & Swinburn, B. (2007). Dissecting obesogenic behaviours: The development and application of a test battery for targeting prescription for weight loss. *Obesity Reviews, 8*(6), 481–486.

Falcini, U. (2014). 'Affordance theory' – A valuable research tool in evaluating children's out-door play environments. *An Leanbh Óg, 8*, 105–121.

Finlay, L. (2003). The reflexive journey: Mapping multiple routes. In L. Finlay & B. Gough (Eds.), *Reflexivity: A practical guide for researchers in health and social sciences* (pp. 3–20). Oxford: Blackwell Science.

Fleer, M., & Ridgway, A. (2013). *Visual methodologies and digital tools for researching with young children: Transforming visuality* (Vol. 10). Cham: Springer Science & Business Media.

Flyvbjerg, B. (2001). *Making social science matter*. Cambridge, UK: Cambridge University Press.

Fraser, H. (2004). Doing narrative research analysing personal stories line by line. *Qualitative Social Work, 3*(2), 179–201.

Fraser, S. (2012). *Authentic childhood: Experiencing Reggio Emilia in the classroom* (3rd ed.). Toronto, ON: Nelson Education.

Gabb, J. (2009). Researching family relationships: A qualitative mixed methods approach. *Methodological Innovations Online, 4*(2), 37–52.

Gabb, J. (2010). Home truths: Ethical issues in family research. *Qualitative Research, 10*(4), 461–478.

Gabb, J., & Fink, J. (2015). Telling moments and everyday experience: Multiple methods research on couple relationships and personal lives. *Sociology, 49*(5), 970–987.

Gabb, J., & Singh, R. (2015). The uses of emotion maps in research and clinical practice with families and couples: Methodological innovation and critical inquiry. *Family Process, 54*(1), 185–197.

Gabbard, C., Caçola, P., & Rodrigues, L. P. (2008). A new inventory for assessing affordances in the home environment for motor development (AHEMD-SR). *Early Childhood Education Journal, 36*(1), 5–9.

Geia, L. K., Hayes, B., & Usher, K. (2013). Yarning/Aboriginal storytelling: Towards an understanding of an Indigenous perspective and its implications for research practice. *Contemporary Nurse, 46*(1), 13–17.

Gibson, J. J. (1977). The theory of affordances. In R. Shaw & J. Bransford (Eds.), *Perceiving, acting, and knowing, toward an ecological psychology*. Hillsdale, NJ: Lawrence Erlbaum Associates.

Gibson, J. J. (1979). *The ecological approach to visual perception*. London: Lawrence Erlbaum Associates.

Given, L., Cantrell Winkler, D., Willson, R., Davidson, C., Danby, S., & Thorpe, K. (2016). Parents as coresearchers at home: Using an observational method to document young children's use of technology. *International Journal of Qualitative Methods, 15*(1), 1609406915621403.

González, N., Moll, L. C., & Amanti, C. (Eds.). (2005). *Funds of knowledge: Theorizing practices in households, communities, and classrooms*. New York: Routledge.

Greenstein, T. N., & Davis, S. N. (2013). *Methods of family research* (3rd ed.). Thousand Oaks, CA/Los Angeles: Sage.

Guillemin, M., & Gillam, L. (2004). Ethics, reflexivity, and "Ethically important moments" in research. *Qualitative Inquiry, 10*(2), 261–280.

Hägglund, S. (2012). Forward. In J. Sarjeant & D. Harcourt (Eds.), *Doing ethical research with children*. Maidenhead: Open University Press.

Harcourt, D. S. (2008). *Constructing ideas and theories about quality: The accounts of young children in two early childhood classrooms in Singapore*. Brisbane: Queensland University of Technology.

Harden, J., Backett-Milburn, K., Hill, M., & MacLean, A. (2010). Oh, what a tangled web we weave: Experiences of doing 'multiple perspectives' research in families. *International Journal of Social Research Methodology, 13*(5), 441–452.

Harding, J. (2006). Questioning the subject in biographical interviewing. *Sociological Research Online, 11*(3), 1–10.

Heft, H. (2010). Affordances and the perception of landscape: An inquiry into environmental perception and aesthetics. In C. Thompson, P. Aspinall, & S. Bell (Eds.), *Innovative approaches to researching landscape and health. Open space: People space 2* (pp. 9–32). London: Routledge.

Iacono, V. L., Symonds, P., & Brown, D. H. (2016). Skype as a tool for qualitative research interviews. *Sociological Research Online, 21*(2), 12.

Irvine, A., Drew, P., & Sainsbury, R. (2013). 'Am I not answering your questions properly?': Clarification, adequacy and responsiveness in semi-structured telephone and face-to-face interviews. *Qualitative Research, 13*(1), 87–106.

James, A., & Prout, A. (2015). *Constructing and reconstructing childhood: Contemporary issues in the sociological study of childhood.* New York: Routledge.

Kvale, S. (1996). *Interviews: An introduction to qualitative research interviewing.* London: Sage.

Kvale, S. (2006). Dominance through interviews and dialogues. *Qualitative Inquiry, 12*(3), 480–500.

Kyttä, M. (2004). The extent of children's independent mobility and the number of actualized affordances as criteria for child-friendly environments. *Journal of Environmental Psychology, 24*(2), 179–198.

Leung, D., & Lapum, J. (2005). A poetical journey: The evolution of a research questions. *International Journal of Qualitative Methods, 4*(3), 1–17.

Lincoln, Y., & Guba, E. (1988, April 5–9). *Criteria for assessing naturalistic inquiries as reports.* Paper presented at the American Educational Research Association, New Orleans, LA.

Little, H., & Sweller, N. (2015). Affordances for risk-taking and physical activity in Australian early childhood education settings. *Early Childhood Education Journal, 43*(4), 337–345.

Lynch, H. (2011). *Infant places, spaces and objects: Exploring the physical in learning environments for infants under two.* PhD, Dublin Institute of Technology.

Macnamara, J. (2015). *Creating an 'architecture of listening' in organizations: The basis of engagement, trust, healthy democracy, social equity, and business sustainability.* Retrieved from Sydney, NSW. https://www.uts.edu.au/sites/default/files/fass-organizational-listening-report.pdf

Madill, A. (2011). Interaction in the semi-structured interview: A comparative analysis of the use of and response to indirect complaints. *Qualitative Research in Psychology, 8*(4), 333–353. https://doi.org/10.1080/14780880903521633.

Markwell, K. (2000). Photo-documentation and analyses as research strategies in human geography. *Geographical Research, 38*(1), 91–98.

McCashen, W. (2005). *The strengths approach.* Bendigo, VIC: St. Luke's Innovative Resources.

Merewether, J., & Fleet, A. (2014). Seeking children's perspectives: A respectful layered research approach. *Early Child Development and Care, 184*(6), 897–914.

Merriam, S., & Tisdall, E. (2016). *Qualitative research: A guide to design and implementation* (4th ed.). San Francisco: Jossey-Bass.

Mori, S., Nakamoto, H., Mizuochi, H., Ikudome, S., & Gabbard, C. (2013). Influence of affordances in the home environment on motor development of young children in Japan. *Child Development Research,* 898406, 1–5. https://doi.org/10.1155/2013/898406.

Palaiologou, I. (2014). 'Do we hear what children want to say?' Ethical praxis when choosing research tools with children under five. *Early Child Development and Care, 184*(5), 689–705.

Patton, M. Q. (2015). *Qualitative research and evaluation methods* (4th ed.). Thousand Oaks, CA: Sage.

Richardson, L., & Adams St. Pierre, E. (2008). Writing: A method of inquiry. In N. Denzin & N. Lincoln (Eds.), *Collecting and interpreting qualitative data materials* (3rd ed., pp. 473–500). Thousand Oaks, CA: Sage.

Rinaldi, C. (2005). Documentation and assessment: What is the relationship? In A. Clark, A. T. Kjorholt, & P. Moss (Eds.), *Beyond listening: Children's perspectives on early childhood services* (pp. 17–28). Bristol: Policy Press.

Rinaldi, C. (2006). *In dialogue with Reggio Emilia: Listening, researching, and learning.* London: Routledge Falmer.

Rizvi, S. (2017). Treading on eggshells: 'Doing' feminism in educational research. *International Journal of Research & Method in Education,* 1–13.

Rose, G. (2016). *Visual methodologies: An introduction to researching with visual methods* (4th ed.). Thousand Oaks, CA: Sage Publications.

Seidman, I. (2013). *Interviewing as qualitative research: A guide for researchers in education and the social sciences* (4th ed.). New York: Teachers College Press.

Stake, R. (2005). Qualitative case studies. In N. Denzin & Y. Lincoln (Eds.), *The Sage handbook of qualitative research* (3rd ed., pp. 433–466). Thousand Oaks, CA: Sage.

Stake, R. (2010). *Qualitative research: Studying how things work.* New York: Guilford Press.

Stark, S., & Torrance, H. (2005). Case study. In B. Somekh & C. Lewin (Eds.), *Research methods in the social sciences* (pp. 33–40). London: Sage.

Stephenson, A. (2009). Horses in the sandpit: Photography, prolonged involvement and 'stepping back' as strategies for listening to children's voices. *Early Child Development and Care, 179*(2), 131–141.

Swinburn, B., Egger, G., & Raza, F. (1999). Dissecting obesogenic environments: The development and application of a framework for identifying and prioritizing environmental interventions for obesity. *Preventative Medicine, 29*(6), 563–570.

Torin, M., & Fisher, J. (2010). Benefits of 'observer effects': Lessons from the field. *Qualitative Research, 10*(3), 357–376.

Tudge, J. (2008). *The everyday lives of young children: Culture, class, and child rearing in diverse societies*. Cambridge, UK: Cambridge University Press.

Warr, D. (2004). Stories in the flesh and voices in the head: Reflections on the context and impact of research with disadvantaged populations. *Qualitative Health Research, 14*(4), 578–587.

Waters, J. (2017). Affordance theory in outdoor play. In T. Waller, E. Ärlemalm-Hagsér, E. Sandseter, L. Hammond, K. Lekies, & S. Wyver (Eds.), *The Sage handbook of outdoor pay and learning* (pp. 40–54). Thousand Oaks, CA: Sage.

6

Considering CHE (Connectivity, Humanness, and Empathy)—Principles for Sustaining Respectful, Authentic, and Dialogical Research with Young Families

Scenario 6: Being Invited in…

Alice, a doctoral student, about to embark on the data collection phase of her research project, sits in her home office, in a regional town west of Brisbane, Queensland, reflecting on the task at hand. She feels very privileged that she has found three young families that have generously offered to partake in her project—each, in their own way, expressing genuine enthusiasm about learning more about the topic of 'Active play for young children', and sharing their insights. Yet, while she has developed a set of loosely structured interview questions, and prompts to enable lines of conversation to hopefully emerge, as well as a set of tools for scanning the environment to collect data to inform the phenomenon being investigated, she feels apprehensive about having the appropriate knowledge and skills required for building rapport and trust with participants in ways that will maximise the potential for these dialogical opportunities.

She appreciates the situated nature of these meetings with young families, and can picture how her introduction, and the process might unfold, and she is determined to enter the research space humbly and respectfully. In the back of her mind, she is also clear that she wants to ensure that her actions and words are authentic, and reflect the deep regard that she has for the strengths

© The Author(s) 2019
A. Brown, *Respectful Research With and About Young Families*, Palgrave Studies in Education Research Methods, https://doi.org/10.1007/978-3-030-02716-2_6

and capacity of family members, and the important role that parents have in raising strong and resilient children. It is also important to her that her actions and words clearly convey that she very much values their time, their capacity, and their lived experiences (Warr, 2004).

However, at this point, she feels ill-equipped for how best to engage in respectful and meaningful relationships with others. This includes concerns related to entering the private lives of these three young families, and the apprehension that they may feel about opening their homes and lives up to the scrutiny that they perceive may occur, such as being judged on their parenting or the tidiness of their house. And, while this is definitely not her intention, Alice wonders how she might set participants at ease, and establish trust and rapport early in the inquiry process, to help to alleviate any concerns participants may have.

She is also unsure to what extent her intentions, and her planned approach to building trust and rapport, might have on broader ethical implications (Galletta, 2013). *For example, she wonders how she might respond if she is offered a cup of tea, or perhaps even a glass of wine during the process of engaging in the inquiry process with families. And, while she appreciates that these offerings and practices might help to relax participants and herself, she is unsure of what her response and actions might mean to the researcher-/research-participant relationship. She is also not sure at this point how her actions, and the ways in which her research is positioned, might potentially shift the power differential, so that all members of young families may feel less threatened, or positioned on a more equal playing field, and comfortable in engaging in collaborative meaning-making.*

Note: This chapter is based on Brown and Danaher (2017).

Chapter Synopsis

This book is framed within a methodological approach to research with young families that is respectful, ethical, and dialogical. Chapter 3 focussed attention on 'storying', and valuing the voice of the other, in order to gain insights into the life events, behaviours, perspectives, and practices of individuals within families. This approach potentially requires researchers to reframe their methodological techniques, and theoretical orientations, in order to ensure authenticity, relevance, and rigour (Palaiologou, 2014), and to best afford for these narratives to be privileged and illuminated (Mannion, 2007). Adopting such an approach also calls on researchers to draw on the mechanics of listening, and engage in dia-logical relations (also raised in earlier chapters), both identified as essential components for engaging in the process of the ethical co-construction of research with family members, and of establishing and maintaining trust, and effective rapport-building (Brown & Danaher, 2017).

What strategies can be employed to shorten the distance between partici-pants and the researcher?

What strategies can be adopted to help to set participants at ease or to help overcome feelings of apprehension, vulnerability, cautiousness, and anxiety, throughout the inquiry process?

How far should we go in terms of blurring the boundaries between our role as a researcher and other roles such as the sharer of information, a confidant, or a friend?

How can we authentically embed practices of reciprocity throughout the research process, including the mutual sharing of information?

Particularly germane to the themes addressed in this chapter are con-siderations regarding going beyond just acknowledging the importance of building rapport, trust, and the relational dimensions of our work and research with young families. This chapter explores an explicit set of strat-egies and tools that are effective in maximising ethical, dialogical, and meaningful research encounters, to achieve mutually beneficial outcomes (Bettez, 2015; Stewart, 2016). While to the novice researcher these con-siderations may seem straightforward, until now qualitative researchers in many respects have been left to their own devices when planning for the relational dimensions of their research. These practices often require researchers to employ a great deal of ingenuity, plus a good deal of emo-tional intelligence and interpersonal skills (Brown & Danaher, 2017; Gill, Stewart, Treasure, & Chadwick, 2008). This is particularly the case in relation to decision-making, pertaining to key elements of rapport-building, and affording for dialogical opportunities with members of young families, including those who may have been marginalised, disen-franchised, or positioned through a pathologised lens (Bermúdez, Muruthi, & Jordan, 2016; Harding, 2006).

This chapter examines a range of these themes and considerations, as well as introducing readers to the CHE principles of Connectivity, Humanness, and Empathy. These principles are robust and rigorous, and guide researchers in analysing and evaluating the effectiveness of their decision-making, and in facilitating and sustaining humanising spaces and authentic relationships with family members (Paris & Winn, 2014). The intent is that these methodological strategies might offer researchers a reflective device to deploy when planning, and evaluating the relational intentions, and outcomes of specific research projects. While not proposed to be a panacea, or the answer, to resolving all relational issues of inquiry, the principles and strategies shared in this chapter potentially provide researchers with a range of tools that are worthy of consideration in their efforts when planning to engage in authentic, respectful, and dialogical relationships with young families.

6.1   Exploring the Relational Dimensions of Research with Young Families

Research That Is Relational, Dialogical, and Humanising

In our quest to engage in meaning-making with others, which often times extends beyond the traditional researcher-participant relationship, interpretivists are often challenged to consider how best to put in place strategies to support a dialogical and relational process (Freire, 1993; Paris & Winn, 2014). This means being conscious of the necessity of adopting a methodological stance framed by a system of relationships that are mutually humanising (understood as "relationships of care and dignity") (Paris, 2011, p. xvi). These actions and considerations will, of course, draw upon and from a particular mindset or stance, and require a degree of "dialogic consciousness raising", and sensitivity to the ways in which we view, enter, and engage with others, in these research spaces and places (Paris & Winn, 2014, p. xvi). Adopting a humanising approach to the relational dimensions of researching with young families may also cause researchers to rethink their methodological stance and associated strategies, in order to ensure that inquiry is ethical, dialogical, respectful, relational, and mutually beneficial (Bettez, 2015; Stewart, 2016).

Humanising research, that is dialogical, ethical, and involves engaging in the storying and co-construction of meaning with participants, can take place in a variety of ways as part of the inquiry process. These dialogical practices may include traditional communication approaches such as face-to-face and telephone, or by employing contemporary approaches such as via electronic mail, or using online platforms and technologies like Skype. Communication and dialogical processes can also draw upon various forms of documentation, such as those referred to in reference to the Mosaic approach outlined in detail in Chap. 5.

Humanising research, which includes relational processes such as these, usually adopts methodological strategies such as in-depth, structured, and semi-structured interviews, or other methodological approaches, such as ethnography, to gain a detailed insight into a phenomenon (Iacono, Symonds, & Brown, 2016). Further, researchers that employ practices such as these aim to maximise trust and rapport with participants, and value dialogical inquiry for the richness of this data (Brown & Danaher, 2017; Paris, 2011). This is particularly the case when there is a genuine desire for honesty, dignity, and transparency to be evidenced in sharing understandings, rather than approaching inquiry like a "somewhat detached, neutral researcher that echoes across the decades from more positivist-influenced versions of qualitative inquiry" (Paris, 2011, p. 139).

Researchers who choose to work within this paradigm understand that their research may take place in communities, and with people, who have experienced a history of being minoritised, marginalised, oppressed, or whose voices have been traditionally silenced (Bergold & Thomas, 2012; Geia, Hayes, & Usher, 2013; Thomas, 2014). As such, those who choose to work within such communities, or who engage in inquiry with others from such a position, embrace practices that reflect relational constructs of dignity, care, and reciprocity, as a means for dialogically framing and engaging in inquiry with individuals and community. Such a frame can be understood as "humanizing research", rather than "colonising inquiry" (Paris, 2011, p. 137 & p. 147; Paris & Winn, 2014). Consequently, in the act of researching, and through our efforts to "understand fully", researchers may need to challenge, or perhaps push against, existing approaches and systems when engaging with others in the research space, in order to reframe the research relationship (Paris, 2011, p. 137).

Paramount in our work in researching with and about young families is fostering trusting relationships. These focussed efforts attempt to make family members feel comfortable in sharing information with us about their everyday practices, and their private and storied lives (note that the concept of 'storying' is addressed in Chap. 3 of this text) (Brown, 2012; Dockett et al., 2009; González, Moll, & Amanti, 2006). However, in the contemporary world in which we live, where families are embedded in a culture of higher scrutiny and increased surveillance, researchers need to be cognisant of how families may be framed or positioned by others, as well as how they might frame or position themselves (see Chap. 2 for further details on positioning and framing). This calls for a certain level of sensitivity in entering these research contexts, and relationships with others, in terms of an awareness of the feelings that families may be experiencing, such as uncertainty, anxiety, or vulnerability (Bratich, 2017; Gabb, 2009).

Whilst we may agree in principle that building rapport and trusting relationships are an important part of the inquiry process, effectively achieving this goal may often prove more challenging than initially anticipated. This is particularly the case where we plan to enter the situated spaces, and private and relational lives of others, or plan to engage in inquiry that may potentially be emotive or sensitive (Fleer & Ridgway, 2013; Gabb, 2010). As such, it may be necessary to adopt an approach, or work within a paradigm that sets a particular tone, in our efforts to afford for safe research spaces, and help participants to feel at ease. Further, working within this type of frame may in fact challenge researchers to go beyond creating safe spaces for inquiry to create "brave spaces" that cultivate and consider issues of social justice, power, privilege, and oppression (Arao & Clemens, 2013, p. 135; hooks, 1994). By being positioned in this way, and engaging in brave conversations, our dialogical relationships become respectful and humanising.

A Rationale for Relationship-Building and Dialogical Inquiry

One recurring theme that continues to emerge in the extensive literature focussed on qualitative research with, or about, others, and that is particularly germane to this chapter, is the centrality and the complexity of establishing and maintaining ethical, respectful, and meaningful relationships (Dockett et al., 2009; Gabb, 2010; Thomas, Tiplady, & Wall, 2014). For instance, in relation to ethical considerations for research, Hammersley (2015) notes that, while there may be debate as to how well-being is defined or interpreted, "respecting people and taking account of their well-being" (p. 436) should define our research. Moreover, Fleer (2013) points out that a critical aspect of our research with families is the active role of "building good relationships", and earning the trust of participants (p. 38). Finally, in a book dedicated to the topic of *Rethinking children and research*, Kellett (2010) dedicates a whole chapter to 'research relationships'.

Critical Elements of Trust and Rapport

Building rapport involves an individual or group feeling comfortable in opening up to, engaging in, communicating, or socialising with another (King & Horrocks, 2010). The crucial elements or strategies of rapport-building have been posited in the relational dimensions of dialogical relationships for nearly a century. This aspect of the inquiry process has been described historically by the likes of Palmer (1928) and Douglas (1985), and more recently by Silverman (2013), who identified specific stages of rapport-building. There is also an emerging specialist field of related scholarship dedicated to more critical understandings of the characteristics and strategies of trust and rapport-building, and to both the limitations and the effects of efforts at rapport-building with research participants (Brown & Danaher, 2017).

For example, in a special themed issue of *Qualitative Inquiry*, Springwood and King (2001) identified rapport "as a methodological trope and relational strategy of the ethnographic habitus" that has nevertheless "too often … simply been ignored", and that elicits varied potential responses, including "the (im)possibility, desirability, ambiguity, and legitimacy of rapport" (p. 403). In another book, entitled *Ethics in qualitative research*, Duncombe and Jessop (2012) dedicated a chapter to relational aspects and authenticity when establishing rapport, or whether it was more just a matter of "faking friendship" (p. 108). In it, the authors state emphatically that "rapport is tantamount to trust, and trust is the foundation for acquiring the fullest, most accurate disclosure a respondent is able to make" (p. 110). They continue by pointing out that as researchers, when we set up strategies and an environment where rapport is created and established, the process opens up participants to being vulnerable.

Paramount at the onset of embarking on the process of the co-construction of meaning with young families, it will be important to prioritise the establishment of trust, and trusting relationships (Gabb, 2010; Yee & Andrews, 2006). This is particularly the case where we enter, or when inquiry potentially takes place in the domestic spaces of young families. In these cases, it is unrealistic to expect families to reveal to the outside world their practices, perspectives, values, and behaviours without feeling safe and trusting the researcher.

As such, it is important that trust-building is established early and upfront as part of the inquiry process, in order for families to feel comfortable in allowing researchers entry into their world (Anandalalakshmy, Chaudhary, & Sharma, 2008). Further, scholars like Bergold (2012) and Paris (2011, 2014) caution that this process needs to develop over time, cannot be rushed, and needs to be approached with honesty and integrity. Bergold (2012) adds that these practices need to be characterised by "closeness, empathy, and emotional involvement", and establishing a "safe space", with great care given to not placing participants in positions where they may be disadvantaged, where they may be re-traumatised, or experience further vulnerability (p. 202).

Being Left to One's Own Devices

Relationality, including building and maintaining trust and rapport with participants throughout the course of an inquiry, is not simply about "good manners" or "common sense" (Stake, 1995, p. 60). While there may

be a fruitful line of argumentation reinforcing the importance of participatory inquiry, and key considerations and assumptions posited about
the importance of relational elements, at this point one could argue that
researchers have been "left to their own devices" (Brown & Danaher,
2017, p. 3), or encouraged to draw upon their 'common sense', talents,
and abilities. Duncombe and Jessop (2012) point out that even those
armed with "a battery of skills in 'doing rapport' ... may find it difficult
to draw neat boundaries around 'rapport', 'friendship' and 'intimacy', in
order to avoid the depths of 'counselling' and 'therapy'" (p. 112). This is
particularly challenging for early career researchers, or others who may
grapple with strategies for authentically and respectfully heightening the
relational elements of the inquiry process (Paris & Winn, 2014).

For example, Brown and Danaher (2017), write about the seemingly
straightforward practice of designing and conducting semi-structured
interviews, but they point out that these practices might "actually entail
the application of highly developed emotional intelligence and require
that researchers have the interpersonal skills necessary for building rapport with research participants" (p. 3). This is particularly the case where
there is value placed on maximising dialogical opportunities with participants, participant voice, and the contribution of participants in the
research project. Yet, at the same time, there is limited guidance offered
as to how this might look, or realistically be approached in terms of
aspects of rapport-building (Warr, 2004).

There is also significant ubiquity, complexity, and diversity regarding
this area of research, with much remaining implicit with the expectation
of intuitiveness, rather than guidelines for explicit and deliberate strategies, considerations, or approaches. For early career researchers, or those
who admit that interpersonal skills may not necessarily be a strong point
in their research repertoire, researchers may experience feeling ill-prepared
or ill-equipped for what may be required of them in their efforts to
maximise dialogical opportunities with others. Furthermore, engaging in
research encounters and interpersonal interactions can be intense, and
requires researchers to draw on their emotional intelligence. The implications of feeling ill-equipped, or unprepared, may have ramifications to
the quality and trustworthiness of the data collected as part of an inquiry,

but may also have a direct or indirect impact on the well-being of the researcher, and the research participants (Gill et al., 2008).

It is against this backdrop of broader absences from, and debates in, qualitative research scholarship that the rest of this chapter is situated. This includes unpacking and providing key examples related to the CHE principles of Connectedness, Humanness, and Empathy (Brown & Danaher, 2012; Brown & Reushle, 2010; Reushle, 2005). These principles may potentially offer researchers of young families a rigorous conceptual framework to refer to when exploring and considering aspects of relationality in inquiry. The CHE principles also offer a useful reference point for reflecting and evaluating the relational intentions and outcomes of an inquiry.

6.2   Maximising Ethical, Dialogical, and Meaningful Research Encounters

Introducing the CHE Principles (Connectivity, Humanness, and Empathy)

Note: This section and earlier sections of this chapter are based on the work and paper by Brown and Danaher (2017).

Philosophically, the CHE principles are positioned within a relativist and post-humanist affective ontology (Mazzei, 2013; Roelvink & Zolkos, 2015). Positioned within this frame, the principles reflect the understanding that human interactions are integrally linked with relationships with multiple others. Epistemologically, the CHE principles align with social constructivist principles that see meaning-making as embedded and situated in social and cultural environments and as being fostered through dialogical relationships with others (Burr, 2015; Keaton & Bodie, 2011). Axiologically, the CHE principles are ethically positioned and framed by principles and strategies based on a perspective that celebrates strengths, and that values diversity, difference, and otherness (Thiele, 2014), but that are also attentive to notions of authenticity and reciprocity (Paris, 2011). In this chapter, reference to the terms 'authentic' and 'authenticity' are understood to be a response that reflects an ethic of care, dignity, and respect, and that embraces a genuine concern for the well-being of others (in this case, research participants) (Pitts & Miller-Day, 2007). This aligns with earlier works of scholars such as Manning (1997) "that eschewed methodological prescriptions, in favour of contextualized applications of philosophical principles such as authenticity" (Brown & Danaher, 2017, p. 2).

I initially came across the scholarly reference of the term 'CHE', through my work and collaboration with a very talented colleague, Associate Professor Shirley Reushle (2005). As part of her doctoral thesis, Reushle employed and made reference to 'CHE', as one of a number of design principles recommended in an educator's efforts to work productively with in-service teacher education students, in order to develop their capacities in online environments. However, the efforts to plan for the dialogical aspects of relationships and rapport-building as part of my own doctoral work (Brown, 2012) led me to the work of Reushle (2005), and inspired me to adopt and in turn adapt the CHE principles of Connectivity, Humanness, and Empathy.

These principles became a framework and a reference point for key considerations and prompts that were employed in my efforts to help to set participants at ease when initially entering the domestic space of the family home. I continued to refer to the CHE principles as a set of techniques and considerations when planning for and engaging in the interview process. These efforts helped to build rapport, and establish productive and empowering relationships between and among myself and family members as research participants (Pitts & Miller-Day, 2007).

Since then, I have collaborated with a number of colleagues to further explore the applications and possibilities of the CHE principles (Brown & Danaher, 2017; Brown & Reushle, 2010). For example, Danaher, in Brown (2012) collaborated with me, and interpreted, and applied the CHE principles retrospectively to his own doctoral project. His study involved engaging with a team of qualitative educational researchers, who examined the educational aspirations, and experiences of the primary or elementary school children and their families travelling with the occupationally mobile Showmen's Guild of Australasia. These families provided entertainment to Australia's agricultural shows with the rides and stalls that constitute sideshow alley.

What became clear in Danaher's and my work together was that, despite the clear differences between our distinctive research projects, our positionality, and the relational approaches that we adopted, were framed and positioned around the desire that we both had in affording participants with multiple opportunities to share their lived experiences and storied lives with us, and the meaning-making associated with their respective environments (Hancox, 2011). Both projects also employed semi-structured interviews as a data-gathering method, where it was necessary to seek out effective relational approaches, and to employ strategies for supporting rapport and trust-building. Further, both foregrounded trustworthiness, and principles of integrity, authenticity, engagement, the ethics of praxis, as an integral part of the inquiry process.

With respect to addressing the three CHE principles articulated in this chapter, the intent is not for these to be a panacea for all the anticipated issues and skills necessary for engaging in respectful, ethical, and relational research with young families. Rather, the intent is that these principles offer an ontological, epistemological, and axiological foundation, or reference point, or perhaps an effective inclusion in a qualitative researcher's armoury or toolkit. As such, the CHE principles are shared in this chapter, as a methodological stance, and a resource that might encourage reflection, consideration, or perhaps a sort of dialogic consciousness-raising. The CHE principles might also provide a guide in the process of data gathering and analysis with the overarching intent of enabling authentic and dialogical relationships with family members, built on dignity and care (Paris, 2011; Rizvi, 2017). The rest of the chapter is now broken into a combined literature review related to the CHE principles, followed by the distinctive application, considerations, and contextualisation of the CHE principles to illustrate the enactment of these principles for inquiry of, with, or about young families. This includes a focus on the broader implications of this analysis for sustaining rapport-building, and for enhancing authentic and dialogical researcher–research participant interactions and collaboration.

Using the CHE Principles (Connectivity, Humanness, and Empathy) to Guide Dialogic Inquiry

Throughout the life of a project, and in the process of planning for and engaging in inquiry with or about young families, we are faced with a complex set of challenges and ethical dilemmas that impact on dialogic inquiry. These issues require researchers to make decisions about a range of matters. These matters include consideration regarding who to involve in inquiry, methodological approaches and strategies to adopt, to considerations regarding issues of interactional constraints, and the interplay between power and agency during all stages of inquiry (Daly, 2007; Roulston, 2014; Vähäsantanen & Saarinen, 2013).

As researchers, how we choose to proceed in our decision-making will impact and have a flow-on effect, on the types of relationships that we have and establish with research participants. These will include their level of engagement with and input into the project, their level of agency, and issues of power (see Chap. 4 for a dedicated chapter on this topic). As such, critical in our efforts will be considering how best to afford opportunities for maximising ethical encounters and practices that reflect respectful and meaningful relationships with others (Hammersley, 2015; Palaiologou, 2014).

All qualitative research, to some degree, involves engaging with 'others' in relational inquiry spaces (Reason & Bradbury, 2008). However, our choices and approaches will be shaped by a range of elements, such as our underlying epistemological, ontological, and axiological positions (the way that we see the world); the type of inquiry and phenomenon being investigated, through to the research questions of the study; the contextual locatedness of the research; and the interpersonal skills of the researcher (such as levels of confidence when engaging with others as part of the process of collecting data) (Daly, 2007; Gabb, 2010; Von Unger, 2012). Setting up positive relational spaces will need to include skills related to the "ethical commitment" for "creating conditions for engagement", and the dialogical process (Palaiologou, 2014, p. 691), as well as other skills such as verbal and non-linguistic communication, 'the art of hearing data', skills of listening, and an adeptness in social perceptiveness (Cousin, 2009; Rubin & Rubin, 2012). The CHE principles of Connectivity, Humanness, and Empathy offer an effective 'check-in' point, for reflecting on how our actions can be authentically embedded in environments and strategies to support dialogical opportunities. These practices offer new possibilities in rendering approaches to interpretivist research being more dialogical.

The worth that readers of this chapter might ascribe to the CHE principles will be dependent on a range of elements, such as the importance placed on the valuing of participants' voices (and their perspectives), and the importance attached to establishing rapport and to building positive and reciprocal relationships between the researcher and the participant, as well as to other important aspects such as the degree of agency and positioning of participants in decision-making within an inquiry, and the confidence and comfort levels in enacting a range of interpersonal skills. At multiple touchpoints throughout the second half of this chapter, you will find reference to a series of reflective questions. The intent is that these questions will serve as prompts, for both emerging and seasoned researchers in guiding engagement with these principles, and assist them to move through an inquiry process that privileges the insights and perspectives of the other, whilst provoking thought for adopting strategies that are mutually humanising, and that maximise dialogue and rapport-building (Paris, 2011).

6.3   Connectivity

The first CHE principle of Connectivity relates to formative relationship matters, such as first impressions, gaining entry to the research space and participant context, seeking participant consent, and negotiating and setting clear expectations and ways of working. Early connections, which can be referred to as 'relationship orientation phase', involve critical matters of initial rapport-building. These include efforts to reduce the distance between the researcher and those participating in the research (Bishop, 2012; Johnson, 2009). This front-ending of the relational process requires a degree of consciousness-raising and sensitivity. This process also requires a willingness by the researcher to invest considerable thought and time in establishing and building relationships of trust, dignity, and care with others, what Paris (2014) and others such as San Pedro and Kinloch (2017) refer to as 'humanisation'.

Early relationships with others, particularly those who are 'inviting us in' to their world, or who are meeting us for the first time, necessitate a particular type of attentiveness to the other. Bishop (2012) refers to the work of Heshusius (1994) and makes the point of the importance of researchers developing a "participatory consciousness" for the other (p. 137). This involves shifting the focus of inquiry from self, to "the other" (p. 137). However, whilst these types of considerations are important, we need to approach these efforts with authenticity, and practice which echoes genuineness, integrity, and honesty, rather than being viewed as a means to an end, or what Duncombe and Jessop (2012) refer to as "faking friendship" (p. 107).

In a practical sense, first impressions matter, so the principle of Connectivity prompts us to consider how we might be initially perceived by participants, as well as how the other might potentially be framed (see Chap. 2 for detail of positionality and framing of 'the other'). This awareness might include being conscious of our own body language, as well as picking up on cues regarding participants' body language (such as body language that reflects openness and acceptance). In entering the private lives of others, we need to be conscious that we are also under scrutiny, no matter how open and friendly we might try to come across. Judgements will be made about the clothes we wear, what we say, and how we say it (our tone of voice) (Pitts & Miller-Day, 2007). Just as importantly, in entering the research space and the research relationship, researchers will need to be cognisant that participants may be apprehensive. They may have reservations in terms of feeling that their environments might be scrutinised or judged. Consequently, researchers should ideally anticipate these types of concerns, and be able to pick up on these cues, and if necessary help to clarify intentions and expectations early, in order to help to set participants at ease.

Given that qualitative research takes place in a system of relationships, which often takes place and is conducted in multiple contexts, researchers may wish to consider adopting a situated and systematic approach to establishing expectations and boundaries related to the inquiry process.

This approach helps to provide transparency around intentions, as well as the opportunity to nuance relational approaches to the associated audience (Dockett et al., 2009). Of course, much of this information shared upfront with participants is conveyed through the participant information sheet and in early conversations as part of the ethical process of informing and seeking participant consent. However, many aspects of an inquiry will still need to be discussed, negotiated, and explicitly communicated.

For example, there may be the need to negotiate with participants clarity around issues such as how they may wish to be referred to, and how they prefer referring to you (e.g. whether their first names will be used during the inquiry). Other aspects which may benefit from clarification could include discussing a safe place or environment where participants would feel most comfortable talking and sharing their story (Bergold & Thomas, 2012). Further, dependent upon the level of participant involvement and participant orientation in an inquiry, Connectivity may include negotiation on matters such as the degree to which they feel comfortable providing input into the inquiry process, and the types of data collection approaches in which they feel most comfortable (Ellis, 2007; Harden, Backett-Milburn, Hill, & MacLean, 2010).

An important aspect of the Connectivity principle is reflecting on how one might enter the research space humbly and sensitively. These efforts might include adopting the associated discourse that reflects these sentiments (Paris & Winn, 2014). For example, in our earliest communications with participants, researchers may wish to convey in an authentic way how privileged they feel about being invited into the private lives of family members, as a "worthy witness" (Paris, 2014, p. xiii). Researchers may also choose to share with participants the value that their insights, storied lives, perspectives, and experiences will have in informing the investigation (Wong & Cumming, 2008). Our early communication might also include conveying the sincere message of the genuine valuing of the opinions, and the skills and capacity that participants bring with them as experts about their own lives to the investigation (Dickson-Swift, James, Kippen, & Liamputtong, 2006; Fenton, Walsh, Wong, & Cumming, 2015; McNeil, 2010). Finally, it is also important that our actions and words convey and reinforce that participants will not be judged or viewed through a pathologised lens (Bermúdez et al., 2016; Uttal, 2009).

Thinking More About 'Connectivity'

• What strategies can be employed to shorten the distance between participants and the researcher?
• What strategies can be adopted to help to set participants or help to overcome feelings of apprehension, or experiences of vulnerability, cautiousness, and anxiety?
• How might the way I am dressed impact on how I am perceived by participants?
• Does the language used in the participant information sheet and consent form sufficiently convey the focus and expectations of the inquiry in a way that is accessible?
• How can I maximise credibility and trust with participants whom I have never met before?
• How can I read the verbal and non-verbal cues/signals of participants to understand how I am perceived, or how they might be feeling?

Connectivity—Contextualisation and Implications for Family Research

The formative stage of rapport- and trust-building with young families will, to a certain degree, be dependent on the level of familiarity family members have with the researcher(s). However, an important part of the orientation relational phase of our work with families will be employing strategies to help set participants at ease. Of course, levels of concern and vulnerability will vary from family to family, and context to context. Therefore, it is important to anticipate concerns that may be felt by families, and proactively address these upfront as part of our early conversations.

For example, in my doctoral project, the first family I made contact with voiced their concerns about being perceived as bad parents, or as not employing the best physical activity practices with their children within the home. Therefore, anticipating that the other families may have the same concerns, I informally broached this topic with other families, and reassured them of my intent, whilst also reinforcing the deep respect I had for them and their parenting, and how much I could learn about the research phenomenon from and with them.

Another important aspect of the Connectivity principle is setting up and negotiating clear expectations with young families, including their level of involvement in the inquiry. These conversations should include discussing how the youngest members of families might participate, and exploring ways in which children will feel most comfortable in communicating their perspectives, as well as ways in which their voices can be privileged. Being explicit about the intent of the inquiry requires greater consideration given to how best to convey this information and process to participants. This includes employing strategies that are accessible, and comprehended by all (including communication regarding the seeking of consent, and an overview and intent of the inquiry).

For example, this might mean that in early conversations with parents, the rationale and intent of the study are verbally shared, along with providing a hard copy of the information sheet. It is also worth using this communication as an opportunity to convey to parents the anticipated value and benefits they might gain from the study. These early conversations should also reinforce to participants that they are encouraged to ask questions, provide feedback, or seek clarification on anything they are unsure of, or wish to seek further information about.

Formatively, Connectivity efforts help to minimise social distance with young families and could include the use of informal banter, easy conversation, and ice-breakers. These conversations might also include the mutual sharing of how the day is going, and what each party has been up to, as well as a genuine interest in the children in the family being researched. Research that takes place within the domestic space of the family home is also conducive to supporting the principle of Connectivity, as it employs a strategy for helping to set family members at ease, as families are already on their own turf, and positioned within an environment where they usually feel more comfortable. However, researching within these environments, particularly in the formative relational stage, also provides researchers with an opportunity to reinforce that they are open and flexible in working around routines, unplanned dramas and schedules, and negotiating with families where they are most comfortable engaging in the inquiry with you. These types of negotiations positively tip the power differential in a family's favour, in terms of the inquiry being positioned in familiar territory (DiCicco-Bloom & Crabtree, 2006).

In our attempts to establish strong Connectivity with families, researchers may be faced with, and challenged by, some unique ethical considerations. For example, in our efforts to establish initial rapport we might be invited to join the family for a meal, a cup of tea, or a glass of wine, and whilst we might see the acceptance of this invitation as an important relational opportunity, others such as Duncombe and Jessop (2012) might caution against engaging in such a social context, referring to it as close to 'faking friendship', and questioning the intent and genuineness of our response. However, I would argue that if our intentions are sincere, and this type of invitation is accepted with integrity, that these social opportunities are critical. In fact, being invited to join family members for a meal or a drink might actually be a reflection of successful Connectivity efforts we have employed, and engaged in with participants.

6.4   Humanness

Founded on the value of reciprocity, or what Pitts and Miller-Day (2007, p. 180) liken to a "reciprocal symbiotic relationship", is the second CHE principle of Humanness. This principle is underpinned by reciprocity, in terms of both the mutual embracing of humane qualities such as dignity and care, that takes place from the onset of the inquiry and interactions between the researcher and participant, and reciprocity in terms of the value placed on the duality of information sharing, where both researcher and participant are recognised as the 'giver' and 'receiver' of information (Johnson, 2009; Paris, 2011; Trainor & Bouchard, 2013). Through the act of research itself, and through our actions in engaging with others, important qualities such as integrity and honesty are evidenced, and are an integral part of the principle of Humanness. This principle is underpinned by the genuine desire to build relationships which often go beyond building rapport and trust. These practices are understood to best be achieved through a genuine openness, self-disclosure, reciprocity, and the sharing of and about oneself (Paris, 2011).

Those wishing to embed the principle of Humanness into their armoury of tools for building trust and rapports with research participants may need to rethink their existing relationship-building strategies, and their role as researcher. These strategies are particularly important when considering ways to minimise, or remove the traditional distance between the researcher and the researched. For example, an integral aspect of adopting this principle is researchers sharing their 'humanness' (Irvine, Drew, & Sainsbury, 2013). This may mean adopting a more informal approach to relationships as part of engaging in inquiry with participants, and understandings of rationality, such as the decision to wear smart casual clothes. Strategies may also include efforts to speak in a more informal tone, the use of light banter, and the reciprocal sharing of personal stories and narratives where appropriate, as part of the inquiry process (Mack, Woodson, Macqueen, Guest, & Namey, 2005).

Another aspect of considering the inclusion of Humanness strategies as part of an inquiry is the mutual dialogical exchange which emerges through an approach that values the "co-construction of meaning, rather than as a monological extraction of information" (Brown & Danaher, 2017, p. 8; Paris & Winn, 2014). Critical to the effectiveness of these exchanges, and being a "worthy witness", are efforts to engage in active listening, "by which voice might be valued, attended to and recognised" (Dreher, 2012, p. 159), or to engage in being 'fully present' in the world of another (Paris & Winn, 2014). There is a dedicated section in Chap. 3 of this text titled, 'Engaging in the act of attentiveness, listening, and hearing', for those readers interested in revisiting the themes. However, the key message to reinforce at this point, is that authentic listening is the act of attentiveness, or attunement to others, which involves being fully present and listening with our whole body (Fedesco, 2015; Geia et al., 2013; Macnamara, 2015; Rinaldi, 2006).

Further, an important aspect of reflecting practices of Humanness is approaching inquiry with others from a position of humbleness. This type of approach reflects a genuine respect and openness to what 'the other' has to say and share. Adopting a position of being humble is also essential, as it reflects the sentiments of feeling privileged that participants are entrusting us with their stories and lived experiences (Paris, 2011). Daly (2007), in referring to the work of family therapists, talks about adopting a position of 'not knowing', where in the case of engaging in inquiry and respectful listening, the researcher admits that their keen interest is hearing about the context of participants, including their willingness to engage in the collaborative process of meaning-making.

However, whilst the mutual sharing of information, referred to as a 'symbiotic relationship' with participants, and the process of reciprocity, and letting down one's guard, may to a certain extent not fit with the traditional persona of a researcher, these are all important aspects of the Humanness principle (Brown & Danaher, 2017; Pitts & Miller-Day, 2007). Yet, to some researchers these aspects and approaches might prove challenging, particularly in relation to the process of self-disclosure and the sharing of self with others. Some researchers might also grapple with the extent to which these types of conversations might blur the boundaries between the role of researcher, and other roles such as confidant or friend (Dickson-Swift et al., 2006; Dockett et al., 2009; Higgs, Moore, & Aitken, 2006). In the end, researchers will embrace the principle of Humanness to varying degrees, dependent upon a number of factors, such as the parameters they set around issues of ethics, interpretations of professional distance, the role they see themselves and participants as having, the type of research being conducted, as well as other factors such as the research context, and the participants involved in the research.

Thinking More About Humanness

- How can I demonstrate humanness and a degree of informality without being seen as unprofessional?
- How can I integrate the separate and shared interests held by the participant(s) and myself?
- How can I avoid making promises or commitments as part of informal communication, particularly regarding how the project might benefit participants?
- How might the employment of Humanness strategies be effective in supporting research participants who may have experienced disadvantage, or marginalisation?

- How might I find a balance between the 'sharing of self' and my dominating a discussion with family members?
- How far should I go in terms of blurring the boundaries between my role as a researcher, and other roles such as the sharer of information, a confidant, or a friend?
- How might I consider the Humanness principle to help overcome emotions expressed by participants such as vulnerability, cautiousness, and apprehension?
- How can I embed Humanness strategies to more appropriately and equitably balance the power in the relationship between myself and the participants?
- What Humanness strategies can I employ to help convey to participants that they are not being judged, and that I am genuinely interested in their stories and the uniqueness of their contexts?

Humanness—Contextualisation and Implications to Family Research

For those who choose to research with, or about, young families, particularly within the context of the family home, there are lots of potential and opportunity for employing strategies to support Humanness. For example, there are opportunities to express a genuine interest in domestic spaces of family members, which might include complimenting parents on parenting practices; complimenting children on a skill or experience; or sharing a genuine interest in the perspectives of family members (Pitts & Miller-Day, 2007). Another way in which the component of the Humanness can be embedded into practice is conveying the message to family members that their insights are valued, and taking a genuine interest in their contexts, voices, and stories. This includes adopting an approach and body language that reflect an openness to their perspectives and opinions. This also includes conveying to participants the fact that we are not wanting to be viewed, or coming across as experts.

Paris and Winn's (2014) collection of work related to 'humanising research', and 'humanising spaces', which are 'dialogical', interconnect and compliment themes related to the Humanness principle outlined in this chapter, particularly considerations and strategies for engaging in authentic relationships with young families who are vulnerable, or from marginalised or minoritised communities. From an interpretivist perspective, approaching and considering idiosyncratic approaches to our relationships with young families helps us to be more responsive to the nuanced spaces and diverse context in which families are located. However, it also encourages us to adopt an authentic level of sensitivity to the vulnerability of the families that we engage with, and a humanising methodological stance, and all that entails (Paris, 2011).

An important aspect of integrating Humanness strategies as part of our communication and relationships with participants, and as part of any inquiry with young families, is the timely sharing of self, and creating an atmosphere of informality. Paris (2011) comments that "we must share of ourselves as we ask people to share of themselves. This is especially true when we are asking our participants to share things that are close to the heart, private, and sometimes painful" (p. 142). This is an effective strategy in our efforts to be mindful of the positioning of family members, and as a strategy to help overcome perceptions of parents feeling they are being judged, or levels of uncertainty or confidence levels in responding to questions being asked.

The 'sharing of self' during our communication with families is usually contextual, and often emerges and is dependent on the interests and topics of communication and conversation we have. For example, Yee and Andrews (2006) provide an example in their paper of a researcher sharing their knowledge of skateboarding, as part of an initial conversation that occurred with a family. This communication helped to establish initial rapport with a "previously uncommunicative 10-year-old boy" in the study (p. 407). In our research with young families, these 'sharing moments' might also afford opportunities for reflecting on our own parenting practices, or upbringing, to parallel an experience, or a point related to the narrative a participant has shared, or a perspective parents or children may have expressed.

Another approach to reciprocity with young families is the timely sharing of a resource, or knowledge we may have on a topic related to the inquiry, or associated with a point related to a conversation (Johnson, 2009). For example, Liamputtong (2007) comments on the importance of researchers being prepared to share or provide information, or to direct participants "to other relevant resources including reading materials or referrals to qualified professionals" (p. 62). Another example highlights the sharing of information, which occurred whilst I was conducting interviews as part of my doctoral studies. Patricia and Mark Calming (one of my participant couples) had been sharing their story of how they were trying to help their daughter Tiffany improve her physical development (which was quite delayed due to learning difficulties). Patricia talked about how she had already been doing some of her own research and reading about ways that particular exercises could help to improve the connections between the left and right brain. In the example to follow, my valuing of reciprocity influenced the dynamics of the interview process regarding the relationship that was formed between myself and parents, and the ease in which I was open to the sharing of information.

Alice   *Left and right brain huh?*

Patricia *Yeah, because we had a bike for her and she couldn't ride it. She always cycled backwards.*

Mark   *She never really took to the bike did she?*

Alice   *Some great examples of helping her to connect the left and right brain is by encouraging her to crawl along with her brother and also encouraging her to climb. They are some of the best ways to connect the left and right brain.*

Patricia *Yeah, so she's gotten a lot better with it but we are still trying to do marching and stuff with her.*

Alice   *Or if you can put a little bit of some great music on and do some aerobics, anything that crosses the midline is really helpful. (I demonstrate some of these movements on the floor), and perhaps you could look up brain gym on the internet for extra ideas.*

Patricia *That's the stuff we've been looking at, yeah the brain gym stuff and just reading about that.*

Alice   *Great to hear Patricia, another really good one is the importance of doing baby massage on young infants and children.*

Reflecting on the principle of Humanness, in our work with young families helps to remind us to reconsider existing practice, and to make explicit the types of strategies that support the building of authentic and respectful relationships with participants, including the building of trust and rapport (Cook, 2012). Whilst doing so, there is also the opportunity to engage in inquiry where, as researchers, we can contribute to the shared creation and construction of knowledge in collaboration with others, which includes reiterating the deep respect we have for their stories and lived experiences (Geia et al., 2013). Of course, adopting such practices comes with its own set of challenges, particularly in treading a fine line between the traditional roles of the researcher, or other issues, such as the sharing of information by the researcher, which might be seen or interpreted by the participants as a sign of endorsement, or might in some way influence the response of participants (Brown & Danaher, 2017). This being said, those who choose to employ humanising practices are motivated by their paradigmatic positioning of a genuine respect for the other, and the value placed on the dialogic process, integrity, and honesty (Brown, 2012; Paris, 2011; Rizvi, 2017). Such an approach to inquiry is underpinned by a union between creating supportive and relational inquiry spaces (Reason & Bradbury, 2008), complimented by an ethics of respect and care (Gabb, 2010).

6.5 Empathy

The third and final CHE principle, Empathy, is closely aligned to the other two CHE principles in terms of paying close attention, and careful consideration, to the practices and strategies we employ in efforts to build authentic relationships with participants, including the development and sustainment of trust and rapport. However, the principle of Empathy has a number of distinguishable characteristics. These include: receptiveness and being prepared to appreciate the perspectives of 'the other'; the practice of compassion, the ability to listen whilst suspending judgement (Dickson-Swift, James, Kippen, & Liamputtong, 2007); and the embedding of relational mutuality (Duncombe & Jessop, 2012; Sanjek, 2015; Watts, 2008). Further, the principle of Empathy is built upon, and emerges from, early efforts evidenced in the inquiry process, involved with establishing authentic relationships built through 'Connectivity'

and 'Humanness'. These efforts provide a foundation for which participants feel comfortable in the presence of someone that is unfamiliar, and
in disclosing and sharing stories of their private lives, behaviours, perspectives, and practices in an environment where they feel safe.

In an edited book titled *The Emotional Nature of Qualitative Research*,
Gilbert (2001) refers to the research process as requiring "an awareness
and intelligent use of our emotions" (p. 11). This is consistent with
embedding and employing 'Empathy' practices and strategies. Such an
approach requires researchers to engage in openness, of being fully present and 'giving of one's whole attention', as part of a 'committed
presence'.

This requires a particular type of listening, one with a focus of "concern and compassion", of being able to feel with, and for, the other, and
being alongside participants as they bravely share their stories (Watts,
2008, p. 9). It also calls on skills of active responsiveness to the narratives
of participants, as well an awareness of the non-verbal cues and messages
participants communicate, referred to as 'attunement' (Dreher, 2012;
Fedesco, 2015). Given the skills and strategies required, researchers may
find it necessary to depart from their traditional role, as simply 'the collector of data', and who practices professional distance, neutrality, and
objectivity. Instead, it may be necessary to adopt a more dialogic interaction style, and the employment of skills to support interpersonal relationships (Sanjek, 2015).

'Relational mutuality' is an important aspect of the principle of
Empathy. It builds upon the orientation phase of relational efforts, which
were the focus of earlier principle of Connectedness. Relational mutuality refers to the genuine and mutual interest individuals have in what
each other has to say. Mutuality reflects a more balanced relationship and
distribution of power, where individuals share information, and where
both are appreciated as being of value, and respected as co-constructors
of meaning (Watts, 2008). Empathy, in this process, reflects efforts to
understand the other, their meaning-making, and their frame of reference (Jordan, 1986). However, in terms of reciprocity, mutuality refers to
the researcher having multiple guises (Watts, 2008), including sharing
the role of giver and receiver of information.

Another similarity to the principle of Humanness is the importance of researchers sharing of themselves. However, the distinction in this case is that researchers are called to draw upon their own emotional experiences and sensitivities in their efforts to communicate and engage with participants (Watts, 2008). This can be referred as the sharing of our 'emotional and affective experiences', such as the sharing of experiences or moments of pleasure, pain, dislike, dread, and the sharing of emotions and moods. This type of sharing of experience effectively promotes empathy and rapport.

Watts (2008) talks about the "verbal and non-verbal components" of empathetic behaviour, all of which are significant in their various capacities and forms (p. 8). She gives the example of 'the power of touch', and how this technique can communicate 'understanding', or comfort, on so many levels, without the use of words. She notes that these types of practices, or exercising of Empathy, are particularly effective if participants are stressed, or are experiencing pain. The employment of these techniques is also a very effective way of making a powerful connection with research participants. Watts (2008) also points out that the 'careful use of language' helps to reflect Empathy, including the use of active, open-ended questioning, and the use of back-channelling, or auditory responses (such as 'Yes', 'Mmmm', 'Uh huh', or 'Okay'). However, a combination of verbal and non-verbal techniques, such as the use of eye contact, with the words 'I understand', is also a very effective technique to reflect Empathy in our engagement with others.

However, while Empathy calls on the skills of employing empathetic behaviour, such as that of the use of verbal and non-verbal communication, Watts (2008) goes on to make an important distinction and refinement to these types of practices, commenting that "empathy is what someone is, not what someone does" (p. 9). This reflects the essence or focus of empathy as very much an intuitive attribute of relationality, or what can be referred to as an "intuitive connectedness to others" (Watts, 2008, p. 9). These efforts call on an affective disposition and connection to our relational self, which may not come naturally to some.

The principle of Empathy and efforts to build trust, rapport, and respectful relationships are particularly important to embed, when engaged in sensitive research. Such inquiry might include inquiry where the focus is on those experiencing illness, those who are incarcerated, in occupations which many might deem inappropriate, or for those who are vulnerable, or who have experienced oppression, disadvantage, disenfranchisement, or marginalisation (Dickson-Swift et al., 2007; Warr, 2004). In these cases, employing practices of Empathy helps us to be more responsive to the emotional stress levels, discomfort, or suffering of others. Watts (2008) talks about this being particularly the case in the field of ethnography, where research may focus on vulnerable subjects (Kontos & Naglie, 2006; Liamputtong, 2007).

And, similar to the other CHE principles, adopting practices and strategies that reflect Empathy may prove challenging to some researchers, who might feel uncomfortable, ill-prepared, or inadequate, in how best to respond to such narrative encounters. Others might experience like "stepping into unfamiliar territory", or walking on eggshells (Watts, 2008, p. 8), particularly at times where, in line with the expectation of reciprocity, one might be called upon to share a personal reflection or account of their own experiences.

Further, as part of employing practices that reflect the principle of Empathy, where researchers attempt to give their whole attention or "committed presence", there may be a risk of experiencing what Watts (2008, p. 3) refers to as "emotion deluge and fatigue". This is particularly the case when engaged in the compelling emotional demands of conversations with potentially vulnerable participants. Watts (2008) talks about this in terms of "treading the narrow path between researcher detachment on the one hand and personal involvement on the other" (p. 5).

For both the participant and researcher who might experience the negative effects of research, it is important in these cases to seek professional support, connect with support networks and agencies, or employ self-care strategies, where feelings can be unloaded (Corden, Sainsbury, Sloper, & Ward, 2005). Finally, Watts (2008, p. 3) cautions about the risk or "propensity for friendship arising from regular contact between researcher and subjects in qualitative social research". She makes an important distinction between empathy and friendship, commenting that "empathy is not synonymous with friendship and avoiding false or insincere friendship contributes to ethical research conduct" (p. 9).

Thinking More About 'Empathy'

- How can I move the inquiry process with young families away from being one of interrogation, to one that is much more in tune with developing enduring relationships with participants, and acknowledging and valuing their contributions and positions?
- How easily can empathy shade into being perceived as 'friendship', or endorsing or critiquing specific attitudes, behaviours, and values on the part of the participants?
- How might my actions and research practices impede or enhance empathy and mutuality with others as part of the inquiry and process of relationality?
- To what extent can and should empathy function as the bridge between self and other/ness?
- How might the embedding of practices of Empathy be instrumental in the data collection phase of research with young families, particularly when engaging in sensitive research?

Empathy—Contextualisation and Implications to Family Research

The development of rapport and trust is a priority, and an essential component of our work and research with young families, particularly if we are to have any hope of gaining rich stories, and shared insights into the lives of those situated within these intimate spaces (Pitts & Miller-Day, 2007). However, rapport is a reciprocal process, and needs to be mutually constructed, in order for each party to empathise with the other, and be willing to bravely engage in shared narrative opportunities. In the telling and retelling of their storied lives, and the sharing of the inner terrain of domesticity, some of the topics young families may engage in could evoke feelings such as anxiety, uncertainty, frustration, or disappointment. These moments and experiences may be emotionally challenging to both the participant and the researcher. In these instances, our closer connections with participants act as an emotional doorway, where we might empathise with participants, offer reassurance, or perhaps step into the role of a 'friend that understands' (Paris, 2011). By adopting practices of empathy in these instances, and in our efforts to enfranchise the other, hopefully researchers are open and accepting of the meaning-making of young families, their stories and understandings, and value their expressions of multiple subjectivities.

From a strengths-based perspective, it is also important to be reminded that not all of our encounters with young families will be negatively charged. On the contrary, many shared moments, and experiences, will be filled with joy, laughter, pride, the warmth of wonderful memories, and even stories of celebration. Adopting practices which support Empathy open us up to the possibilities and potentialities of authentically sharing in emotions attached to these narratives, but also the richness that these stories offer to providing insight into the phenomenon being investigated. These moments will offer opportunities to employ empathetic practices, which in doing so contribute to continuing to build strong and respectful relationships with family members.

Efforts to reflect Empathy with young families might mean doing less talking and more listening. It may mean having less of a focus on direct questioning, and instead adopting practices and techniques that enable conversations to flow and evolve organically. In the end, if family members feel safe and comfortable in our company, they will be more inclined to expand on points, and take conversations further, including going beyond the directions we had initially anticipated. In these instances, we have opportunities to build upon authentic relationships that are genuinely warm and empathetic, to a useful, respectful, and ethical "counterbalance" (Watts, 2008, p. 9).

6.6   Conclusion

Our research with young families can be so rewarding and insightful, but doesn't come without its challenges. This is particularly the case in entering and building trust and rapport with others in spaces such as the family home, or with families who are vulnerable or marginalised. In our conversations and inquiry with family members, emotions will vary along a continuum from fear and concern, to joy and pride, as part of them sharing their lived experiences. An awareness of the CHE principles offers a reflective tool, and supports an increased sensitivity, for how we might respond humanely, ethically, and empathetically. Each of these elements are critical to the success of building strong and respectful relationships with participants, as well as the success of the data that is collected as part of our inquiry. These aspects and elements of our practice require ongoing reflection, problematising, and refinement, in terms of our methodological approaches and the tools we employ. In the words of Paris (2014), it is about an "ongoing process of 'becoming'" (p. xiii), as we grapple with the tensions, and straddle the fine rope of how far we are prepared to go to embrace the principles of CHE, in order to help us build dialogical, respectful, and ethical relationships with participants.

References

Anandalalakshmy, S., Chaudhary, N., & Sharma, N. (Eds.). (2008). *Researching families and children*. Thousand Oaks, CA: Sage.

Arao, B., & Clemens, K. (2013). From safe spaces to brave spaces: A new way to frame dialogue around diversity and social justice. In L. Landreman (Ed.), *The art of effective facilitation: Reflections from social justice educators* (pp. 135–150). Sterling, VA: Stylus Publishing.

Bergold, J., & Thomas, S. (2012). Participatory research methods: A methodological approach in motion. *Historical Social Research/Historische Sozialforschung, 13*(1), 191–222.

Bermúdez, J. M., Muruthi, B., & Jordan, L. (2016). Decolonizing research methods for family science: Creating space at the centre – Decolonizing research practices. *Journal of Family Theory & Review, 8*(2), 192–206.

Bettez, S. C. (2015). Navigating the complexity of qualitative research in postmodern contexts: Assemblage, critical reflexivity, and communion as guides. *International Journal of Qualitative Studies in Education, 28*(8), 932–954.

Bishop, R. (2012). Indigenous methods in qualitative educational research. In S. Delamont (Ed.), *Handbook of qualitative research in education* (pp. 126–142). Cheltenham, UK: Edward Elgar Publishing.

Bratich, J. (2017). Observation in a surveilled world. In N. Denzin & N. Lincoln (Eds.), *The Sage handbook of qualitative research*. Thousand Oaks, CA: Sage.

Brown, A. (2012). *The new frontier: A social ecological exploration of factors impacting on parental support for the active play of young children within the micro-environment of the family home.* PhD, University of Southern Queensland, Toowoomba, QLD.

Brown, A., & Danaher, P. A. (2012, December 2–6). *Respectful, responsible and reciprocal ruralities research: Approaching and positioning educational research differently within Australian rural communities.* Paper presented at the joint international conference of the Australian Association for Research in Education and the Asia Pacific Educational Research Association (AARE 2012): Regional and Global Cooperation in Educational Research, Sydney, NWS.

Brown, A., & Danaher, P. A. (2017). CHE Principles: Facilitating authentic and dialogical semi-structured interviews in educational research. *International Journal of Research & Method in Education,* 1–15. https://doi.org/10.1080/1743727X.2017.13799.

Brown, A., & Reushle, S. (2010). People, pedagogy and the power of connection. *Studies in Learning, Evaluation, Innovation and Development,* 7(3), 37–48.

Burr, V. (2015). *Social constructionism.* London: Routledge.

Cook, T. (2012). *Where participatory approaches meet pragmatism in funded (health) research: The challenge of finding meaningful spaces.* Paper presented at the Forum Qualitative Sozialforschung/Forum: Qualitative Social Research.

Corden, A., Sainsbury, R., Sloper, P., & Ward, B. (2005). Using a model of group psychotherapy to support social research on sensitive topics. *International Journal of Social Research Methodology,* 8(2), 151–160.

Cousin, G. (2009). *Strategies for researching learning in higher education: An introduction to contemporary methods and approaches.* New York: Routledge.

Daly, K. J. (2007). *Qualitative methods for family studies and human development.* Thousand Oaks, CA: Sage.

DiCicco-Bloom, B., & Crabtree, B. (2006). The qualitative research interview. *Medical Education,* 40(4), 314–321.

Dickson-Swift, V., James, E., Kippen, S., & Liamputtong, P. (2006). Blurring boundaries in qualitative health research on sensitive topics. *Qualitative Health Research,* 16(6), 853–871.

Dickson-Swift, V., James, E., Kippen, S., & Liamputtong, P. (2007). Doing sensitive research: What challenges do qualitative researchers face? *Qualitative Research,* 7(3), 327–353.

Dockett, S., Perry, B., Kearney, E., Hamshire, A., Mason, J., & Schmied, V. (2009). Researching with families: Ethical issues and situations. *Contemporary Issues in Early Childhood,* 10(4), 353–365.

Douglas, J. D. (1985). *Creative interviewing*. Beverly Hills, CA: Sage.

Dreher, T. (2012). A partial promise of voice: Digital storytelling and the limits of listening. *Media International Australia Incorporating Culture and Policy: Quarterly Journal of Media Research and Resources, 42*, 157–166.

Duncombe, J., & Jessop, J. (2012). Doing rapport' and the ethics of 'faking friendship'. In T. Miller, M. Birch, M. Mauthner, & J. Jessop (Eds.), *Ethics in Qualitative Research* (2nd ed., pp. 108–121). London: Sage.

Ellis, C. (2007). Telling secrets, revealing lives: Relational ethics in research with intimate others. *Qualitative Inquiry, 13*(1), 3–29.

Fedesco, H. N. (2015). The impact of (In)effective listening on interpersonal interactions. *The International Journal of Listening, 29*(2), 103–106.

Fenton, A., Walsh, K., Wong, S., & Cumming, T. (2015). Using strengths-based approaches in early years practice and research. *International Journal of Early Childhood, 47*(1), 27–52.

Fleer, M., & Ridgway, A. (2013). *Visual methodologies and digital tools for researching with young children: Transforming visuality*. Cham, Switzerland: Springer.

Freire, P. (1993). *Pedagogy of the oppressed*. New York: Continuum.

Gabb, J. (2009). Researching family relationships: A qualitative mixed methods approach. *Methodological Innovations Online, 4*(2), 37–52.

Gabb, J. (2010). Home truths: Ethical issues in family research. *Qualitative Research, 10*(4), 461–478.

Galletta, A. (2013). *Mastering the semi-structured interview and beyond: From research design to analysis and publication* (Qualitative studies in psychology). New York: University Press.

Geia, L. K., Hayes, B., & Usher, K. (2013). Yarning/aboriginal storytelling: Towards an understanding of an Indigenous perspective and its implications for research practice. *Contemporary Nurse, 46*(1), 13–17.

Gilbert, K. R. (2001). Introduction: Why are we interested in emotions? In K. R. Gilbert (Ed.), *The emotional nature of qualitative research*. Boca Raton, FL: CRC Press.

Gill, P., Stewart, K., Treasure, E., & Chadwick, B. (2008). Methods of data collection in qualitative research: Interviews and focus groups. *British Dental Journal, 204*(6), 291–295.

González, N., Moll, L. C., & Amanti, C. (Eds.). (2006). *Funds of knowledge: Theorizing practices in households, communities, and classrooms*. Mahwah, NJ: Routledge.

Hammersley, M. (2015). On ethical principles for social research. *International Journal of Social Research Methodology, 128*(4), 433–449.

Hancox, D. (2011). Stories with impact: The potential of storytelling to contribute to cultural research and social inclusion. *The Journal of Media and Culture, 14*(6).

Harden, J., Backett-Milburn, K., Hill, M., & MacLean, A. (2010). Oh, what a tangled web we weave: Experiences of doing 'multiple perspectives' research in families. *International Journal of Social Research Methodology, 13*(5), 441–452.

Harding, S. (2006). *Science and social inequality: Feminist and postcolonial issues.* Champaign, IL: University of Illinois Press.

Heshusius, L. (1994). Freeing ourselves from objectivity: Managing subjectivity or turning toward a participatory mode of consciousness? *Educational Researcher, 23*(3), 15–22.

Higgs, P., Moore, D., & Aitken, C. (2006). Engagement, reciprocity and advocacy: Ethical harm reduction practice in research with injecting drug users. *Drug and Alcohol Review, 25*(5), 419–423.

hooks, b. (1994). *Outlaw culture – Resisting representations.* New York: Routledge.

Iacono, V. L., Symonds, P., & Brown, D. H. (2016). Skype as a tool for qualitative research interviews. *Sociological Research Online, 21*(2), 12.

Irvine, A., Drew, P., & Sainsbury, R. (2013). 'Am I not answering your questions properly?': Clarification, adequacy and responsiveness in semi-structured telephone and face-to-face interviews. *Qualitative Research, 13*(1), 87–106.

Johnson, N. (2009). The role of self and emotion within qualitative sensitive research: A reflective account. *Enquire, 4*, 23–50.

Jordan, J. (1986). *The meaning of mutuality: Stone Center for Developmental Services and Studies.* Wellsley, MA: Wellesley College Wellesley.

Keaton, S. A., & Bodie, G. D. (2011). Explaining social constructivism. *Communication Teacher, 25*(4), 192–196.

Kellett, M. (2010). *Rethinking children and research: Attitudes in contemporary society.* London: Continuum International Publishing.

King, N., & Horrocks, C. (2010). *Interviews in qualitative research* (1st ed.). Los Angeles: Sage.

Kontos, P., & Naglie, G. (2006). Expressions of personhood in Alzheimer's: Moving from ethnographic text to performing ethnography. *Qualitative Research, 6*(3), 301–317.

Liamputtong, P. (2007). *Researching the vulnerable.* London: Sage.

Mack, N., Woodson, C., Macqueen, K., Guest, G., & Namey, E. (2005). *Qualitative research methods: A data collector's field guide.* Research Triangle Park, NC: Family Health International.

Macnamara, J. (2015). *Creating an 'architecture of listening' in organizations: The basis of engagement, trust, healthy democracy, social equity, and business sustainability*. Retrieved from Sydney, NSW. https://www.uts.edu.au/sites/default/files/fass-organizational-listening-report.pdf

Manning, K. (1997). Authenticity in constructivist inquiry: Methodological considerations without prescription. *Qualitative Inquiry, 3*(1), 93–115.

Mannion, G. (2007). Going spatial, going relational: Why "listening to children" and children's participation needs reframing. *Discourse: Studies in the Cultural Politics of Education, 28*(3), 405–420.

Mazzei, L. (2013). A voice without organs: Interviewing in posthumanist research. *International Journal of Qualitative Studies in Education, 26*(6), 732–740.

McNeil, T. (2010). Family as a social determinant of health: Implications for governments and institutions to promote the health and well-being of families. *Healthcare Quarterly, 14*(Special Issue, Child Health Canada), 60–67.

Palaiologou, I. (2014). 'Do we hear what children want to say?' Ethical praxis when choosing research tools with children under five. *Early Child Development and Care, 184*(5), 689–705.

Palmer, V. (1928). *Field studies in sociology: A student's manual*. Chicago: University of Chicago Press.

Paris, D. (2011). 'A friend who understand fully': Notes on humanizing research in a multiethnic youth community. *International Journal of Qualitative Studies in Education, 24*(2), 137–149.

Paris, D., & Winn, M. (Eds.). (2014). *Humanizing research: Decolonizing qualitative inquiry with youth and communities*. London: Sage.

Pitts, M., & Miller-Day, M. (2007). Upward turning points and positive rapport-development across time in researcher—Participant relationships. *Qualitative Research, 7*(2), 177–201.

Reason, P., & Bradbury, H. (2008). Introduction. In P. Reason & H. Bradbury (Eds.), *The Sage handbook of action research. Participative inquiry and practice* (2nd ed., pp. 1–10). London: Sage.

Reushle, S. (2005). *Inquiry into a transformative approach to professional development for online educators*. PhD/Research, University of Southern Queensland, Toowoomba, QLD.

Rinaldi, C. (2006). *In dialogue with Reggio Emilia: Listening, researching, and learning*. London: Routledge Falmer.

Rizvi, S. (2017). Treading on eggshells: 'Doing' feminism in educational research. *International Journal of Research & Method in Education*, 1–13.

Roelvink, G., & Zolkos, M. (2015). Affective ontologies: Post-humanist perspectives on the self, feeling and intersubjectivity. *Emotion, Space and Society, 14*, 47–49.

Roulston, K. (2014). Interactional problems in research interviews. *Qualitative Research, 14*(3), 277–293.

Rubin, H., & Rubin, I. (2012). *Qualitative interviewing: The art of hearing data* (3rd ed.). London: Sage.

San Pedro, T., & Kinloch, V. (2017). Toward projects in humanization: Research on co-creating and sustaining dialogic relationships. *American educational research journal, 54*(1_suppl), 373S–394S.

Sanjek, R. (Ed.). (2015). *Mutuality: Anthropology's changing terms of engagement.* Philadelphia, PA: University of Pennsylvania Press.

Silverman, D. (2013). *Doing qualitative research: A practical handbook.* Thousand Oaks, CA: Sage.

Springwood, C., & King, C. (2001). Unsettling engagements: On the ends of rapport in critical ethnography. *Qualitative Inquiry, 7*(4), 403–417.

Stake, R. (1995). *The art of case study research.* Thousand Oaks, CA: Sage.

Stewart, V. C. (2016). More than words in a text: Learning to conduct qualitative research in the midst of a major life event. *International Journal of Qualitative Studies in Education, 29*(4), 573–593.

Thiele, K. (2014). Ethos of diffraction: New paradigms for a (post) humanist ethics. *Parallax, 20*(3), 202–216.

Thomas, R. (2014). Honouring the oral traditions of my ancestors through storytelling. In S. Strega & L. Brown (Eds.), *Research as resistance: Revisiting critical, Indigenous and anti-oppressive approaches to research* (2nd ed., pp. 177–198). Toronto, ON: Canadian Scholars Press.

Thomas, U., Tiplady, L., & Wall, K. (2014). Stories of practitioner enquiry: Using narrative interviews to explore teachers' perspectives of learning to learn. *International Journal of Qualitative Studies in Education, 27*(3), 397–411.

Trainor, A., & Bouchard, K. (2013). Exploring and developing reciprocity in research design. *International Journal of Qualitative Studies in Education, 26*(8), 986–1003.

Uttal, L. (2009). (Re)visioning family ties to communities and contexts. In S. A. Lloyd, A. L. Few, & K. R. Allen (Eds.), *Handbook of feminist studies* (pp. 134–146). Thousand Oaks, CA: Sage.

Vähäsantanen, K., & Saarinen, J. (2013). The power dance in the research interview: Manifesting power and powerlessness. *Qualitative Researcher, 13*(5), 493–510.

Von Unger, H. (2012). *Participatory health research: Who participates in what?* Paper presented at the Forum Qualitative Sozialforschung/Forum: Qualitative Social Research.

Warr, D. (2004). Stories in the flesh and voices in the head: Reflections on the context and impact of research with disadvantaged populations. *Qualitative Health Research, 14*(4), 578–587.

Watts, J. H. (2008). Emotion, empathy and exit: Reflections on doing ethnographic qualitative research on sensitive topics. *Medical Sociology Online, 3*(2), 3–14.

Wong, S. M., & Cumming, T. (2008). *Practice grounded in theory: The theoretical and philosophical underpinnings of SDN's Child, Family and Children's Services Programs. The second of eight reports investigating SDN's Child, Family and Children's Services Program.* Retrieved from Sydney, NSW. https://www.uts.edu.au/sites/default/files/fass-organizational-listening-report.pdf

Yee, W. C., & Andrews, J. (2006). Professional researcher or a 'good guest'? Ethical dilemmas involved in researching children and families in the home setting. *Educational Review, 58*(4), 397–413. https://doi.org/10.1080/00131910600971859.

7

The 'Retelling' of Stories Through Sense-Making of Data

Scenario 7—Custodian of the Story…

He wished to honour their stories, tell their stories, each story, shared stories. He had spent so many hours in their company, in their homes, in their neighbourhoods, in the lifespaces of young families. Each family so generously investing time, and emotional energy on describing, reliving, and sharing their experiences, and the strategies they had employed in an attempt to rebuild their lives again, and move forward from the natural disaster of an inland tsunami that had so tragically struck their community a year ago.

He now hesitated, as he anticipated the next step in his research journey. As he considered his role and the task ahead of him as a qualitative researcher, he wondered how he might best make sense of the data he had collected. He had a clear goal of developing rich, thick descriptions of his findings, to inform the phenomenon he had chosen to investigate. And, while he appreciated the privileged position he was in, as a 'custodian of the stories of others', he was also aware that he needed to seriously consider the most effective approach to capture the richness, meaning, and reconstruction of these stories. He knew it was critical now to find an approach that would somehow afford him the ability to piece together the data he had collected, while cognisant to preserve the integrity of these stories, and the dignity of the teller of each story (Kim, 2016).

© The Author(s) 2019   **229**
A. Brown, *Respectful Research With and About Young Families*, Palgrave Studies in
Education Research Methods, https://doi.org/10.1007/978-3-030-02716-2_7

He was overcome by the deep respect that he had for these families and their community, their resilience, and the way they had rallied together; of how they had so openly and genuinely given of themselves in efforts to support the rebuilding process.

Now he needed to adopt an approach to the analysis of this data that would somehow reflect these efforts, support the process of restorying, and in doing so create coherent narratives. The intent of this process being to capture the hardship, adversity, and the significant impact these life events had had on the families in this community, while also committed to somehow honouring these people by the ways that these stories were shared and key messages conveyed (Kiser, Baumgardner, & Dorado, 2010). *He was conscious of the intent not to portray members of the community solely as victims, but as strong adversaries. A community with great resilience, and perseverance, able to draw on, and from, not only their own capital, but also a range of social and collective capital, in order to rebuild, to overcome, and to move forward towards a hopeful future. As a custodian of the stories of others, he was aware of the great responsibility, and onerous task he had ahead of him. A task that required him to adopt an approach for the retelling and the sharing of these stories (his findings) with others (his audience).*

Chapter Synopsis

One of the most important parts of any inquiry is reporting on the data collected and the insights gained. The intent of our findings is not only to inform the research questions identified, but also to contribute to broader discipline, methodological and conceptual knowledge. Unfortunately, while engaged in the research process, there is a potential to lose sight of another important responsibility we have, that of being 'custodians of the story', and honouring the lived experiences and narratives that others have generously shared with us.

Making sense of qualitative data can be a daunting and somewhat onerous task. There is often great complexity evidenced in our efforts to merge and include shared stories, with other forms of data, in order to create thick, rich descriptions (Elsbach & Kramer, 2016; Mason, 2018). However, while challenging, this part of the inquiry process is one of the most important and exciting aspects of our research journey. For it is in the retelling of these stories that we are able to communicate and share the great insights we have amassed in relation to the lives and contexts of others, while at the same time honouring those stories.

What does it mean, and what responsibilities do we have, as 'custodians of the story'?

How might adopting the role of custodian of the story impact on the analysis tools and methods we adopt?

How might being a custodian of the story impact on the stories we choose to tell and privilege, as well as those stories we choose to ignore?

What responsibility do we have as custodians of the story in the reconstruction of each story; the piecing together of data: preserving the integrity of the data; and honouring the dignity of the teller of the story?

What potential is afforded to participants in the retelling of their stories, and in conveying their stories to others?

How might our retelling of stories be instrumental in improving the world of the participants we represent? As 'custodians', how might we serve?

In order to achieve such a task, we need to draw on a particular skill set as well as an appreciation of the context of the inquiry. Great consideration also needs to be invested in the selection of authentic and trustworthy methods to make sense of our findings. At this point, many choose to go down the path of analysis methods already well established and respected. Others opt instead to embrace innovative adaptations, or new approaches for the task of the 'sense-making' of data.

The process of choosing tools or an approach for analysing data can be a complex balancing act for the researcher. Such a task involves weighing up a range of factors, including revisiting the intent of the inquiry (a study's research questions and goals); and how the employment of an approach might also honour the perspectives and artefacts shared by others. Qualitative researchers also face decisions with respect to strategies that will best reflect the authenticity and integrity of our efforts, while also juggling the advice of others, and existing and established conventions of data analysis practices espoused by experts in the field.

Qualitative researchers are spoilt for choice, in terms of the overwhelming array of literature, and advice on offer, on the topic of data analysis, and the sense-making process. Experts include Denzin and Lincoln (2008, 2017), Miles, Huberman, and Saldana, (2014), Tisdall, Davis and Gallagher (2008), Merriam and Tisdall (2016), Clandinin, Huber, Menan, Murphy and Swanson (2016), and many others (Daly, 2007b; Elsbach & Kramer, 2016; Mason, 2018). As such, this chapter offers quite a different approach to the topic of analysis, understood in this chapter as the 'sense-making' of data. Key themes woven throughout this chapter reflect the importance of honouring and respecting participants' voice, stories, and lived experiences.

The chapter reinforces the privileged position of researchers in being 'invited in' to the contexts and lifespaces of families, and the need to approach our role with integrity and humbleness. Just as importantly, readers are reminded that with this privilege come responsibilities. This includes the implications this responsibility has through the lens of being 'custodians of the story' and consideration given as to how the stories of others are shared and passed on.

Given this, rather than starting this chapter by introducing and discussing a range of analysis methods, the chapter starts by revisiting the role of 'researcher as storyteller', initially addressed in Chap. 3 of this text. The reasoning behind this is to offer the reader a different lens in which to consider and view data. 'Data' in this case is referred to as 'stories', and understood to represent the narratives collected from participants, through methods such as interviews. However, 'stories' are also understood in broader terms, to include other types of data that captures the lived experiences, contexts, and environments of participants (see Chap. 3 on the topic of storying).

At various junctures throughout this chapter, readers have an opportunity to take a moment to pause, and to reflect on the role of custodians of the story, particularly the implications this role may have on the practices and strategies they adopted for such an important task. Readers are also invited to explore how this role might reflect the decolonising nature of our research sites, such as the domestic spaces of young families, and other spaces families occupy. Finally, researchers are encouraged to think about the role of custodians of the story, in terms of how this role might reflect humanising components and responsibilities.

The second part of Module 7 shifts attention to factors influencing researcher decision-making, in relation to the process of analysis and the retelling of participant stories. These decisions include consideration given to the ways stories may be told, which stories might be privileged, and which stories might be ignored or overlooked. Finally, given that data encompasses a range of forms, and serves multiple purposes, a series of questions are presented, and information shared, to guide custodians' thinking and decision-making around approaches, frameworks, and processes that may best serve the task of sense-making and the retelling of stories. Eisner (1998) refers to these methods as one's 'artistry' of the tools that support us in privileging the stories of others.

7.1   Representing and Conveying What We See and Hear

An important responsibility of those engaged in qualitative research is gathering enough data to inform the phenomenon being investigated (Creswell, 2013). Interpretivists are aware of the multiple realities in which individuals view their world, their multiple ways of knowing and meaning systems, and the nuances and idiosyncratic nature of individuals in context (Merriam & Tisdall, 2016). Those who choose to adopt such a world view appreciate that people's experiences, perspectives, and practices are inextricably connected to social worlds, social networks, as well as constructed across systems, and through time, rather than individuals being viewed in isolation or removed from context (Brown, 2012; Denzin & Lincoln, 2011; Walter, 2013). As such, in the process of co-constructing meaning, it is an interpretivist's mission not to extract one truth, nor attempt to generalise findings to a broader audience, but to illuminate most effectively and respectfully the accounts of people's lives and contexts (Berg, 2016; Mannion, 2007).

7.2   Custodians of the Story—The Responsibility Attached to the 'Retelling'

In Chap. 3 the important act of 'storying' was discussed. This included exploring the role the researcher plays in these events. In this role, the storyteller endeavours to authentically, and respectfully, pass on to others the practices, history, values, and meaning that individuals attribute to their contexts and life events (Hampton & Toombs, 2013; Kiser et al., 2010). Efforts to describe or capture the honour and responsibility associated with the 'restorying' process and co-construction of meaning are reflected in terms such as 'custodians of the data' or 'custodians of the story'. The task of custodians include processes such as documenting, sense-making (analysing and interpreting), re-presenting, and, finally, communicating research findings to a wider audience through various mediums (traditionally being in a written form, but may also include visual or oral re-presentations).

Considering the Responsibility of 'Custodian's' in the Sense-Making and Retelling of Others' Stories

Many a researcher would like to tell the whole story but of course cannot; the whole story exceeds anyone's knowing, anyone's telling (Stake, 2003, p. 144).

'Custodians of the story' are intent in seeing the world through the perspectives or eyes of another. However, in doing so they are required to make important decisions regarding how to make sense of, to retell, or to best re-present the stories, perspectives, behaviours, and contexts of others. These types of considerations are also balanced up with other decisions, such as how to stay true to the study, while also reflecting the interests and rights of participants. This task becomes even more challenging when the lived experiences of others continue to unfold, shift, change, and evolve as new events, new characters, and new settings are explored.

At some stage during this process, or perhaps as part of an ongoing research cycle, researchers may need to shift modes, from interpreter, to other roles, such as storyteller, each role requiring a different skill set, such as the role of storyteller requiring communication or narrative skills that will aid in conveying these stories to an audience in ways that capture the meaning people attribute to their contexts and experiences. This shift between roles requires a degree of fluidity and flexibility, including the ability of the researcher being open to data unravelling before us, while also keeping in mind the situatedness of this data (Stake, 2010; Walter, 2013). For the role of storyteller is one that is integrally linked to being co-constructors of meaning in context (Clark & Moss, 2011; Grbich, 2004).

An important task associated with being a custodian of the story is the retelling of stories, and the re-presenting and presenting of our findings to others in ways that attempt to capture and convey the worlds, experiences, and meaning-making of others. Such a task calls on researchers to be humble, as well as cognisant that the practices and processes we adopt for making sense of, and conveying these stories, are authentic, and approached in ways that honour and reflect the rights and dignity of participants (Dockett et al., 2009; Fiese, 2013; Harcourt & Einarsdóttir, 2011). Further, custodians have a range of additional responsibilities associated with the retelling of stories, such as deciding on what to do with the stories collected and the ownership of these stories.

Moreover, custodians face decisions regarding who deserves to hear about these stories and findings. Finally, in the retelling of stories, custodians need to give great consideration to the image adopted to reflect 'the other', and how the other is re-presented, and portrayed in the restorying process. For in the process of restorying, custodians can potentially be emancipatory, and instrumental in improving the world and lives of those we represent. It is in the images we portray, and the stories and messages we share, that we have the opportunity to privilege the perspectives of individuals, particularly those who have to this point been historically marginalised or disenfranchised.

It is this array, and many other significant considerations, associated with the responsibility of being a custodian of the story, that adds an additional layer of complexity to the analysis and sense-making process for custodians. This additional layer of complexity and responsibility may, in fact, be referred to a 'lens' or frame, in which to view our approach to both the analysis and information dissemination process—a frame which reflects the responsibility of being custodians; a frame that reflects the decolonising and humanising aspects of our role.

For example, in the scenario shared at the beginning of the chapter, it was evidenced that the researcher was very conscious of the responsibility attached to being a custodian of the story, in the research he conducted within the community and with families. The researcher was conscious that the restorying process had the potential to present a particular image of participants. There was also evidence that the researcher had clear expectations, and ways in which he intended to portray and capture the dignity of others. In doing so, he wished to convey, through storying, an image of community members not as victims, but as strong and capable. They were people with great resilience, who had at their disposal, and were able to draw upon, personal and collective capital (Kim, 2016). As a custodian of the story, it was clear that the researcher's intent was to frame the stories and experiences of others in ways that reflected their commitment to embrace a hopeful future (Miles, Chapman, & Francis, 2015).

This interpretation of custodians of the story potentially shifts researchers beyond some of the traditional roles associated with appropriating and making sense of data, to one of being 'the teller of powerful stories'. Such a shift calls not only on a different level of commitment to the 'sense-making' process, but also to the type of narratives shared and the way these stories are retold. This approach not only gives shape to, and translates the thoughts, actions and perspectives of others in all their complexity, subtlety, and nuances, but also does so in ways which attempt to capture their richness and potentiality (Clandinin, 2007). This understanding of 'custodians' reflects the great responsibility and honour associated with such as role. Researchers are responsible for thinking carefully about going beyond simply the retelling of stories, to that of illuminating the thoughts, lives, and meaning-making of others (Gubrium, Holstein, Marvasti, & McKinney, 2012; Harden, Backett-Milburn, Hill, & MacLean, 2010).

Considering the Filters Custodians Bring to Restorying

In efforts to elicit a version of participants' lived experiences and constructions of reality, qualitative researchers recognise that we are co-constructors in the creation of meaning. We are integrally embedded in the framing of meaning (Grbich, 2007). As such, we bring with us to the task of meaning-making a range of filters such as our past experiences, our perspectives, positionality, and the literature we have immersed ourselves in or chosen to embrace. We also acknowledge that we are not value-neutral in these efforts, and that the filters we adopt will be embedded in the task of conveying the stories of others (our findings), as well the stories we choose to privilege (Daly, 2007a). (You may wish to refer to Chap. 2 that addresses the topic of positionality in detail.)

As part of the task of the retelling of stories, custodians need to ensure a level of transparency, in terms of explicitly identifying and stating the impact that our positioning, the filters imposed, as well as our interests and bias have on framing our restorying. This will include being transparent in the way that we choose to reflect and reconstruct another's reality (Sutton & Austin, 2015). Custodian recognise that even with the best of intentions to represent the stories and contexts of others accurately. We will adopt a particular lens (or several) when presenting the perspectives, images, contexts, and stories of others. In doing so, we present our own constructions and understandings of that reality. Custodians of the story are very aware of these filters and the power that comes with purposefully choosing to portray the other, and their storied lives, in a way that is respectful and ethical.

For example, the understandings, meaning-making, and interpretations of those positioned, or who choose to work within a strengths-based paradigm when researching with young families, will not only view a phenomenon through this lens, but will choose to re-present findings and the stories of others through a strengths-based paradigm. The choice of intentionally adopting such a filter will also be evidenced in how research findings are conveyed. This might include choosing to focus on positive observations and messages of potentiality and hope, rather than restorying through a deficit lens. These re-presentations are likely to celebrate and privilege the stories of families in ways that reflect the 'funds of knowledge' evidenced and the various types of social capital that emerge from the data collected. Further, in retelling the stories of others and the findings of their inquiry with young families, researchers are likely to present a strong image of the other. This image might reflect and profile the various affordances evidenced, such as their culture, skills, resources, capacities, and various types of capital.

Time for Some Personal Reflection
Consider a lens or perspective that you choose to adopt and work within as part of an inquiry:

• How might this perspective influence the way you view your data?
• How might this perspective influence the data you choose to privilege, or the data you overlook?
• How might this perspective influence the way that 'the other' is framed, privileged, or re-presented?
• How might this perspective influence the stories you choose to privilege, or how these stories are told?

7.3   Making Sense of Data—Deciding on What Is 'Data', and Which Data Is Important

A popular methodological approach that interpretivist researchers employ is to use multiple data collection techniques in order to gather layers of meaning to afford for rich, thick descriptions, and understandings of a phenomenon (Creswell, 2013; Merriam & Tisdall, 2016). However, such an approach leaves us with a plethora of data to wade through and interpret. This may present a practical challenge, one that for some may seem daunting, overwhelming, and onerous. It also presents an epistemological challenge in terms of deciding what we choose to recognise as data, and the tools we employ to make sense of the data (Mason, 2018).

Retracing the Steps and Original Intent of Our Inquiry

In order to see more clearly the forest from the trees, in terms of what constitutes data, and before we approach and engage in the sense-making process, it may be worth pressing the pause button. In doing so, we have an opportunity to regroup and take time out to reflect more deeply on questions related to the data we have, and factors that might inform our decision-making. In reference to the process of making sense of our data, Merriam and Tisdall (2016) recommend that rather than leaving this process till the end of a qualitative study, that researchers adopt a more strategic approach to efforts of analysis and interpretation, suggesting that this process occurs concurrently with the data collection phase of an inquiry. This process would include researchers moving back and forth through and across the data.

Time for Some Personal Reflection

An effective approach for those wishing to engage in this process is to retrace the steps of an inquiry, starting by revisiting the original problem identified, and the goals and motivations for the study (Merriam & Tisdall, 2016). At the very least, this process should involve carefully reviewing the questions originally posed, and what the study sought to explore and uncover. Of course, this should be an inherent and ongoing process that all researchers engage in as part of the cycle of inquiry. At this point, it is also worth revisiting the motivations for pursuing the focus of the study, and the positionality and filters that frame the study (including the epidemiology, ontology, and axiology of the researcher). It is also timely to revisit the image we hold of the other, and how we might choose to reflect this image in the process of analysis. This will include deciding on the filters we use to make sense of and engage in the restorying process. You may wish to reflect on the types of questions outlined below to aid in this process:

- What problems or concerns were identified at the beginning of my study?
- What did the study aim to explore, uncover, or reveal?
- What did the study propose to communicate and share with others?
- What filters, paradigms, or perspectives are adopted, reflected, and integrated throughout the study (including my epidemiology, ontology, and axiology)?

7.4   Sense-Making: Deciding Which Tools to Use, and What Strategies to Employ

While we may be armed with rich thick data, and a renewed sense of vision, as custodians of the story, deciding which data to keep, which stories to tell, which to winnow, and which to consolidate is easier said than done (Miles et al., 2014; Stake, 2003). It is at this point in an inquiry process that researchers are faced with many possibilities and options for interpreting the rich and vibrant worlds of others. Further, each approach offers different ways to understand and interpret the stories of others, in turn influencing which data are privileged and which stories are told (Gabb, 2010).

Custodians may choose to employ one style of 'rendering' or analysis, while others may decide to deploy a range of analytical strategies. However, whichever the approach, the intent, metaphorically, is to find different pieces of the puzzle that together will help create a particular type of picture (Mason, 2018). This re-creating, or restorying, will, of course, call on the skills of piecing together, in an attempt to make a 'best fit'.

For custodians of the story, adopting the process of concurrently sifting through the data, while retracing the original intent of the study, affords us with an opportunity to examine the data more closely, in order to differentiate the value of the various data. And, while there may be multiple ways of interpreting the data, rather than hoping to produce "the right knowledge", or, indeed, "one truth", at the forefront of custodian decision-making will be the intent of deploying analysis strategies that are respectful to the stories of others (Denzin & Lincoln, 2017; Fraser, 2004, p. 195). Further, custodians will be cognisant that through the analysis process, efforts are focussed on not losing sight of intent of these stories, and that the data used in reconstructing the powerful and liberating stories of other.

Considerations for Adopting Established and Well-Used Methods

Due to the messiness and complexity of the sense-making process, it is common for researchers to choose to adopt a traditional or established methodological lens that has already been tried and tested (Gersick, 2016). Others choose to deploy a combination of several established approaches for the process of analysis (Daly, 2007a, 2007b). These approaches might include interpretative analysis, thematic/content analysis, ethnography, grounded theory, phenomenology, discourse analysis, or interpretivist analysis. With a plethora of approaches, frameworks, and strategies available for analysing data, rather than attempt to detail or cover well-established territory, the intent of this section of Chap. 7 is to explore several of the analytical approaches that most closely align with the themes reflected in this chapter—these being analytic approaches that might best serve the purposes of custodians of the story.

Interpretative Analysis

Those who choose to collect the stories of others, through methods that might include interviews as one of the data collection methods employed, often favour an analytic approach that embraces the interpretation of these narratives. Interpretative analysis is one such approach, and attempts to examine, detail, and produce accounts of the personal lived experiences of others. Interpretative analysis supports the process of examining, detailing, and finally producing accounts of the personal lived experiences of others. These efforts are primarily idiographic, with a commitment to examine the uniqueness of each case, rather than to produce more general claims (Matua & Van Der Wal, 2015). Custodians of the story may find this approach to analysis attractive, as efforts focus on the balance between the meaning-making of the researcher and those of the participant (Daly, 2007a).

An interpretative approach to analysis usually starts by dividing the data into 'meaning units', consisting of aspects of the text that stand out, and which help capture and convey "significant pieces of meaning to the reader" (Elliott & Timula, 2008, p. 153). These meaning units become the basis for analysis. The next step of the analysis process focusses on the creation of categories and assigning codes, and themes to the identified meaning units. This tends to be a balancing act between the researching making efforts to be respectful of the data, and adopting labels that reflect the original language of participants, while also drawing upon "previous theorising" (Elliott & Timula, 2008, p. 156). Techniques adopted at this point of analysis process often overlap with the analytic approach of thematic and content analysis.

Thematic and Content Analysis

Thematic analysis draws from a number of methodologies and positioning, including grounded theory, interpretivism, and phenomenology.

The approach involves searching for patterns in the data, the goal of which is to reveal points of interest, while informing understandings related to the topic of research and associated research questions. Thematic analysis is of value for the focus it offers in identifying key themes unique to a particular context, or a number of sites, or settings.

Custodians of the story may find that thematic analysis offers a powerful analytic approach for making sense of and presenting compelling narratives to their audience, comprised of key themes that emerge from the data. Such an approach would afford custodians the opportunity to find patterns or cluster data from the artefacts, anecdotes, and stories collected, as a way of re-presenting and retelling the stories of others. Using the narratives created offers custodians a way of providing the reader with some sense of the characters and contexts of the research, while also sharing insights and directly linking these stories to examples and themes relevant, and that related to the associated research questions (Braun & Clarke, 2013; King & Horrocks, 2010). Finally, this analytical approach offers custodians opportunities to exemplify, give shape to, and hone in on key themes which emerge from the stories of others. However, just as importantly, these types of strategies help set the tone for the information conveyed and portrayed, such as presenting a sense of hope, respect, or adopting a strengths-based perspective.

Rather than adopting a positivist approach to content or thematic analysis, which would involve counting of the number of instances related to an associated 'coding', interpretivists engage in subjective decision-making regarding the themes chosen, and the interpretation of the themes that emerge from coding (Stake, 2013). There are range of ways to move through the process of coding and theming of the stories of others to support the process of meaning-making. Each approach involves moving through the data and making notes within the data in terms of the patterns, ideas, and concepts that emerge (Sutton & Austin, 2015). Researchers then cluster or 'chunk' data, ideas, and concepts into categories that fit loosely into themes, and associate a name to each theme (usually chosen to reflect the concepts of the theme). The identification of themes is also informed and related to key topics from the research questions of an inquiry (Guest, MacQueen, & Namey, 2011).

For custodians of the story, Braun and Clarke (2006) present an excellent suggestion regarding considerations for embedding anecdotes and direct quotes of participant stories to powerfully present key points. They suggest that "extracts need to be embedded within an analytic narrative that compellingly illustrates the story you are telling about your data, and make an argument in relation to the research question" (p. 93). An example of this is made in reference to adopting a Mosaic approach for inquiry (see Chap. 5 of this text for an overview). Referring to this approach, Clark and Moss (2001) combine the data from interviews with other types of data (such as that of observations, images, and artefacts) to help reveal and reflect a more holistic and contextual accounts when sharing the stories of others (Baird, 2013; Clark & Moss, 2011). Provided below is an excerpt from my doctoral thesis, which illustrates efforts to embed an anecdote to reinforce a key point:

Fences—Great for Keeping Children Safe, Not So Great for Supporting Active Play with Neighbours

The Hampton family included Lucy (28), George (28), Susan (4), and Simon (18 months). A key feature that existed as part of the outdoor environment at the Hampton's was a high fence and hedge that surrounded their house on three sides. I was keen to explore how this feature impacted on opportunities for Susan and Simon to actively play outdoors.

Sarah   *This space is actually a really good area for us, and we put the grass in deliberately. During the worse part of the drought, we had a paper bark tree in the back yard and all the grass that was under it just died off and there was nothing. We realised that Helen really didn't know what grass was when we had her at the park when she was just starting to walk at 12 months of age and she'd put her feet down. And yet our other friends would put their kids down and they would crawl all over and have handfuls of dirt and grass and we were really horrified. We ripped out the tree and we put in turf so that she would have soft grass to play on.*

Alice	Do they have any friends that come over from around the neighbourhood?
Lucy	Well, next door they have two kids that are about a year older than mine, but we do have a bit of a policy that because we all (the parents) work, they can talk to each other at the fence there, but they can't come over. We get together at Christmas time and what have you.
Alice	So, on the week-ends can they go over?
Lucy	No, to be honest, I'm pushed. Having the other kids over here would be too much. We have other people coming over here quite regularly. I think it was a shared agreement with the neighbours.
Alice	Simon and Sally are comfortable with that? They don't push that boundary?
Lucy	I mean, yeah, Sally has asked, and we say no. They're not at that age. They still need constant surveillance. Maybe when they are 5, 6 or 7 they will be more independent.
Alice	So a lot of it has to do with the fact that both of you work during the week and therefore value 'you time, child time and family time'? It is additional work to supervise as well?
Lucy	We are probably not close enough to be able to trust them. It's not the same familiarity with them; we have been here 2 years. But in saying that, we're always talking and chatting. I think it just comes down to more a coping mechanism, I feel pushed.

The sharing of this important story helps reinforce a very important point that reflects the changing play experiences in the suburbs for many families, where the environments are increasingly spaces of increased surveillance and control by parents. This means that for many children in contemporary times, playing with neighbours and engaging in social play with local families are more strategically considered and planned (O'Connor & Brown, 2013).

And while, even at a young age, Simon and Susan often engaged in unsupervised outdoor play within their own backyard environment, their playing with neighbours still reflected a trend of being highly regulated and controlled by parents, influenced by parental behaviours, as well as in the way that the environment was designed (high fences and hedges). This 'control' over the environment helped give the Hamptons peace of mind, with the children playing in the well-fenced-in yard where they could play freely, while also knowing that fence would stop the children going onto the street.

Finally, before we leave this approach to analysis, it is important to note that an important step in adopting an interpretivist approach to thematic analysis is the researcher (and their team, or critical friends), clearly identifying the factors that have informed decisions and judgements. This process helps ensure rigour regarding the process for determining data identified as important, and the data that might be discarded. This part of the process of thematic analysis is referred to as 'audibility', or the process of being transparent, in terms of the researcher clearly articulating the processes intentionally undertaken for arriving at the themes identified for analysis. This includes providing "reflexive excerpts about how categories or themes were generated" and "discussion of the interpretive meaning making process". As part of this transparency, it is also important to communicate to participants how our decision-making is influenced by our positioning and perspectives.

Using a Framework for Analysis

Analytic frameworks offer researchers a valuable tool, and a systematic and flexible methodological approach to manage and organise data. Adopting a framework for analysis provides a structure for the sense-making process, with the aim of shedding light on the phenomenon investigated (Gale, Heath, Cameron, Rashid, & Redwood, 2013). The framework method can be used in conjunction with other analysis methods, such as that of thematic analysis, or content analysis. A framework is an effective tool to aid researchers in focussing on the relationships that exists within the data.

For custodians of the story, employing a framework for analysis may contribute to developing narratives that offer descriptive and explanatory conclusions, related to themes associated with the research. Utilising a framework method would be particularly valuable, when combined with other methods, such as thematic analysis of textual data, or the collection of the stories of 'others'. Finally, adopting a framework for analysis may help custodians with the authenticity and integrity of data, particularly in terms of efforts to show the relationship between data and the situatedness of the data in the context in which the stories and the lived experiences of others originally occurred.

The process of adopting a framework for analysis often starts after initial coding is complete and agreed upon by the research team. Codes can then be grouped into categories and clearly defined. These categories are then able to form the development of an analytical framework in an iterative process. However, another way of employing a framework as part of the analysis process is to start with an existing framework, inspired by or borrowed from elsewhere (Snilstveit, Oliver, & Vojtkova, 2012). This approach can be referred to as employing a paradigmatic framework (such as an ecological or social ecological framework), where there is commitment and value in working within a paradigmatic position, which includes an associated framework. This type of approach is usually adopted quite early in an investigation and flows through to then being employed as a framework for analysis. In this case, categories can either emerge from the data, or can be designed and developed around the existing framework.

For example, very early in my doctoral research I saw value in understanding a phenomenon through an ecological lens, and later a social ecological lens, due to the importance I placed on my positioning and on the 'valuing of context'. This paradigm influenced all aspects of the research project, from the way my research questions were framed, right through to adapting a social ecological framework to help make sense of data collected, related to parent values, understandings, and support of active play opportunities with their young children. In my case, this position helped to clarify the type of conceptual framework that was necessary to provide direction to my inquiry, and, later, to support the interpretation of the data that was collected.

An important point to note, particularly for custodians of the story, is that while using a framework for analysis may be effective in making sense of data, there is still a need to be cognisant that in systematically reducing the data into themes, and providing structure around these themes through the use of a framework, that we do not lose sight of the idiosyncratic nature of the voices and the context of participants. Further, if the data are rich enough, the stories generated through this process offer researchers the opportunity to go beyond purely descriptions of particular cases, but to include details and an explanation and "reasons for the emergence of a phenomena", or how a phenomenon is evidenced, understood, and interpreted in particular contexts, as well as across contexts (Gale et al., 2013, p. 5).

For example, in reference to the social ecological perspective (Stokols, Grzywacz, McMahan, & Phillips, 2003) and framework adopted for my doctoral study, it was appreciated that the contexts and systems in which members of young families were positioned were complex and idiosyncratic. As such, adopting an interpretivist paradigm and approach to analysis with young families opened up a type of inquiry that was able to peel back some of this complexity afforded for the layers of context and meaning to be exposed (Miles et al. 2015, #3046). Further, by adopting this method of analysis, I was able to pursue an in-depth insight into the lives of families with young children, and to explore their commonly held assumptions. As such, rather than the pursuit of numbers, statistics, or the desire to generalise, adopting a social ecological framework for analysis helped me to capture the details, richness of context, accounts, nuances, and social situations of others in an ever-changing world (Daly, 2007a, 2007b).

Narrative Analysis

Narrative analysis serves the purpose of providing a means to gain insight into the active construction of meaning-making of others, and the processes of their sense-making (Bamberg, 2012). For custodians of the story, narrative analysis affords us the opportunity to move beyond surface-level accounts and restorying. There is an expectation with this analysis approach to dig below the surface in order to fully explore and identify the perspectives, motivations, values, and emotions of others in order to gain a "deeper understanding of the data that have been gathered" (Braun & Clarke, 2013, p. 174; Fivush & Merrill, 2016). As custodians, we are in a position to not only give more consideration to the stories collected and shared by others, but to give consideration to these the stories, experiences, and environments of others are conveyed or revealed.

In the study of young families, narrative analysis can serve in the examination of a range of aspects of family life, including: family members' perspectives, values, relationships, as well as the meaning-making they associate with the environments in which they spend a significant time. Further, narratives are invaluable for researchers interested in exploring sites of identity (Bamberg & Georgakopoulou, 2008) and matters of positioning that may otherwise remain unnoticed (See Chap. 2 for further details on this topic) . Accordingly, for researchers of young families, narrative analysis serves as a critical strategy in affording for the identities of the storytellers to emerge. This is achieved by paying close attention to how individuals and groups actively position themselves, as well as their understandings of how they may be positioned by others.

An important aspect of narrative analysis is a focus on how the narrative is constructed, cognisant that 'the story' is a representation of a person's life, experiences, values and cultural norms, and context at a given moment in time. The focus of narrative analysis can be approached by studying how others make sense of their experiences, events, and contexts, or in terms of different extensions of time. However, others have chosen to focus on broader narrative practices, such as examining the spatial sequences for "organizing and perceiving human action" (Hyvärinen, 2008, p. 455). Finally, another lens in which to analyse stories is by exploring how others' identity evolve across time and place, and within contexts (Daly, 2007a). The focus of this analysis may, or may not, include the main themes that emerge in the sense-making of the individual, familied experiences, or through the lens of their ecological or 'temporal structures' (Daly, 2007a).

Fivush and Merrill (2016) outline the employment of an ecological systems approach to family narrative. Fivush and Merrill (2016) drew from an established ecological systems approach for making sense of the data, because of the value this framework placed on "family narratives at the juncture of the individual and culture" (p. 306). They continue by pointing out that "an ecological systems approach to family narratives provides a coherent framework for understanding how various types of family narratives are shared and brought into the individual's developing identity and well-being" (p. 312).

For custodians of the story, the use of ecological frameworks is powerful in terms of providing a lens for focussing attention on the restorying, and by locating these stories in context. However, it also offers custodians opportunities to focus the lens on the embedded 'layers of ecological niches' that exist in lived experiences, storied lives, and environments in which families move and live, and the idiosyncratic nature of these niches (Fivush & Merrill, 2016). Finally, adopting an ecological framework helps ensure that the narrative accounts of the family are "embedded within social and cultural systems that inform and infuse every interaction", as well as their meaning-making (Fivush & Merrill, 2016, p. 307).

The Importance of Staying True to the Vision of the Study

As essential as it is to use and learn from the established analysis methods, frameworks, and tools, there may be times when existing and traditional analytic approaches may not align or be consistent with the paradigmatic positioning of the researcher, or the requirements of a study. Attempting to embrace such methods may, in fact, be like trying to fit a square peg into a round hole, in terms of being ineffective in helping to make sense of data or offer strategies for gaining insight into the questions an inquiry seeks to investigate, At these times, it is important that researchers stay true to their vision, and not lose sight of the focus and goals of their inquiry.

For custodians of the story, decisions for whether to adopt a traditional lens to data analysis, or new and innovative methods, call on us to consider how to best stay true to the stories of others. This usually means locating oneself in a brave space, a space where we are able to stand back and consider issues such as social justice, power, privilege, and the agency and voice of others (Arao & Clemens, 2013; hooks, 1994). In doing so, hopefully the decisions we make are based on the importance we place on dialogical narratives that reflect respectful and humanising relationships with others (Bergold & Thomas, 2012; Harden et al., 2010). Along these lines, Gersick (2016) suggests that it is "a mistake to be intimidated by precedent" (p. 331). She advocates for qualitative researchers being "open to new discoveries", and inventive with their analysis process (p. 331).

Of course, in doing so, Gersick (2016) points out, in reference to her own experience, that this process is not necessarily one of 'taking the easy road', and quite possibly will require a lot of trial, error, and discovery. An effective approach to adopt at this point may be researchers spreading data out; shifting it around; circling and highlighting key themes, words, and phrases; and summarising ideas, as well as making continual notes and comments of what they see, and their sense-making.

Like a detective may put together their notes to solve a case, and spread these multiple notes all over a wall or whiteboard, researchers may wish to adopt a similar style of approach, in efforts to map out a visual data display of their findings (Gersick, 2016). The emergence of an innovative analysis method may also occur through the process of drawing upon, and testing out one's own ideas and meaning-making, along with conversations with peers and co-researchers. Of course, it is important to note that in adopting an innovative approach to analysis, it will still be important to identify the theory and research that has inspired or informed this approach. This will include providing a strong rationale for the chosen approach including the adopted approach supporting the purposes, integrity, and idiosyncratic nature of the study.

7.5   Deciding Which Stories to Tell and How to Tell Them

We circle back at this point in the chapter to revisit the issue that many of us face regarding which stories to tell, and how to present the data, particularly the importance of revisiting the role of being custodians of the story. This includes care being taken to present a "faithful rendition" of our encounters and to not lose sight of the integrity of these materials and stories (Warr, 2004, p. 579).

For example, decisions will need to be made about how to assess the value and usefulness of these stories (our data), and consider ways that these narratives might be synthesised and shaped in an attempt to retain the integrity, complexity, and nuances of the stories (Daly, 2007a). Care will also need to be taken to represent our findings in ways which are not devoid of "context", or "empty of people, feeling and experience", but which attempt to bring "concepts into a relationship with the messiness of ordinary life" (Willis, 2000, p. xi). Further, in our efforts to capture the social worlds, and to tell the stories of others, researchers may also wish to consider how they might situate these stories and findings.

Warr (2004) writes about this task requiring the preservation of "situational details", and the stories of others, in efforts to preserve the contextual information, and capture the richness and complexity of our research encounters (p. 579). Others, such as Flyvbjerg (2006), refer to this approach as capturing context-dependent details of people's lives, and the experiences and contexts which frame them. In doing so, we present these stories in ways which intensify important elements and experiences of others, in efforts to capture the emotion, feelings, and sensations of participants, as well as providing rich contextual details of the environments, or places in which participants are embedded and positioned (Warr, 2004).

Researchers may wish to approach the process of restorying by selecting data that will provide a context-dependent understanding of a phenomenon (Stake, 2010). Researchers achieve this by drawing on different types of data they have collected, such as observations, photodocumentation, and interviews. This approach might include a combination of extracts of direct quotes of others, and balance this with rich contextual details in which these stories were situated and the voices of others were positioned. Our efforts to restory will also need to attempt to capture the meaning-making and deliberations of others in ways which are authentic and respectful.

For example, in my doctoral thesis I was intrinsically interested in the situated nature of human behaviour (Brown, 2012). As such, it was important that the analysis and presentation of parents' stories were organised in such a way that others could relate to the people and contexts vicariously (Mills, Durepos, & Wiebe, 2010). So as well as capturing the stories and context of each family in the form of dedicated chapter in my thesis, I also integrated a range of what I referred to as 'heartfelt stories' (Brown, 2012; Dey, 1993; Warr, 2004).

Drawing on my personal and sensory experiences allowed me to tell a different, more personal type of narrative of individual contexts. This included seeing the delight in the eyes of Helen, Tom, and Sarah Mason, walking and playing with their dogs in the local park, or the fear in the eyes of the Calming family as they talked about their concern in leaving their children play in the backyard without supervision, or the wonderful family atmosphere and valuing of family time shared that came across so strongly in the Hampton family (Brown, 2012). Note, I have included a number of these stories already in the text, so will not include another at this point.

These 'heartfelt stories' linked closely to the axiological perspective and frame in which my study was positioned, which viewed parents through a 'strength-based lens'. As such, parents were recognised as a child's first teacher, and as playing a critical role in influencing children, and supporting secure attachments, healthy behaviours, values, and participation in active play (Campbell et al., 2008; Spurrier, Magarey, Golley, Curnow, & Sawyer, 2008). This step in the analysis process required me to reread the original transcriptions, and rather than adopting an approach similar to that of a reporter, discussing facts from a distance, there was a need to adopt a more personal lens to capture a very individual and 'real side' of each family's approach to supporting active play.

7.6 Conclusion

There is great responsibility associated with being custodians of the stories, including making choices for how we make sense of the stories we have, and how these stories are then shared with others. As highlighted in this chapter, this task goes far beyond simply coding or clustering data into themes. It calls on a particular type of commitment, which includes thinking deeply about the types of stories we wish to share, and the messages we wish to convey.

Given the variety of ways for making sense of data, custodians may be tempted or are at risk of falling into the trap of choosing a safe and easily accessed analytical option. Yet, if we are to take our role seriously, great consideration needs to be given to the rationale behind, and effectiveness of, the approach or framework we choose to adopt to retell the stories of others (Sandelowski, 1991). This same level of consideration will also need to be given to the ways we re-represent the stories of others, how these stories might portray a strong image of the other, and present a powerful message of their contexts, lived experiences, and life events.

References

Arao, B., & Clemens, K. (2013). From safe spaces to brave spaces: A new way to frame dialogue around diversity and social justice. In L. Landreman (Ed.), *The art of effective facilitation: Reflections from social justice educators* (pp. 135–150). Sterling, VA: Stylus Publishing.

Baird, K. (2013). Exploring a methodology with young children: Reflections on using the Mosaic and Ecocultural approaches. *Australasian Journal of Early Childhood, 38*(1), 35–40.

Bamberg, M. (2012). Narrative analysis. In H. Cooper (Ed.), *APA handbook of research methods in psychology* (Vol. 2). Washington, DC: American Psychological Association.

Bamberg, M., & Georgakopoulou, A. (2008). Small stories as a new perspective in narrative and identity analysis. *Text & Talk, 28*(3), 377–396.

Berg, B. (2016). *Qualitative research methods for the social sciences* (9th ed.). Boston: Pearson.

Bergold, J., & Thomas, S. (2012). Participatory research methods: A methodological approach in motion. *Historical Social Research/Historische Sozialforschung, 13*(1), 191–222.

Braun, V., & Clarke, V. (2006). Using thematic analysis in psychology. *Qualitative Research in Psychology, 3*(2), 77–101.

Braun, V., & Clarke, V. (2013). *Successful qualitative research: A practical guide for beginners.* Thousand Oaks, CA: Sage.

Brown, A. (2012). *The new frontier: A social ecological exploration of factors impacting on parental support for the active play of young children within the micro-environment of the family home.* PhD, University of Southern Queensland, Toowoomba, QLD.

Campbell, K., Hesketh, K., Crawford, D., Salmon, J., Ball, K., & McCallum, Z. (2008). The infant feeding activity and nutrition trial (INFANT) an early intervention to prevent childhood obesity: Cluster-randomised controlled trial. *Bio Med Central, 8*(103), 1–9.

Clandinin, J. (2007). *Handbook of narrative inquiry: Mapping a methodology.* Thousand Oaks, CA: Sage.

Clandinin, J., Huber, J., Menan, J., Murphy, M., & Swanson, C. (2016). Narrative inquiry: Conducting research in early childhood. In A. Farrell, S. Kagan, & E. Tisdall (Eds.), *The Sage handbook of early childhood research* (pp. 240–254). Los Angeles: Sage.

Clark, A., & Moss, P. (2001). *Listening to young children: The Mosaic approach.* London: National Children's Bureau for the Joseph Rowntree Foundation.

Clark, A., & Moss, P. (2011). *Listening to young children: The Mosaic approach* (2). London: National Children's Bureau and Joseph Rowntree Foundation.

Creswell, J. (2013). *Qualitative inquiry and research design: Choosing among five approaches* (3rd ed.). London: Sage.

Daly, K. J. (2007a). Analytical strategies. In K. J. Daly (Ed.), *Qualitative methods for family studies and human development* (pp. 209–242). Thousand Oaks, CA: Sage.

Daly, K. J. (2007b). *Qualitative methods for family studies and human development.* Thousand Oaks, CA: Sage.

Denzin, N., & Lincoln, N. (Eds.). (2011). *The Sage handbook of qualitative research* (4th ed.). Thousand Oaks, CA: Sage.

Denzin, N., & Lincoln, N. (2017). *The Sage handbook of qualitative research* (5th ed.). Thousand Oaks, CA: Sage.

Denzin, N. K., Lincoln, Y. S., & Smith, L. T. (Eds.). (2008). *Handbook of critical and indigenous methodologies.* Thousand Oaks, CA: Sage.

Dey, I. (1993). *Qualitative data analysis: A user-friendly guide for social scientists.* London: Routledge.

Dockett, S., Perry, B., Kearney, E., Hamshire, A., Mason, J., & Schmied, V. (2009). Researching with families: Ethical issues and situations. *Contemporary Issues in Early Childhood, 10*(4), 353–365.

Eisner, W. (1998). *The enlightened eye: Qualitative inquiry and the enhancement of educational practice.* Upper Saddle River, NJ: Merrill.

Elliott, R., & Timula, L. (2008). Descriptive and interpretive approaches to qualitative research. In J. Miles & P. Gilbert (Eds.), *A handbook of research methods for clinical and health psychology* (pp. 147–159). Oxford, UK: Oxford University Press.

Elsbach, K. D., & Kramer, R. M. (2016). *Handbook of qualitative organizational research: Innovative pathways and methods.* New York: Routledge.

Fiese, B. (2013). Family context in early childhood. In O. Saracho & B. Spodek (Eds.), *Handbook of research on the education of young children* (3rd ed., pp. 369–384). New York: Routledge.

Fivush, R., & Merrill, N. (2016). An ecological systems approach to family narratives. *Memory Studies, 9*(3), 305–314.

Flyvbjerg, B. (2006). Five misunderstandings about case-study research. *Qualitative Inquiry, 12*(2), 219–245.

Fraser, H. (2004). Doing narrative research analysing personal stories line by line. *Qualitative Social Work, 3*(2), 179–201.

Gabb, J. (2010). Home truths: Ethical issues in family research. *Qualitative Research, 10*(4), 461–478.

Gale, N. K., Heath, G., Cameron, E., Rashid, S., & Redwood, S. (2013). Using the framework method for the analysis of qualitative data in multi-disciplinary health research. *BMC Medical Research Methodology, 13*(1), 117.

Gersick, C. (2016). Adventures in qualitative research. In K. D. Elsbach & R. M. Kramer (Eds.), *Handbook of qualitative organizational research: Innovative pathways and methods* (pp. 311–317). New York: Routledge.

Grbich, C. (2004). *New approaches in social research*. London: Sage.

Grbich, C. (2007). *Qualitative data analysis: An Introduction*. London: Sage.

Gubrium, J., Holstein, J., Marvasti, A., & McKinney, K. (2012). *The Sage handbook of interview research: The complexity of craft*. Thousand Oaks, CA: Sage.

Guest, G., MacQueen, K. M., & Namey, E. E. (2011). *Applied thematic analysis*. Thousand Oaks, CA: Sage.

Hampton, R., & Toombs, M. (2013). Culture, identity and Indigenous Australian people. In R. Hampton & M. Toombs (Eds.), *Indigenous Australians and health: The wombat in the room* (pp. 3–23). South Melbourne, VIC: Oxford University Press.

Harcourt, D., & Einarsdóttir, J. (2011). Introducing children's perspectives and participation in research. *European Early Childhood Education Research Journal, 19*(3), 301–307.

Harden, J., Backett-Milburn, K., Hill, M., & MacLean, A. (2010). Oh, what a tangled web we weave: Experiences of doing 'multiple perspectives' research in families. *International Journal of Social Research Methodology, 13*(5), 441–452.

hooks, b. (1994). *Teaching to transgress: Education as the practice of freedom*. New York: Routledge.

Hyvärinen, M. (2008). Analyzing narratives and story-telling. In P. Alasuutari, L. Bickman, & J. Brannen (Eds.), *The Sage handbook of social research methods* (pp. 447–460). Los Angeles: Sage.

Kim, J. (2016). *Understanding narrative inquiry: The crafting and analysis of stories as research*. Thousand Oaks, CA: Sage.

King, N., & Horrocks, C. (2010). *Interviews in qualitative research* (1st ed.). Los Angeles: Sage.

Kiser, L. J., Baumgardner, B., & Dorado, J. (2010). Who are we, but for the stories we tell: Family stories and healing. *Psychological Trauma: Theory, Research, Practice, and Policy, 2*(3), 243–249.

Mannion, G. (2007). Going spatial, going relationational: Why "listening to children" and children's participation needs reframing. *Discourse: Studies in the Cultural Politics of Education, 28*(3), 405–420.

Mason, J. (2018). *Qualitative researching* (3rd ed.). London: Sage.

Matua, G., & Van Der Wal, D. (2015). Differentiating between descriptive and interpretive phenomenological research approaches. *Nurse Researcher, 22*(6), 22–27.

Merriam, S., & Tisdall, E. (2016). *Qualitative research: A guide to design and implementation* (4th ed.). San Francisco: Jossey-Bass.

Miles, M., Chapman, Y., & Francis, K. (2015). Peeling the onion: Understanding others' lived experience. *Contemporary Nurse, 50*(2–3), 286–295.

Miles, M., Huberman, M., & Saldana, J. (2014). *Qualitative data analysis: A methods sourcebook* (3rd ed.). Thousand Oaks, CA: Sage.

Mills, A., Durepos, G., & Wiebe, E. (Eds.). (2010). *Encyclopedia of case study research*. Thousand Oaks, CA: Sage.

O'Connor, J., & Brown, A. (2013). A qualitative study of 'fear' as a regulator of children's independent physical activity in the suburbs. *Health & Place, 24*, 157–164. Retrieved from https://doi.org/10.1016/j.healthplace.2013.09.002i

Sandelowski, M. (1991). Telling stories: Narrative approaches in qualitative research. *Journal of nursing scholarship, 23*(3), 161–166.

Snilstveit, B., Oliver, S., & Vojtkova, M. (2012). Narrative approaches to systematic review and synthesis of evidence for international development policy and practice. *Journal of Development Effectiveness, 4*(3), 409–429.

Spurrier, N., Magarey, A., Golley, R., Curnow, F., & Sawyer, M. (2008). Relationships between the home environment and physical activity and dietary patterns of preschool children: A cross-sectional study. *International Journal of Behavioral Nutrition and Physical Activity, 5*(31), 1–12.

Stake, R. (2003). Case studies. In N. Denzin & Y. Lincoln (Eds.), *Strategies of qualitative inquiry* (pp. 134–164). Thousand Oaks, CA: Sage.

Stake, R. (2010). *Qualitative research: Studying how things work.* New York: Guilford Press.

Stake, R. (2013). *Multiple case study analysis.* New York: Guilford Press.

Stokols, D., Grzywacz, J., McMahan, S., & Phillips, K. (2003). Increasing the health promotive capacity of human environments. *American Journal of Health Promotion, 18*(1), 4–13.

Sutton, J., & Austin, Z. (2015). Qualitative research: Data collection, analysis, and management. *The Canadian Journal of Hospital Pharmacy, 68*(3), 226–231.

Tisdall, K., Davis, J. M., & Gallagher, M. (2008). *Researching with children and young people: Research design, methods and analysis.* Thousand Oaks, CA: Sage.

Walter, M. (Ed.). (2013). *Social research methods* (3rd ed.). Melbourne, VIC: Oxford University Press.

Warr, D. (2004). Stories in the flesh and voices in the head: Reflections on the context and impact of research with disadvantaged populations. *Qualitative Health Research, 14*(4), 578–587.

Willis, P. (2000). *The ethnographic imagination.* Cambridge, UK: Polity Press.

8

Forging Frontiers—Reframing, Methodological Innovation, and Possibilities for Research with, and of, Young Families

"And so she forges towards the new frontier, although confident, she steps tentatively, for little does she know what is to become of her."
(Brown, 2008, p. 152)

Chapter Synopsis

Those willing to break new ground, face new challenges, explore unchartered waters, or extend their research into spaces defined as 'innovative' do so willingly, with the understanding that they will be moving out of a safe space into a brave space. Such practices may require individuals to take a risk, to seize an opportunity, to look at a problem differently, or to be prepared to challenge established research practices, paradigms, and perspectives. Yet, with a clarity of vision, those who choose to venture down this unworn path do so with the belief that what they are doing is important and necessary, if they are to more effectively understand a problem, a phenomenon; to embrace more inclusive practices; or to achieve a particular research goal.

© The Author(s) 2019   **259**
A. Brown, *Respectful Research With and About Young Families*, Palgrave Studies in
Education Research Methods, https://doi.org/10.1007/978-3-030-02716-2_8

How might innovative inquiry lead to changing dominant modernist discourse, or positive social change for minority, marginalised, or disenfranchised families whose voices have traditionally been silenced?

How might innovation in reframing social ecological frameworks translate to more fully accounting for the contextual nuances of factors that exist within young families and impact on their practice and behaviours?

How might innovative practice pay closer attention to ways in which to engage in humanising relationships with young families?

Evidenced in the many pages of this book are examples of researchers prepared to undertake such endeavours; researchers willing to reframe, or think otherwise about practice; researchers ready to take on a challenge, and in doing so have 'forged methodological frontiers'. For example, Django Paris (2011) writes, "We can be friends with our participants. We can, in small ways, come to understand. We can inspire them as they inspire us. We can humanize through the act of research" (p. 147). In these words, Paris (2011) illustrates efforts to reframe and adopt a different lens that challenges us to shift our thinking about 'the other', and the impact this thinking may have on our approach to inquiry.

Examples such as Paris's view on humanising research, while appearing deceptively simple with the mention of just a few words on a page, can in fact have a profound impact on those open to listening, to learning, and for being prepared to approach research with an open mind. Researchers, inspired by ideas and perspectives, such as those shared by Paris (2011, 2014) on humanising research, may potentially give more thought to the level of family involvement, and participant engagement in research; or may give greater consideration to aspects such as power differential, or the degree of participant agency evidenced in inquiry.

Those willing to engage in the important process of reflexivity, focussed on questioning and adapting their existing practices, are in a strong position for innovative methodological approaches to emerge—practices that may potentially disrupt the status quo, and in doing so afford for more respectful and effective ways to understand families. Further, researchers challenged, or inspired by the likes of Bermúdez, Muruthi, and Jordan (2016), may be motivated to reframe the type of inquiry adopted, to reframe the image of the other, or to more deeply consider the footprint or potential legacy that they leave when an inquiry is complete. 'Custodians of the story', open to exploring new ideas and perspectives, may be motivated to present a stronger image of the other, through the ways in which stories are communicated and conveyed.

For those committed to better understanding the lived experiences, environments, and perspectives of young families, this chapter offers a final opportunity within this text to peek into the future of the innovative and contemporary ideas, research practices, and methodological approaches currently on the radar; an opportunity to consider how the ideas shared on these final pages may have application to existing research methods, and approaches; an opportunity to see the possibilities and potentialities for how future inquiry with young families may be reframed and conducted.

8.1   Retracing Our Tracks

To embark on a task such as that of reframing practice, or deeply considering one's existing approach to inquiry, is no easy feat. Nor is it necessarily the most comfortable, or easy, path to travel down. However, innovative practice often requires a certain level of discomfort and openness, and a willingness to take a risk. It may even require some of us to work within and negotiate through brave spaces, where there may be the need to adapt existing methodological approaches or practice, or invent new ways of doing research with young families.

For those up to the challenge, there is the opportunity to engage in a different type of inquiry that can be potentially more dialogical, or to consider more equitable distributions of power—inquiry that might challenge prevailing and dominant discourse. There is an opportunity for researchers to give greater consideration to the very privileged position that we are in, in terms of families allowing us entry into their domestic spaces, and entrusting us with their life stories, and the implications this has on the methodological approaches we employ.

Interpretivist researchers of young families have a passionate commitment to gain insights into the narratives and lifeworld of family members, and their behaviours, practices, perspectives, and environments. There is also the genuine intent of affording individuals with the opportunity to share their perspectives on issues which impact on their lives, and on matters which concern them (McCarthy, Doolittle, & Schlater, 2012). Further, it is the vision of many scholars who choose to research within an innovative space that, directly or indirectly, their findings will make a difference to the individuals at the heart of an inquiry (Greenstein & Davis, 2013).

The Importance of Being Open to the Possibilities

In the complex and shifting landscapes in which social research is positioned, there is an increasing need for researchers to listen, to learn and taking inspiration from the work of others, and to be prepared to challenge established practices, methodologies, and discourse. This could mean seeking to better understand and consider the implications that decolonisation and humanising perspectives have on inquiry with young families, or to more deeply consider the implications that adopting critical feminist, post-structuralist, or indigenous methodologies and knowledge constructs might have on inquiry (Foster & Young, 2015; Greenstein & Davis, 2013; Palaiologou, 2014; Pascal & Bertram, 2012; Tuck, 2016).

Those willing to question or challenge existing ways of knowing and doing are in a unique position to potentially look at, explore, or investigate phenomenon, environments, or the relationships that we have with participants through a different lens. The results of such efforts may potentially lead to an increased awareness and sensitivity to the legacy of colonising inquiry. Or, inspire researchers' to engage in methodological approaches which deeply and authentically embed practices of respect, social justice, and democracy. Quite often, the goal of these endeavours is to afford for a greater level of dialogical practice, while also being cognisant of participants' rights and agency (Paris, 2011).

For example, those open to adopting a strengths-based perspective in which to position their research may choose to reframe the lens through which a phenomenon is viewed. Others may be inclined to reshape the goals and questions of an inquiry, where greater emphasis is placed on uncovering the potentials and strengths of a phenomenon, rather than focussing solely on deficits. Or, as a result of researchers choosing to work within a social ecological paradigm, methodological practices may have the potential to harness the knowledge, insight, and meaning-making that family members bring with them to the research relationship (Harden, Backett-Milburn, Hill, & MacLean, 2010). Others who choose to embrace methodological practices that reflect dignity, respect, and value the knowledge of young families may potentially enter these spaces more humbly, with a heightened sensitivity of the other (Bermúdez et al., 2016; Dockett et al., 2009; McNeil, 2010).

Finally, for 'custodians of the story', there is great potential to engage in innovative practice, which could include a focus on strategies for more effectively re-presenting and co-creating stories with and about others—stories which convey the richness, honour, insight, and diversity of young families (Fiese, 2013; McHale, Booth, & Amato, 2014). Custodians committed to portraying a strong image of 'the other' may set a new precedence in methodological practice, to narratives that convey a powerful a message of respect, possibility, optimism, and hope—stories which thoughtfully reflect, celebrate, and capture the richness and diversity that individuals, groups, and communities bring to the table (Brown, 2012; Dockett et al., 2009; McNeil, 2010; Tesoriero, Boyle, & Enright, 2010).

8.2   Pushing Methodological Boundaries— The Importance of Reframing and Challenging the Normative Yardstick

Restrained by a 'Mindset Myopia'

While the potential for innovative research and pushing the boundaries of existing discourses practices and paradigms may be aspirational, unfortunately 'mindset myopia' is one of the greatest challenges faced by many of today's researchers. Mindset myopia describes the constrained or narrow focus that researchers may experience, or work within, that impacts on their ability to step out of, look beyond what they see in front of them, or the ability to think otherwise. One reason that may account for this phenomenon is individuals being unavoidably positioned, or 'framed' in context, such as epistemological discourse, paradigms, ways of seeing the world, and established ways of knowing (Moss, 2015) (see Chap. 2 for further details on this topic).

The word 'frame', referred to in this instance, is inspired by, and loosely based on, Goffman (1974) and cognitive scientist Lakoff's (2014) work. Lakoff (2004) is known for the example he frequently refers to as 'the elephant frame'. He points out that as soon as we hear the word 'elephant', we automatically have a frame of the elephant that we identify with, which includes being a large animal; having a long trunk, large floppy ears; and living in Africa.

In this text, a frame is understood as a conceptual structure, case, idea, boundary, or context. Each frame has a schema, which includes a range of associated elements that define and create the frame, such as discourse, visual cues, practices, understandings of the frame, values, and metaphors associated with the frame. The characteristics and elements associated with a frame are learned or built up by individuals (as a series of mental filters), through and across context, culture, time, and place. As such, individuals automatically make sense of their world by recalling a frame, and by drawing upon the elements, or the schema associated with the frame, as a 'mental shortcut', when referring to, or interpreting, a frame.

For researchers, these frames are ones which we automatically refer to, and respond with, in defining a problem, or seeing, understanding, and exploring a phenomenon. The associated words and metaphors used in reference to a 'frame' automatically conjure a particular image, or way of approaching an investigation, in our mind. Within a research space, the individuals and groups who join us are also 'framed'. These 'frames' influence the way in which researches view, engage with, and respond to 'the other'.

For example, as interpretivist researchers, we work within an 'interpretivist frame'. This frame has an associated discourse, suggested ways of working, right through to the recommended methods for making sense of research findings, and communicating these findings to others. (See

Chap. 3 dedicated to 'Interpretivism' and its value for unfolding the lives and stories of young families.) As such, it can be difficult, or near-impossible, to move into a creative space, or a space in which innovation can be cultivated if we engage within the existing interpretivist frame unquestionably, or automatically.

Shifting Beyond a 'Mindset Myopia' by Engaging in a Frame Audit

Those researchers interested in shifting beyond a 'mindset myopia' may wish to consider engaging in a frame audit. This process is a way for interrogating the frames which are associated with an anticipated inquiry (see Chap. 2 for further details on this process). A frame audit moves researchers through a process of raised consciousness of the frames which they are currently positioned (Paris & Winn, 2014). This includes taking stock of the frames which exist, and are embedded in the spaces in which an inquiry will conducted, as well as considering the frames in which the other may be positioned. Engaging in a frame audit offers researchers an opportunity to point a critical lens on the impact that existing frames have on themselves, and the other (Darder, 2015; Milner, 2007). An increased awareness of these frames offer the researcher an opportunity to make a conscious decision as to whether to continue working within, and accepting these frames, or to 'reframe'.

'Reframing'—A Strategy for Opening Up Innovation and Creative Potential

For researchers seeking to engage in methodological innovation with young families, 'reframing' can be an effective strategy. Reframing has the potential to shift inquiry from automatically defaulting to an existing way of working and seeing the world, to one that seeks to question the existing frames that bind us. This is achieved by challenging the elements located within an existing frame, and disrupting normative discourse and existing research practices, approaches, and methodologies.

The conscious choice to reframe potentially moves the researcher into a creative space, in turn unlocking the door to new research spaces new ways of seeing problems, rethinking research questions, right through to seeing a whole new set of possibilities and solutions for investigating a problem (Seelig, 2011). Engaging in the act of reframing triggers researchers to explore alternative forms of knowledge and ways of theorising about young families. Reframing can expand the possibilities and potentialities for engaging with families in and of context, with the possibility of leading to more emancipatory results, or as a powerful vehicle for activism, by purposely reframing the other.

Moving Through a Process of Reframing

One effective strategy for those wishing to reframe is to identify existing discourse (words, phrases, language) associated with a frame, and then to reframe by purposely changing the discourse and using a new or nuanced discourse. This may include the conscious intent of adopting, consistently embedding, and integrating a different set of words into the inquiry process. For example, the words adopted could purposefully capture the way in which participants and practice are framed as part of an inquiry.

In introducing and consistently employing an adapted or new discourse, when referring to, engaging in research, and when communicating our research to others, we purposely reframe and covertly influence and alter existing frames. For example, Seelig (2011) shares an analogy of 'planning for a birthday party'. She points out that these words automatically conjure up particular set of default practices and images in our mind, about what the practice and behaviours of planning for the party might look like. An example of 'expanding the frame' is then shared, where Seelig (2011) suggests that rather than planning for a birthday 'party', that we plan for a birthday 'celebration'. The replacement of 'party' with the word 'celebration' automatically changes the frame reference point in our minds, as well as different set of images, and associated processes, practices, and behaviours.

Lakoff (2004, 2014) points out that a metaphor, or a set of metaphors, are often associated with the frame, or when describing a frame. As such, for those wishing to reframe, a powerful approach is to adopt and employ a different metaphor, or a set of metaphors. If approached thoughtfully, consistently, and authentically, efforts to introduce and embed a new metaphor has the potential to effectively, and covertly, increase our own consciousness of the new frame, or altered frame. The new metaphor may also effectively impact on others ways of seeing, and evoke a new imagery of the frame we wish to create.

Another strategy to support reframing is one which Seelig (2011) refers to as the ability to reframe the problem and the question. Seelig points out that by engaging in the process of looking at a problem differently, we increase the potential to unlock an array of creative solutions. This requires researchers to engage in the practice of looking at the problem, or phenomenon from a range of different angles (i.e. to pan in and pan out, to pan left and pan right). In doing so, researchers have the potential to open up the frame, in turn reframing not only the questions we ask, but also the problem we choose to focus on. Looking at a problem from different angles also extends the possibility for ways in which to explore the problem, and conduct an inquiry.

Examples of Reframing

There are many examples of researchers who demonstrated efforts to reframe practice, and who have, in their own ways, sought to break methodological boundaries. For example, researchers who have challenged traditional research practice focussed on 'children as users of services', 'children's voice', and 'child participation in the context of children's health, education and welfare (Mannion, 2007). Or, researchers who have demonstrated efforts to reframe inquiry practices by introducing a new lens, a new set of elements, a new approach, such as moving from 'family-centred care' to 'child-centred care', or a new paradigm based on associated philosophy and discourse (Coyne, Hallström, & Söderbäck, 2016).

The work of Reid (2013) and her team illustrates this type of practice. Over a period of 18 years, their team have focussed on reframing and rethinking practice, in order to better reflect a person-centred approach, and a more 'whole of child' philosophy. This resulted in more interdisciplinary work; and promoting 'innovation in data collection methodology built around an innovative holiday activity format experienced as fun and games by child participants, rather than as tedious testing', as well as changes to their "data analytic approach to include interest in individual cases as well as group differences" (p. 340).

Reid and her teams' (2013) efforts to reframe and refocus the lens of inquiry meant reconnecting with those at the heart of their inquiry, and efforts to "hold the person at the centre" of their "research thinking" (p. 337). Informed by the framing of a "person-centred perspective", the team were better able to increase researcher interest in "the child's experience of their academic, health or mental health difficulties as well as the experience of their parent and family as a way of contextualising our data" (p. 341). Reframing inquiry to that of "person-centred" influenced the "process, purpose and practices" of their methodologies, how they engaged with their "participant clients", how they collected their data, "illuminated their data" to "to include interest in individual cases as well as group differences" (p. 339).

In another example, Mannion (2007), concerned with the way that the rights of the child were being interpreted and translated into contemporary paradigms and post-structuralist discourse, chose to challenge this paradigm. Mannion noted that existing frames, which included the "discourse of listening", were evidenced and reflected in policy, practice, and research, and had "grave deficiencies" (p. 405). Mannion and his team (2007) attempted to reframe this paradigm, by adopting practice and perspectives where "policy and practice and research on children's participation" were "better framed as being fundamentally about child/adult relations" (p. 405).

A 'frame audit' ensued, with Mannion (2007) arguing that in order to reframe, it was first important to put under the spotlight current practice that relate to 'child as participant', and 'child voice'. The audit included identifying the role that government, organisations, and children's rights agendas, such as United Nations Convention (1989), played in the framing of these terms. What became evident to Mannion (2007), by engaging in this process, was that while researchers and professionals focussed on attending to children's health and welfare, and may have in principle supported the idea of 'child voice', in reality a range of factors such as that of culture, adult interpretations, and adult agendas had the potential to distort child voice, and not match intent with delivery (Mannion, 2007). Mannion (2007) suggested that reframing should include being "more sensitive to how place and space are implicated in identity formation" (p. 410). Finally, others such as Bermúdez, et. al. (2016) are challenging understandings of "involvement" in terms of "troubling interpretations of family", beyond the normative yardstick of traditional, and or Western-centric perspectives (p. 197), instead seeking to reframe practice by going beyond colonising views of 'family' in inquiry. In these ways, the intent is to advance theory and practice in ways that seek to challenge traditional frames of family research, to research that could potentially involve different types of families that go beyond the nuclear family.

Reframing participant involvement has so much potential to open up new ways of inquiry, inquiry that can generate more productive and transformative understandings, and pay closer attention to relationships with others, as well as authentic consideration to the inclusion of 'voice', and 'agency'. Such efforts require reexamining and reevaluating existing axiological perspectives, established regimes of truths, and dominant discourse, and moving beyond simply descriptive, prescriptive, and surface-level participant involvement. Such a task also requires researchers adopting an approach to inquiry that reframes participants in a more positive and empowering light, or reframes inquiry in ways that have the potential to generate more productive and transformative understandings and relationships with others, perhaps even engaging in inquiry that seeks to investigate the "micro-ethical dimensions" of participant involvement, and scrutinise notions such as power, and participant agency (Guillemin & Gillam, 2004, p. 278; Palaiologou, 2014).

8.3 The Value of Embeddedness and Recognition of Context

Regardless of what else we do during our time on this planet we do one thing fully and uniquely: we live our life. And we live it in context. (Ricci, 2003, p. 593)

As Stokols (2018) points out in his current writing on social ecology, 'in the digital age', the world that we live in now sees great complexity between 'people's relationships with their environments'. This reference to ecological complexity recognises that the reach of factors that sit within ecological systems extends far beyond the virtual wall of the micro-environments that contemporary families are located and move within, with each family evidencing their own idiosyncratic diversity and contextual nuances (Brown, 2012; Brown, Stokols, Sallis, Hiatt, & Orleans, 2013). As such, in this final chapter on 'forging frontiers and methodological innovation', it would be remiss of me not to include a section on the important place that 'pervasiveness of context' has in future research with young families. This includes the necessity of researchers seeking alternative methodologies and frameworks for understanding family life, and the intersections that exist with history, identity, culture, community, and context (Uttal, 2009, p. 141). Such an interpretation of 'context' is rooted in a particular way of thinking of social practices, beliefs, and values, all of which are integrally linked to systems, and of humans moving within and amongst the immediate microsystem, broader systems, and milieu of people's everyday lives, as well as through and across time.

Taking inspiration from pioneers and early adopters, such as Stokols (1992, 1996, 2018), and Binder (1972) and Binder, Stokols and Catalano (1975), there are opportunities for innovative practice, for those willing to challenge and extend on dominant frameworks, or willing to pursue investigations to explore the bi-directional influence that context and social practices have on family life and human behaviour. There is great potential for researchers ready to explore alternative methodologies that are more effective in understanding the contextual embeddedness of phenomena. Others may choose to investigate methods that are effective in better understanding and accounting for the connectedness of individuals to their community, history, kinship networks, and ancestry "both past and present", and "interwoven through intergenerational systems of belief, history, tradition, and relational processes" (Bermúdez et al., 2016, p. 198; McCubbin, McCubbin, Zhang, Kehl, & Strom, 2013).

Taking inspiration from the art of cartography, and infinite possibilities of maps to represent place, ground-breaking research and practice may emerge from those motivated to explore ways to adapt ecological frameworks to more effectively account for the locatedness of families within contexts and systems. Others may choose to adapt models in ways robust enough to account for the ecological niche of the family environment, the complexity of determining factors that impact on behaviour, practices, and values. For some, creativity might emerge from the necessity to gain greater insight into the idiosyncratic micro-context of families, including the unique set of conditions and circumstances that operate on, and are embedded in, the lives of family members, and that give meaning to their thoughts and actions. These are only some of the possibilities for innovation in the area of social ecology and research with young families for those willing to challenge existing ecological frameworks in order to better account for the holistic nature of human behaviour.

While these endeavours may sound, or appear, ambitious, the result for those committed to working within these brave and innovated spaces will be the opportunity to gain greater insight into the unique set of ecological factors that can influence family practices, behaviours, and values—*the New Frontier*. As a result, research findings have the potential to contribute to strategically targeting the specific factors that impact on a phenomenon, and improving the health, wellbeing, and positive outcomes for children, and their families (Brown, 2009; Stokols, Grzywacz, McMahan, & Phillips, 2003). Innovative practice in the field of social ecology has the potential to identify critical leverage points, enabling support services and multiple stakeholders from different sectors to adopt a more targeted approach to working with young families to build collective capital.

8.4   Towards Decolonisation and Humanising Inquiry

Adopting a decolonising or humanising lens to inquiry offers an opportunity for researchers to consider alternative ways in which to engage in inquiry (Zavala, 2013). Researchers may be motivated to pay closer attention to individual rights and choice, as well as methodological approaches. This could include affording participants more equitable levels of input into all aspects of an inquiry, from identifying the focus and process for the inquiry, right through to the ownership of the data, and how the findings may be shared with others (Bermúdez et al., 2016). Others may seek to engage in practice that pays closer attention to ways in which to engage in humanising relationships with young families; or to embed authentic decolonising and humanising practices in ways that can potentially shift the legacy of modernist discourse and definitions of family, family values, and behaviours; or explore ways in which restorying can be embraced as an instrument for social change. For some, innovation may emerge framing inquiry in ways that reflect respect, dignity, and care. This paradigm could translate to a raised consciousness for 'the other', including greater consideration given to the ways we enter and engage with others in domestic spaces. Great consideration could also be given to those who may have already experienced marginalisation and disenfranchisement historically, as a ramification of engaging in social research (Brown & Danaher, 2017; Gabb, 2010; Paris, 2011).

For 'custodians of the story', motivated to embrace humanising and decolonising agendas, there are opportunities to construct narratives in ways which challenge traditional binaries. Others may seek out opportunities to challenge 'deficit discourse', commonly adopted to describe or frame young families (such as 'oppressed', or 'needy') (Swadener & Mutua, 2008). Custodians may potentially adopt a different form of storying that purposely shifts the lens off a colonising discourse, to narratives which reflect and celebrate the dignity and identity of the other—stories which intentionally reframe young families by celebrating their lived history, shared history, alternative views, perspectives, and representations (Bermúdez et al., 2016).

There is also the potential of innovation to emerge from researchers motivated to apply humanising and decolonising epistemologies to reexamine and rethink 'child voice', and the place of the voice of children, particularly young children in research with young families (Clark, 2011; Mannion, 2007). This includes researchers willing to work within a brave space that challenges existing practice and discourse on children's participation and involvement in decision-making, or researchers willing to explore methodologies and research tools that better account for children within families as active agents, important social actors, skilled communicators, and as co-researchers (Bushin, 2009; McDowell, 2015; Pascal & Bertram, 2012).

Others may be inspired by 'participant-centred' methodologies, and how research practices can authentically embed practices that honour and privilege the perspectives and experiences of children (Palaiologou, 2014; Qvortrup, 2005). This may include new research spaces for understanding how young families construct and engage in their social worlds, or research agendas that better account for the capacity of children as "competent interpreters of their everyday" (Mason & Danby, 2011, p. 186). Such an agenda may include implementing methodologies that better afford for child voice and perspectives, in order to better understand their place and lived experiences in domestic spaces, and other environments in which young families move. Consequently, there is scope, and innovative potential, to embed rights-based practices throughout the inquiry process to prioritise participant voice (Kellett, 2010), including affordances for co-constructing meaning with all members of young families (Fargas-Malet, McSherry, Larkin, & Robinson, 2010; McTavish, Streelasky, & Coles, 2012).

Future humanising and postcolonial research requires a level of activism, and "an explicit action orientation" focus (Bermúdez et al., 2016, p. 198; Swadener & Mutua, 2008). It is important that these pursuits are grounded in ethical, respectful, and reciprocal practice, and adopt a level of commitment and responsibility for participants that extends beyond the outcomes of inquiry and knowledge production. As such, those endeavouring to engage in innovative inquiry with young families need to give greater consideration to their responsibility in research, including how, as a result of conducting a study, a project has the potential for transformative action (Ishimaru & Bang, 2015). Finally, it is important that researchers are able to provide evidence of how research directly or indirectly can enhance the lives or social context of young families (Shahjahan, 2011). As a result, there is catalytic potential that inquiry offers for social change and for opening up doors "for diversity within social and political systems" (Bermúdez et al., 2016, p. 196).

8.5 Opportunities for Multi-disciplinary and Collaborative Research

Factors that influence the behaviours, values, practices, and 'lived experiences' of young families are diverse, complex, and occur in a dynamic manner. As such, there is a critical imperative in seeking to better understand, effectively work with, and provide targeted support for young families. These types of opportunities, and methodological innovation, emerge from and through collaboration with multiple disciplines.

Collaborations with those from multiple disciplines and areas of expertise have the potential for a more focussed understanding of the dynamics, needs, practices, and behaviours of young families. Innovative multi-disciplinary research with young families opens up opportunities for creating a new paradigms, new ways of working together, and more effective and respectful ways of sharing theories, findings, and productive models for collaboration (Poulton, Moffitt, & Silva, 2015). Further, these ways of working represent unique opportunities to engage in open dialogue, and a process of learning and seeing phenomena through the 'eyes of others'. Multi-disciplinary collaboration affords for new ways of working with, supporting, and strengthening the trajectory of health, development, and children in families. Moving forward, multi-disciplinary research requires agencies, organisations, and researchers from various fields, with a vested interest in young families, to be more strategic of the types of research to target and focus on.

The complexity of contemporary young families requires multipronged and strategic research agendas that have the potential to holistically understand and consider the range of factors influencing parenting and family behaviour. This approach requires the removal of sector-imposed boundaries to afford for more integrated approaches to research with young families. This approach would draw from and incorporate a range of experts and disciplines including professionals such as social workers, the health sector and clinicians, educators, town planning experts, and local government. These types of approaches offer those engaged in inquiry the opportunity to look at problems or a phenomenon from varying perspectives and angles, to identify the existing frames in which they work within, and to draw from extensive and varied expertise, knowledge, and skills (Shonkoff, 2012). For example, instead of working in silos, or competing teams to explore factors that challenge the health and wellbeing of today's young families, valuable insight can potentially emerge from multi-disciplinary discussions and research.

There is also so much potential for creative and innovative multi-disciplinary research with young families to more fully explore and track the results of place-based interventions. This would ideally be informed and build upon existing research and insights (Moore & Fry, 2011; Moore, McDonald, McHugh-Dillon, & West, 2016). However, this approach could also potentially add to the strong body of research informed by a range of research expertise, to offer insight into understandings of effective strategies for building the capacity and skills of parents and significant carers in young families, particularly those in vulnerable communities and adverse living conditions (Moore et al., 2014; Shonkoff, 2017). The benefits of this type of research would see a greater focus on understanding environmental factors that influence families and the home environment implicit within the various systematic levels and multiple interpretations on intervention strategies.

Aligned with a social ecological paradigm, future research considerations may benefit from broadening the scope of the family micro-environment in order to more contextually and comprehensively explore indicators of health and other behaviours of young families (Brown, 2012). There is also potential for future research to investigate other interrelated dimensions of a family's overall wellness orientation. This broader conceptualisation of family research could explore multi-faceted, multi-level conceptualisations of aspects such as family wellness orientations. This type of inquiry would potentially include investigating factors such as physical activity levels, nutritional practices of the family in the home and beyond, emotional tone or climate of the family, safety of the home environment, crime potential, and social capital that exists and could be accessed within communities.

Finally, but just as importantly, multi-disciplinary family research offers great potential for exploring feminist-post-structuralist themes from a range of perspectives and lenses. It is an exciting opportunity of exposing "more mainstream scholars to feminist and gender-sensitive approaches (hooks, 2000)" (Kaestle, 2016, p. 75). Unfortunately, so often, this important research sits within a very specific discipline and set of frames.

As such, adopting a multi-disciplinary approach affords possibilities for identifying and challenging existing frames, approaches to families' scholarship, and entrenched ideologies, in reference to areas such as gender consciousness, social norms, and different types of family, family relationships, and existing power structures (Kaestle, 2016). There is also potential for methodological innovation, for those willing to rethink and reframe traditional social science research in ways that are sensitive to exploring phenomenon such as: 'othering and un-othering'; of 'motherhood' (Henderson, Harmon, & Newman, 2016); fatherhood; and patriarchal ideals (Doucet, 2016; Fulcher, Dinella, & Weisgram, 2015; Swenson & Zvonkovic, 2016). Or sensitive and respectful ways in which inquiry could potentially be framed more inclusively which extend beyond those of 'traditional' family types, to include non-traditional relationships and families, in order to better understand their complexity, and relational contexts (van Eeden-Moorefield, Malloy, & Benson, 2016).

Multi-disciplinary research teams, which include feminist family research, offer the potential for inquiry to explore 'the lived experiences of diverse families in their own right', and to afford for research to cast off "a residual binary structure of normal versus other established by academia's historical embrace of comparative positivist scholarship" (Kaestle, 2016, pp. 72–73). Adopting such an approach creates a unique research space for empowering social change, and the potential to reframe family research, the discourse used, and associated metaphors. Working collaboratively within this paradigm of research with young families, feminist scholars, as well as those from a range of disciplines and areas of expertise, have the potential to act as a force of positive transformative social change, in terms of both the language we use and the way we view, understand, and refer to 'family' (Bermúdez et al., 2016).

8.6   Final Words—Forging Forward, We Are Still Learning

As researchers, we are all still learning, and indeed need to continue to do so, particularly if we are to negotiate and manoeuvre around and through a research space that is shifting feast. It is also increasingly evident that the young families we are researching are positioned, negotiate, and move within dynamic contexts. This is particularly evidenced when we encounter diverse ethical issues, which emerge from different settings, cultures, and the idiosyncratic practices, and domestic environments of young families.

So, in 'forging new frontiers' and forging forward, it is important that as researchers, we are open to new learnings in order to be responsive to these changes. In doing so, we open ourselves up to the potential for fresh thinking to emerge, where creativity and innovation are possible. It is hoped that the words, concepts, and ideas shared in this text have in some way contributed to this learning, and has opened the door a little further to the possibilities and potentialities of ethical and respectful ways to research with, and of, young families.

As raised earlier in this chapter, if we are to challenge what is be deemed 'legitimate knowledge' (hooks, 2000), taken-for-granted assumptions and paradigms, problematise existing methodologies, or push methodological boundaries, we first need to reflect deeply (which may include engaging in a 'frame audit') (Bermúdez et al., 2016). While this process may be tough, or deemed ambitious (Pascal & Bertram, 2009), it may be necessary, particularly if our intent is to expand definitions of family, and to privilege their voices and stories; or to consider more deeply authentic and respectful methodological approaches for better understanding their lived experiences, and the places and domestic spaces in which members of young families are embedded.

As researchers forging forward, there is so much potential to learn from and with others, as well as through experimentation. There is so much more potential to learn about, and explore strategies which better reflect a decolonising agenda, or ways to better represent the voices, cultures, and lived experiences of others, particularly those who have been traditionally ignored or silenced (Bermúdez et al., 2016). There is also potential to learn about, and to explore ways to redistribute, or to decentre traditional positions of power evidenced in social research, or approaches to inquiry.

As we forge forward, there is so much potential for our learning to include ways to engage in more participatory methods, where participants are positioned within, rather than apart from inquiry (Christensen & James, 2008). For researchers brave enough to venture into new and innovative spaces there are opportunities to engage in Strategies that afford for our encounters with young families to be more democratic, more open to dialogue, open to diversity, and open to active listening. To embrace practices that would support inquiry with young families underpinned by ethical praxis that unfolds at all stages of an inquiry (Palaiologou, 2014).

We have the potential for our 'learnings' to position us in new research spaces that better consider ways to engage with, and respond to, young families, their circumstances, their idiosyncrasies, and their diversity, particularly those most vulnerable (Shonkoff & Fisher, 2013). This learning has the potential to extend beyond the goal of simply publishing our findings in peer-reviewed journals. This would include researchers considering more deeply the role they might play as catalysts for transformational thinking, and extend into the other social or ethical responsibilities that research with young families might entail.

As researchers we have so much to learn, and to think more about, in terms of ways in which our contribution to research may help inform strategies for reducing excessive adversity. And, while engaging in such deliberations, perhaps our learnings and ambitions may extend to considering ways in which the interventions and information shared with stakeholders could potentially strengthen the capacities of parents and significant caregivers in young families. This vision extends beyond short-term goals, to more enduring goals, where the intent could potentially include building capacity through, and across the life course.

What becomes evident by being open to this type of learning is the responsibility we have as researchers of young families. For example, 'custodians of the story' that are open to deep reflection might seek to learn more about the implications of the trust that is bestowed upon them, and in the way that the contexts and life stories of others are shared. There is potential to learn so much more about how we might best privilege these stories, and the impact these stories may have not only on participants, but also on others we choose to share these stories with. There is also so much to learn about potential new technologies, new methods, tools, and strategies that may help us in our efforts to better capture, retell, and share these stories.

We are reminded of the words of Daly (2007) that "families are at the center of this changing world, and it is the stance of openness associated with inductive qualitative inquiry that puts us in a strategic position to understand and communicate about these changes" (p. xiii). As such, researchers of young families have so much to learn about ways in which our choice of instruments and methodological approaches might leverage and challenge existing practice, in terms of questioning better ways to engage in authentic, respectful, and dialogical research. As researchers, we have enormous potential to provoke, to nudge, and to inform future research agendas.

We have so much to learn about how we might reclaim utopian imagination and possibilities, and mobilise robust hope in a research-based approach that frames inquiry, and the ways we communicate our research with others. This might include considering ways in which to better work within, and present a discourse of optimism, in researching with young families, rather than reinforcing a deficit paradigm. Or embrace a form of dialogue which is able to re-narraterise, in efforts to counter colonialisation, alienation, and injustice (Ritchie & Rau, 2010). Or, to reflect on how, through the communicating of our findings and stories, researchers can offer a vision of hope, particularly for those marginalised, or socially disadvantaged.

Therefore, in forging forward, I invite you to continue learning, and to continue to look at this very important area of research as a journey of ongoing discovery. A journey of 'forging frontiers' in a legitimate space that still has so far to go. But also a journey of forging frontiers so as to unleash the untapped potential that awaits those willing to reframe. Those with an uncompromising conviction to pursue legitimate, respectful, and ethical research with young families.

So, be bold. Be brave. Have courage, and don't be afraid of standing out in a research space that needs to embrace efforts to advance forward. Here's to our continued learning journey.

Alice ☺

References

Bermúdez, J. M., Muruthi, B., & Jordan, L. (2016). Decolonizing research methods for family science: Creating space at the centre – Decolonizing research practices. *Journal of Family Theory & Review, 8*(2), 192–206.

Binder, A. (1972). A new context for psychology: Social ecology. *American Psychologist, 27*(9), 903–908.

Binder, A., Stokols, D., & Catalano, R. (1975). Social ecology: An emerging multidiscipline. *Journal of Environmental Education, 7*(2), 32–43.

Brown, A. (2008). Towards a new frontier in understanding the contextual influences on paediatric inactivity. In R. Henderson & P. A. Danaher (Eds.), *Troubling terrains: Tactics for traversing and transforming contemporary educational research* (pp. 149–168). Teneriffe, QLD: Post Pressed.

Brown, A. (2009). *South Burnett early movement and stimulation project.* Retrieved from Toowoomba, QLD. https://eprints.usq.edu.au/22536/1/Brown_2012_whole.pdf

Brown, A. (2012). *The new frontier: A social ecological exploration of factors impacting on parental support for the active play of young children within the micro-environment of the family home.* PhD, University of Southern Queensland, Toowoomba, QLD.

Brown, A., & Danaher, P. A. (2017). CHE Principles: Facilitating authentic and dialogical semi-structured interviews in educational research. *International Journal of Research & Method in Education*, 1–15. https://doi.org/10.1080/1743727X.2017.13799.

Brown, A., Stokols, D., Sallis, J., Hiatt, R., & Orleans, T. (2013). *The possibilities and potential of social ecological frameworks to understand health behaviours and outcomes.* Paper presented at the proceeding of symposium (24) presented at the 34th annual conference of the Society of Behavioral Medicine, San Francisco. http://www.sbm.org/UserFiles/file/Symposium_24_Stokols.pdf

Bushin, N. (2009). Researching family migration decision making: A children-in-families approach. *Population, Space and Place, 15*(5), 429–443.

Christensen, P., & James, A. (Eds.). (2008). *Research with children: Perspectives and practices* (2nd ed.). Milton Park, Oxon: Falmer Press.

Clark, A. (2011). Breaking methodological boundaries? Exploring visual, participatory methods with adults and young children. *European Early Childhood Education Research Journal, 19*(3), 321–330.

Coyne, I., Hallström, I., & Söderbäck, M. (2016). Reframing the focus from a family-centred to a child-centred care approach for children's healthcare. *Journal of Child Health Care, 20*(4), 494–502.

Daly, K. J. (2007). *Qualitative methods for family studies and human development.* Thousand Oaks, CA: Sage.

Darder, A. (2015). Decolonizing interpretive research: A critical bicultural methodology for social change. *The International Education Journal: Comparative Perspectives, 14*(2), 63–77.

Dockett, S., Perry, B., Kearney, E., Hamshire, A., Mason, J., & Schmied, V. (2009). Researching with families: Ethical issues and situations. *Contemporary Issues in Early Childhood, 10*(4), 353–365.

Doucet, A. (2016). Is the stay-at-home dad (SAHD) a feminist concept? A genealogical, relational, and feminist critique. *Sex Roles, 75*(1–2), 4–14.

Fargas-Malet, M., McSherry, D., Larkin, E., & Robinson, C. (2010). Research with children: Methodological issues and innovative techniques. *Journal of Early Childhood Research, 8*(2), 175–192.

Fiese, B. (2013). Family context in early childhood. In O. Saracho & B. Spodek (Eds.), *Handbook of research on the education of young children* (3rd ed., pp. 369–384). New York: Routledge.

Foster, V., & Young, A. (2015). Reflecting on participatory methodologies: Research with parents of babies requiring neonatal care. *International Journal of Social Research Methodology, 18*(1), 91–104.

Fulcher, M., Dinella, L. M., & Weisgram, E. S. (2015). Constructing a feminist reorganization of the heterosexual breadwinner/caregiver family model: College students' plans for their own future families. *Sex Roles, 73*(3–4), 174–186.

Gabb, J. (2010). *Researching intimacy in families.* Basingstoke, UK: Springer.

Goffman, E. (1974). *Frame analysis: An essay on the organisation of experience.* Cambridge, MA: Harvard University Press.

Greenstein, T. N., & Davis, S. N. (2013). *Methods of family research* (3rd ed.). Thousand Oaks, CA/Los Angeles: Sage.

Guillemin, M., & Gillam, L. (2004). Ethics, reflexivity, and "ethically important moments" in research. *Qualitative Inquiry, 10*(2), 261–280.

Harden, J., Backett-Milburn, K., Hill, M., & MacLean, A. (2010). Oh, what a tangled web we weave: Experiences of doing 'multiple perspectives' research in families. *International Journal of Social Research Methodology, 13*(5), 441–452.

Henderson, A., Harmon, S., & Newman, H. (2016). The price mothers pay, even when they are not buying it: Mental health consequences of idealized motherhood. *Sex Roles, 74*(11–12), 512–526.

hooks, b. (2000). *Feminist theory: From margin to center* (2nd ed.). London: Pluto Press.

Ishimaru, A., & Bang, M. (2015). *Toward a transformative research and practice agenda for racial equity in family engagement: 2015–2016 family leadership design collaborative white paper.* Retrieved from University of Washington. http://familydesigncollab.org/wp-content/uploads/2017/03/FLDC-Convening-Report-Fin-033117.pdf

Kaestle, C. (2016). Feminist perspectives advance four challenges to transform family studies. *Sex Roles, 75*(1), 71–77.

Kellett, M. (2010). *Rethinking children and research: Attitudes in contemporary society.* London: Continuum International Publishing.

Lakoff, G. (2004). *Don't think of an elephant! Know your values and frame the debate: The essential guide for progressives.* White River Junction, VT: Chelsea Green Publishing.

Lakoff, G. (2014). *The all new don't think of an elephant!: Know your values and frame the debate.* White River Junction, VT: Chelsea Green Publishing.

Mannion, G. (2007). Going spatial, going relational: Why "listening to children" and children's participation needs reframing. *Discourse: Studies in the Cultural Politics of Education, 28*(3), 405–420.

Mason, J., & Danby, S. (2011). Children as experts in their lives: Child inclusive research. *Child Indicators Research, 4*(2), 185–189.

McCarthy, J. R., Doolittle, M., & Schlater, S. D. (2012). *Understanding family meanings: A reflective text.* Bristol, UK: The Open University.

McCubbin, L. D., McCubbin, H. I., Zhang, W., Kehl, L., & Strom, I. (2013). Relational well-being: An indigenous perspective and measure. *Family Relations, 62*(2), 354–365.

McDowell, T. (2015). *Applying critical social theories to family therapy practice.* New York: Springer.

McHale, S., Booth, A., & Amato, P. (Eds.). (2014). *Emerging methods in family research.* London: Springer.

McNeil, T. (2010). Family as a social determinant of health: Implications for governments and institutions to promote the health and well-being of families. *Healthcare Quarterly, 14*(Special Issue, Child Health Canada), 60–67.

McTavish, M., Streelasky, J., & Coles, L. (2012). Listening to children's voices: Children as participants in research. *International Journal of Early Childhood, 44*(3), 249–267.

Milner, H. R. (2007). Race, culture, and researcher positionality: Working through dangers seen, unseen, and unforeseen. *Educational Researcher, 36*(7), 388–400.

Moore, T., & Fry, R. (2011). *Place-based approaches to child and family services: A literature review*. Retrieved from Parkville, VIC. http://www.rch.org.au/uploadedfiles/Main/Content/ccch/Place_based_services_literature_review.pdf

Moore, T., McDonald, M., McHugh-Dillon, H., & West, S. (2016). *Community engagement: A key strategy for improving outcomes for Australian families*. Retrieved from Melbourne, VIC. https://aifs.gov.au/cfca/sites/default/files/cfca39-community-engagement.pdf

Moore, T., McHugh-Dillon, H., Bull, K., Fry, R., Laidlaw, B., & West, S. (2014). *The evidence: What we know about place-based approaches to support children's wellbeing*. Retrieved from Parkville, VIC. https://www.rch.org.au/uploadedFiles/Main/Content/ccch/CCCH_Collaborate_for_Children_Report_The_Evidence_Nov2014.pdf

Moss, P. (2015). Where am I? Position and perspective in researching early childhood education. In A. Farrell, S. Kagan, E. Tisdall, & M. Kay (Eds.), *The Sage handbook of early childhood research*. Thousand Oaks, CA: Sage.

Palaiologou, I. (2014). 'Do we hear what children want to say?' Ethical praxis when choosing research tools with children under five. *Early Child Development and Care, 184*(5), 689–705.

Paris, D. (2011). 'A friend who understand fully': Notes on humanizing research in a multiethnic youth community. *International Journal of Qualitative Studies in Education, 24*(2), 137–149.

Paris, D., & Winn, M. (Eds.). (2014). *Humanizing research: Decolonizing qualitative inquiry with youth and communities*. London: Sage.

Pascal, C., & Bertram, T. (2009). Listening to young citizens: The struggle to make real a participatory paradigm in research with young children. *European Early Childhood Education Research Journal, 17*(2), 249–262.

Pascal, C., & Bertram, T. (2012). Praxis, ethics and power: Developing praxeology as a participatory paradigm for early childhood research. *European Early Childhood Education Research Journal, 20*(4), 477–492.

Poulton, R., Moffitt, T. E., & Silva, P. A. (2015). The Dunedin Multidisciplinary Health and Development Study: overview of the first 40 years, with an eye to the future. *Social Psychiatry and Psychiatric Epidemiology, 50*(5), 679–693.

Qvortrup, J. (2005). Varieties of childhood. In *Studies in modern childhood* (pp. 1–20). New York: Springer.

Reid, C. (2013). Developing a research framework to inform an evidence base for person-centered medicine: Keeping the person at the centre. *European Journal for Person Centered Healthcare, 1*(2), 336–342.

Ricci, R. (2003). Autoethnographic verse: Nicky's boy: A life in two worlds. *The Qualitative Report, 8*(4), 591–596.

Ritchie, J., & Rau, C. (2010). Countercolonial narratives of early childhood education in Aotearoa2. In G. Cannella & L. Soto (Eds.), *Childhoods: A handbook* (pp. 355–373). New York: Peter Lang Publishing.

Seelig, T. (2011). *inGenius: A crash course on creativity.* New York: Harper Collins.

Shahjahan, R. A. (2011). Decolonizing the evidence-based education and policy movement: Revealing the colonial vestiges in educational policy, research, and neoliberal reform. *Journal of Education Policy, 26*(2), 181–206.

Shonkoff, J. P. (2012). Leveraging the biology of adversity to address the roots of disparities in health and development. *Proceedings from the National Academy of Science of the United States of America, 109*(Supp 2), 1–6.

Shonkoff, J. P. (2017). Breakthrough impacts. What science tells us about supporting early childhood development. *Young Children, 72*(2), 8–16.

Shonkoff, J. P., & Fisher, P. (2013). Rethinking evidence-based practice and two-generation programs to create the future of early childhood policy. *Development and Psychopathology, 25*(4), 1635–1653.

Stokols, D. (1992). Establishing and maintaining healthy environments. Toward a social ecology of health promotion. *American Psychologist, 47*(1), 6–22.

Stokols, D. (1996). Translating social ecological theory into guidelines for community health promotion. *American Journal of Health Promotion, 10*(4), 282–298.

Stokols, D. (2018). *Social ecology in the digital age: Solving problems in a globalised world.* San Diego, CA: Academic.

Stokols, D., Grzywacz, J., McMahan, S., & Phillips, K. (2003). Increasing the health promotive capacity of human environments. *American Journal of Health Promotion, 18*(1), 4–13.

Swadener, B., & Mutua, K. (2008). Decolonizing performances: Deconstructing the global postcolonial. In N. K. Denzin, Y. S. Lincoln, & L. T. Smith (Eds.), *Handbook of critical and indigenous methodologies* (pp. 31–43). Los Angeles: Sage.

Swenson, A. R., & Zvonkovic, A. M. (2016). Navigating mothering: A feminist analysis of frequent work travel and independence in families. *Sex Roles, 74*(11–12), 543–557.

Tesoriero, F., Boyle, F., & Enright, L. (2010). Using strengths-based ways to build community and contribute to social inclusion. *New Community Quarterly, 8*(4), 33–37.

Tuck, E. (2016). In conversation with Michelle Fine. Inner angles: Of ethical responses to/with indigenous and decolonizing theories. In N. D. M. Giardina (Ed.), *Ethical futures in qualitative research: Decolonizing the politics of knowledge, International congress of qualitative inquiry series* (pp. 145–168). London: Routledge.

United Nations. (1989). *Convention on the rights of the child.* Retrieved from New York. https://www.humanrights.gov.au/convention-rights-child

Uttal, L. (2009). (Re)visioning family ties to communities and contexts. In S. A. Lloyd, A. L. Few, & K. R. Allen (Eds.), *Handbook of feminist studies* (pp. 134–146). Thousand Oaks, CA: Sage.

van Eeden-Moorefield, B., Malloy, K., & Benson, K. (2016). Gay men's (non) monogamy ideals and lived experience. *Sex Roles, 75*(1–2), 43–55.

Zavala, M. (2013). What do we mean by decolonizing research strategies? Lessons from decolonizing, Indigenous research projects in New Zealand and Latin America. *Decolonization: Indigeneity, Education & Society, 2*(1), 55–71.

Index

© The Author(s) 2019   **287**
A. Brown, *Respectful Research With and About Young Families*, Palgrave Studies in
Education Research Methods, https://doi.org/10.1007/978-3-030-02716-2